MW00617611

THE GOD OF TWO TESTAMENTS

Who was Jesus of Nazareth:

fraud, prophet, or God Himself?

And what is the relationship of

Jesus and the Trinity?

THE GOD OF TWO TESTAMENTS

Who was Jesus of Nazareth:

fraud, prophet, or God Himself?

And what is the relationship of

Jesus and the Trinity?

R. Brent Graves

The God of Two Testaments

by R. Brent Graves

Cover Design by Paul Povolni

ISBN 1-56722-045-2

Paperback edition: 1982
Reprint history: 1985, 1986, 1990, 1991, 1994, 1996
Revised edition: 2000

Printed in United States of America

Printed by

WORD AFLAME® PRESS
8855 DUNN ROAD
HAZELWOOD, MO 63042-2299

This book is gratefully dedicated to the author's loved ones and friends. A special note is expressed to four people:

Jim and Marianne Turner
Robert Sabin
Nathaniel Urshan

I know that this book would not have been written if it had not been for my dear Christian friends Jim and Marianne Turner. Furthermore, by becoming acquainted with Robert Sabin and Nathaniel Urshan, two great evangelists, at a crucial time, I became even more convinced that I had to complete this task that God has given me.

As this second edition is being prepared for the presses, I wish to thank the editorial staff and everyone else at Word Aflame Press for their consistent commitment and valuable assistance. This second edition, like the first, has truly proven to be a team effort.

Contents

Preface to the Second Edition

This expanded edition has been written with both a real sense of burden and a genuine feeling of thankfulness since I am aware that the nature of God and the identity of Jesus are two related issues of supreme importance to every individual. When I first began to consider another edition of *The God of Two Testaments*, I first had in mind primarily minor corrections of typographical errors and refinement of language. However, as I thought about how a second edition could be a significant improvement over the first, it did not take me long to realize that I would not be satisfied unless a discussion of crucial passages of Scripture was expanded considerably—particularly concerning questions that have arisen over the years.

Immediately after I began this revised edition, I came across a book entitled *The Oneness of God* by David K. Bernard (like my own, also published by Word Aflame Press). What is interesting is that I found this book in a small secular library (having less than a half dozen Christian books) on a military housing compound in the mountains of western Saudi Arabia only about forty miles from Mecca! It is ironic that a book that glorifies Jesus Christ so magnificently could be found so close to the center of Islam. I have no idea how *The Oneness of God* made its way to this location, but it was a source of much encouragement since I was able to read the book at a time when I was evaluating my own book. I personally accept it as divine providence.

Although *The Oneness of God* and *The God of Two Testaments* are very different in many ways, they are also very similar in other ways. One book was written by an author who grew up in what is known as a Oneness religious heritage, while the other book was written by an author who grew up in what is known as a trinitarian heritage. Although the two books have different emphasis in places, they complement one another. Despite the authors' diverse backgrounds, the two books reach exactly the same conclusions about the nature of God in general and the identity of Jesus in particular. In short, *The Oneness of God* is well written, balanced, comprehensive, scholarly, and yet readable, inspirational, and—most important of all—Scriptural.

While *The God of Two Testaments* often discusses the original, inspired languages, a constant effort has been made to keep the discussion both readable and relevant. In this regard, many exciting points are presented that should benefit everyone.

What about the Biblical languages of Hebrew, Aramaic, and Greek? Does one have to be a scholar in these languages to learn the truth about the nature of God—or any doctrinal truth? Most definitely not! While a knowledge of the original languages of the Bible is often helpful, many Christians down through the centuries with absolutely no knowledge of the Biblical languages have understood the truth of the oneness of God's nature and other basic doctrines, even though their only source was a translation of the Bible, such as the King James Version.

I am convinced that the basic truths of God's Word

can be seen by the diligent believer no matter which translation is used. However, it is obvious that some versions are more accurate than others, especially since several of the twentieth-century translations (1) frequently depend on unreliable, corrupt manuscripts and (2) often give an unjustifiable, loose paraphrase and interpretation because of doctrinal presuppositions, instead of a literal translation of what was written in the original, inspired languages.

Both the King James Version and the similar New King James Version are generally faithful in translating the Hebrew, Aramaic, and the Greek. And as far as the New Testament is concerned, the KJV and the NKJV have the advantage of relying primarily on the Byzantine family of manuscripts. For many years now, Biblical scholars have been steadily recognizing more and more the consistency and the integrity of these manuscripts, and the result is that the Byzantine family is now respected by scholars much more than it is ridiculed—a situation far different than what it was only twenty years go.

It is significant that the deity of Jesus has been more faithfully preserved in the Byzantine manuscripts (e.g., I Timothy 3:16)—and hence in the KJV and the NKJV, which have relied upon these Greek manuscripts. But it is interesting that even when other versions used corrupt manuscripts, the deity of Jesus can still be seen also in those translations of the New Testament. In other words, our Lord has not left Himself without witness even in the liberal English translations of our modern era!

Regarding *any* Biblical doctrine, it is important that we use Scriptural terminology, since unscriptural terms are often related to unscriptural doctrines. It was only natural for the Roman Catholic Church to come up with unscriptural terms such as "trinity," "triune God," and "three persons" in order to try to explain an unscriptural doctrine. The word "person" is a term that is normally used for a *human being*. Therefore, it is appropriate to use this word for Jesus if reference is being made to His *human* nature and His physical Sonship as a human being; however, it is best *not* to use "person" for God in general or for Jesus' divine nature in particular—the eternal Spirit of God that dwelt *in* Him. Again, the word "person" implies a human being, and our Lord God is far more than a physical human being.

The trinity is an important doctrine of papal Rome. Although I have absolutely no doubt of the Roman origin of the trinity, I hold no personal animosity against either Roman Catholics or those Protestants who are trinitarian. On the contrary, I respect all devout Catholics and sincere Protestants for their faith, however misguided it may be. I had the great blessing of growing up in a conservative Christian home in which my parents tried to be practicing believers, and their Christian faith was a great blessing to me, my sister, and my two brothers. I will always be thankful for that Christian heritage.

Although my religious heritage is strongly trinitarian, it is a heritage that sought to honor God and His Word in many ways. In addition to attending three state universities and two foreign universities, I have been educated in four conservative Christian institutions (three regionally accredited universities and one regionally accredited seminary)—all of which are trinitarian and all having dedicated scholars that I highly respect. Although I also attended a prominent Jewish institution for several years of Ph.D.

studies (at which time it became financially insolvent), I had dropped my trinitarian belief long before that period. Today, I have wonderful Christian friends and beloved relatives, both by blood and by marriage, who are either devout Roman Catholics or evangelical trinitarian Protestants.

Because of my background, I have much empathy for the sincere Christian who has been taught that the Christian God is a trinity of three persons. Because this doctrine is about the very nature of God Himself, trinitarian Christians are *conditioned* to think that it is blasphemous even to consider believing in a God who is not a God of three divine persons. As a result, the trinitarian believer is told not to question this belief, even though the Bible says that we are to "prove all things" and "hold fast that which is good" (I Thessalonians 5:21).

Naturally, there is much about God that the human mind cannot comprehend, let alone prove; however, the Bible reveals much about God's nature and being. Consequently, every individual has the opportunity and the responsibility to prove or confirm what the Word of God teaches concerning the nature of God Himself. Certainly, one should be able to prove to himself or herself whether or not the Bible teaches that God is a trinity. This is not too much to ask. The basic concept of deity is simply too important to ignore, and we can be grateful that the Bible has given us many clear passages of Scripture that explain both the nature of God's being and the identity of Jesus of Nazareth.

As dominant as it is throughout the Christian world, trinitarianism is in a no-win situation as far as the Word of God is concerned. The doctrine itself is a self-contradictory, non-Biblical, pagan belief that has its roots and development in the church of Rome. And because of its origin, it has confused and blinded millions of people for many centuries.

The doctrine of the trinity not only misrepresents the basic being of God Himself, but it also misrepresents who Jesus really is. No true trinitarian can fully appreciate the *complete* deity of Jesus that the New Testament claims for Him. No trinitarian can fully appreciate that *God Himself was in Jesus Christ* (II Corinthians 5:19), despite that this is the consistent message of the New Testament revelation.

For over fifteen hundred years, Matthew 28:19 has been misrepresented as a trinitarian baptismal statement. That is indeed ironic since this verse of Scripture shows the oneness of God's being in a very clear manner. By associating the Father, the Son, and the Holy Spirit with *one* name, Jesus was identifying this name with three roles of one God—and certainly not with three distinct persons of a trinity. The context of Matthew 28:16-20 indicates that the glorified, risen *Christ*, who was worshiped according to verse 17, is being exalted throughout the entire passage.

A comparison of Matthew 28 with the parallel verses in the latter part of the other Gospels substantiates that "the name" of the Father, the Son, and Holy Spirit in Matthew 28:19 is none other than the name of Jesus Himself! (Compare Matthew 28:19 with Mark 16:15-17; Luke 24:47; John 20:31.)

Furthermore, throughout the Book of Acts, the early converts were consistently baptized in the name of the Lord Jesus Christ, *not* in the name of a trinity. In plain fact, the New Testament Christians were *always* baptized in the name of "Jesus" and *never* in the name of "the Father, the Son, and the Holy Spirit" as a trinitarian baptismal formula.

This is the tragic dilemma of all who try to interpret Matthew 28:19 as a trinitarian statement. This is the tragic dilemma of all trinitarians. No trinitarian Christian, no trinitarian minister, and no trinitarian scholar has ever been able to explain *why* the name of Jesus, and not a trinity, is exalted in all the post-resurrection passages of the Gospels. No trinitarian scholar has ever been able to explain *why* the Christians in the Book of Acts were always baptized in the name of Jesus and *why* they were never baptized in the name of a trinity. The important issue of Matthew 28:19 is expanded in the last chapter of this new edition, and in this discussion it is vital for us to remember that the Word of God reveals a wonderful truth—not simply a clever argument from a self-deceived, modern, human author.

The annals of church history indicate that there have always been Christians who believed in one God of different manifestations and roles, instead of a God of three distinct persons. And today, human beings are still coming to the marvelous truth that our Lord Jesus Christ *is* "our great God and Savior" (Titus 2:13).

There is no doubt that Bible-believing, evangelical Christians have done much good in the proclamation of the gospel of Christ. There is no question that Jesus Christ has been honored and exalted even in the trinitarian churches whenever Jesus is in the foreground, as He is throughout the New Testament. Unfortunately for the trinitarian, the doctrine of the trinity is always lurking in the background and often intrudes into the foreground, pushing out Jesus, because of the fundamental nature of the doctrine itself. The result is that the trinity continues to be a confounding confusion and a dangerous distraction for every Christian who attempts to believe in it and tries to understand it.

This book is an invitation for both Christian leaders and lay members from all walks of life in all of the churches to accept the simple, wonderful truth about Jesus. This is an invitation for ministers, elders, deacons, Bible class teachers, seminary professors, and all Christians (both Catholic and Protestant) to believe and teach that our Creator God came to this earth to live as a human being, to die on a cross, and to rise from the grave in order to become *both* our Lord and our Savior. This is an invitation for all people everywhere to believe in and worship Jesus, "the true God" (I John 5:20), instead of the gods of man's imagination and speculation.

Introduction

Several years ago a bewildered believer wrote to Billy Graham that he was seriously considering denying Jesus Christ. He informed Mr. Graham that he had the impression that Christianity is a religion of tritheism, in other words, a belief in three gods: Father, Son, and Holy Spirit. In short, the inquirer was dismayed and confused, and because of his confusion he was ready to give up his Christian faith and accept the clear monotheism of Judaism. The inquirer was deeply troubled about a question that has disturbed more than a few.

This is the question: Is the God of the New Testament a different God from the God of the Old Testament? Is the Lord of the apostle Paul (who was a Hebrew Christian) a different Lord from the Lord of Abraham (who was the first Hebrew)? The objective of this study is to show that the Christian God is the same as the Hebrew God—the same God with the same attributes.

Unfortunately, a wide divergence of opinion can be observed among the various sectors of Christendom. But that divergence of opinion is not the fault of the Bible, for the Bible is quite explicit concerning the matter.

In spite of the clear testimony of John 20:28-29 and other verses of Scripture, Unitarians proudly refuse to accept Jesus as their Lord and God. The sect known as Jehovah's Witnesses also denies the full deity of Jesus Christ.

In remarkable similarity to the Mormon faith, Herbert W. Armstrong's Worldwide Church of God and his son

Garner Ted Armstrong's Church of God International have likewise expounded polytheistic tendencies, for these two religious movements have taught that God the Father and Jesus the Son are two completely separate and distinct divine beings.

At the other end of the religious spectrum, Christian Science and other religious groups teach that God does not have a distinct personality or individuality at all but that He is simply a divine "principle."

Millions of professing Christians affirm a belief in the trinity. What about the doctrine of the trinity? What does the phrase "Father, Son, and Holy Spirit" mean in the Biblical sense? Is the Christian God a trinity of three divine persons? Those Christians who advocate a belief in the trinity differ widely in their views of God. Apparently many Catholics and Protestants do have tritheistic leanings, professing a belief in a trinity of three distinct persons in the strictest sense.

On the other hand, the religious heritage of some Protestants is "economic trinitarianism," by which they mean a belief in one God who has revealed Himself in three different manifestations as Father, Son, and Holy Spirit. They reject the claim that the Christian God is a trinity of three distinct "persons." Today many Presbyterians and other Christians among various Protestant churches have this view of God.

There are Christian groups that do not use trinitarian terminology at all and are known as Oneness churches. These religious movements, of which the United Pentecostal Church International is the largest, believe that one indivisible God has revealed Himself in different manifestations and roles, not in three persons. This concept—that the Lord God is indeed one Lord—is the approach taken in the following pages.

It may come as a shock to some, but the terms "trinity," "trinitarian," "three persons," and "triune God" are not found in the Bible. If nothing else, this fact alone ought to cause us to ask ourselves (and our ministers) where such terminology did come from.

Martin Luther was quite frank about it; he openly declared that he disliked such terms since they could not be found in the Scriptures. For non-Biblical terminology leads to confusion, and confusion can lead to heresy.

In order to combat confusion and heresy, let us strive to call Bible things by Bible names, to speak where the Bible speaks, and to be silent where the Bible is silent. The theologians and the philosophers might wish to speculate about the Godhead, but ultimately the individual Christian must choose for himself what he is to believe concerning the fundamental questions he is to hold so dearly. With regard to our basic concepts of the God we worship, may we simply accept what the Bible teaches, no more and no less.

We are not expected to speculate concerning something so sacred as the nature of God Himself. In fact, we are not privileged to do so. However, we *are* expected to study the Scriptures in order to have a reliable foundation upon which to place our Christian faith. Jews in Berea were considered "more noble" when they searched the Scriptures daily in trying to decide whether or not they should accept Jesus of Nazareth as the prophesied Messiah (Acts 17:11). They were considered noble not because they blindly accepted the apostle Paul's words; they were so considered because they accepted Paul's *challenge*, going to their own Scriptures and proving to themselves what was the truth.

Jesus reminded us that the Word of God is truth (John 17:17). What does God teach us about Himself through His Word? This should be our concern. We can be thankful that the God of the Bible has not left us without testimony and that we can consult and reflect upon this testimony whenever we choose to ponder the evidence in the Bible. We are especially blessed that the Biblical evidence is not only available, but that it is evidence that one really cannot ignore if he believes that the Bible is God's Word for humanity. For the Bible majestically reveals to us two great, related truths: (1) the essential oneness in being of the Hebrew and Christian God and (2) the complete deity of Jesus Christ as the incarnation of that God.

To emphasize that the Bible is the Word of God, throughout this book I have chosen to capitalize not only the words "Bible" and "Scripture" but also the adjective forms "Biblical" and "Scriptural," even though the more common practice today is not to capitalize the latter. While I recommend the use of the King James Version and New King James Version, I have occasionally made my own direct translation in order to identify a Hebrew title or name of God or bring out the full force of a certain phrase.

In certain Biblical quotations I have added italics or another contrasting font for emphasis. Perhaps some scholars might question the propriety of such usage, but this book, *The God of Two Testaments*, is not primarily addressed to the intellectuals (even though they might receive some benefit from reading it). It is not necessarily addressed to the atheists or the skeptics (even though they, too, could receive some clarification from reading it).

Why was this book written? Because of honest, seeking individuals who feel hopelessly confused. Because of sincere Christian people who are searching for Biblical answers to important questions.

Because of some people's religious heritage and background, it may take courage to accept what is read—and to act upon it—in spite of the Biblical evidence that is presented.

If one accepts the Biblical testimony of the following pages and commits his life to his Creator and Savior, he will undertake an important spiritual adventure. And one thing is certain: any price paid will be worth it, as many past and present faithful believers have demonstrated by the witness of their lives. And the best is yet to come, because we have the promise of eternal life with Jesus as a sure inheritance if we are "faithful unto death" (Revelation 2:10).

If the reader is challenged in the following chapters, it is my earnest prayer that this challenge will lead to a continual, honest investigation of the Bible, the Word of God. For the basic goal of this study has been to declare the counsel of God, the whole counsel of God, and only the counsel of God, from the Scriptures.

May our God richly bless us as we embark upon a most sacred journey, a journey into the very nature and character of God Himself, a journey that should have as its only map and signposts the Scriptures, which God has given us. The following chapters are simply an attempt to present what God has stated concerning Himself through His Word, for this is a Biblical study of God, the Hebrew and the Christian God—the God of two Testaments.

Chapter 1

Elohim: Mighty God

The creation . . .
In the beginning there was chaos—like an ocean of
seething oil—shapeless.
At the command of the celestial deities, the god
Izanagi and the goddess Izanami stood upon the
Floating Bridge of Heaven and plunged a jewel-
bedecked spear into the ocean of chaos.
They stirred it until the liquid thickened and coag-
ulated.
Then they withdrew the spear, and the drops that
fell from its tip formed the tiny island of Onokoro that
nestled in the waves like an emerald.
Pleased with their creation, they descended upon
a rainbow to the newly formed island and made it the

Central Pillar of earth! (Kojiki)

Thus we have an account of the creation according to Japanese mythology. Scholars normally use the word *myth* to mean either a story of "unknown origin" that is at least partially traditional or a story invented to explain a truth, religious belief, or practice. Whether we turn to Africa, South America, North America, Europe, South Asia, the Far East, or the Middle East, the mythologies of the nations have their dashing heroes and villains—both gods and goddesses. Such deities, we are told, are responsible for the creation of the world and everything in it. One famous version explains the heaven and the earth as nothing less than the corpse of a goddess slain in battle! Small wonder that scholars commonly refer to these mythologies as "creation myths," for so they are. All the creation accounts of antiquity read like the inventions of demented minds with vivid imaginations.

That is, all except one. One ancient version ranks far superior to the others—the account of the creation in the first chapter of Genesis. Unlike the pagan versions with their many gods and goddesses, the Bible simply states: "In the beginning God created the heaven and the earth" (Genesis 1:1).

In striking contrast to the world's religions, the Bible informs us that there is but *one* God responsible for the creation. No divine villains here! No jealous deities here! No capricious gods and goddesses here! Only one God— the Creator. Commenting on the unique claim of the Old Testament, an authoritative Jewish source reminds us: "Completely new . . . was Israel's idea of God. . . . Paganism is challenged in all its aspects. God is One;

there is no other (Deuteronomy 6:4; Isaiah 45:21; 46:9)."[1]

Let Us Make Man

Despite the testimony of Jewish scholarship, despite the consistent record from the Bible itself that "God is One: there is no other," some have stepped forward to offer a challenge. They have turned to the first chapter of Genesis for the basis of that challenge:

"And God said, Let us make man in our image, after our likeness" (Genesis 1:26).

According to some Christian writers, this verse indicates that God is one Being—but a Being composed of more than one divine person. In discussing the clause, "Let us make man," one commentator suggested that "the three persons of the Trinity, Father, Son, and Holy Ghost, consult about it and concur in it."[2]

If this conjecture is accurate, then we have a serious challenge to the strict statements of other Old Testament Scripture. But *is* the above conjecture accurate? And what does *Hebrew* scholarship say about Genesis 1:26? With regard to the latter question, Dr. Ephraim A. Speiser wrote that even though plural pronouns are used, a singular *sense* is meant. In his own words: "Here God refers to himself, which may account for the more formal construction in the plural."[3]

The statement in Genesis could be a kind of "literary plural." And according to Dr. Speiser's translation of the Hebrew idiom, we should have in the English: "Then God said, I will make man in my image, after my likeness."[4]

There may be more merit for this rendering than some might think, for Speiser calls our attention to the fact that "the very next verse uses the singular throughout." Here is the next verse: "So God created man in His own image; *He* created him in the image of God. *He* created them male and female" (Genesis 1:27).

If the Lord is trying to reveal a plurality of persons in the Godhead by using plural pronouns in verse 26, it is strange that He not only uses singular pronouns in the next verse (which is simply a summary of verse 26) but that He also uses singular pronouns in verses 29, 30, and 31. It is enlightening that the Bible regularly uses singular pronouns in referring to God, and this is the case in literally thousands of instances throughout the Scriptures from Genesis through Revelation. Genesis 1:26 most likely uses the literary plural since in this verse God is speaking (hence the plural), whereas in the next verse God is not speaking (hence the singular).

The literary plural (using "we" for "I") is a device of speakers and writers in all languages. Distinguished Greek scholar A. T. Robertson has noted that the apostle Paul used the literary plural on several occasions in his epistles.[5]

A responsible Hebrew source has expanded the above explanation as follows: "The use of the plural, 'Let *us* make man,' is the Hebrew idiomatic way of expressing deliberation as in [Genesis] xi,7; or it is the plural of Majesty, royal commands being conveyed in the first person plural, as in Ezra iv,18."[6]

In addition to the competent testimony of Jewish linguistic scholarship, even Christian scholars have challenged the trinitarian interpretation. The popular *Oxford Annotated Bible* of the Revised Standard Version has suggested: "The plural *us, our* ([Gen.] 3.22; 11.7) probably refers to the divine beings who surround God in his heavenly court (I Kings 22:19; Job 1:6; Isaiah 6:8; compare Psalm 29:1) and in whose image man was made."[7]

Besides the linguistic explanation of either the literary plural or the plural of majesty, which both Jewish and Christian scholars give, the foregoing statement about Genesis 1:26 by the Oxford Annotated Bible is also credible for two reasons: (1) One Spirit-Being called *God* has identified Himself as the Creator. And if the Creator was speaking to others, He was definitely speaking to others who were *not* God. For the verse states, "And *God* said . . ." (2) God *may* have been informing His angels of His intentions of the creation, because angelic beings do surround Him; according to the Bible, the angels are there.

For example, a prophet of God once told of a vision he had seen: "I saw Yahweh sitting on *His* throne, and all the host of heaven standing beside Him at His right hand and at His left" (I Kings 22:19). The use of the singular pronouns here attests that the prophet saw *One* (not three) seated on the throne—with the angelic host in His presence.

Likewise, a king of Israel prayed: "O Yahweh the God of Israel, the One who is enthroned above the cherubim, You are God, even You alone, of all the kingdoms of the earth; You have made heaven and earth" (II Kings 19:15). Thus we learn that King Hezekiah prayed to a God who was "One" enthroned above His cherubim. And the Bible informs us that this God answered Hezekiah's prayer in a mighty way.[8]

To summarize, I believe that we are to understand

Genesis 1:26 as a literary plural or a plural of majesty—
or both.

The Hebrew Intensive Plural

Many people appear to be confused about the
Godhead question; and one thing that has led to this confusion is a misapplication of the Hebrew word *Elohim*, a
regular term for "God" in the Old Testament Scriptures.

Since *Elohim* is a plural form, some Christian authors
have emphasized that the name signifies "the plurality of
persons in the Godhead, Father, Son, and Holy Ghost."[9]

Those writers who point to *Elohim* as a "plurality of
persons in the Godhead" usually do not have very much
to say about the Hebrew language itself—the language in
which the word is found. In Hebrew, many words appear
in the plural form but have a *singular connotation*. The
following are some examples:

mayim: water
shamayim: heaven
panim: face
sarim: court official
milium: consecration
megurim: dwelling place
bethulim: virginity
tamin: honest, perfect
rachamim: compassion
tzaharaim: noon
orim: light, brightness
urim: enlightenment
Mitsrayim: Egypt
Yerushalayim: Jerusalem

bechurim: the age of youth
biuthim: terror, anguish
hathulim: mockery, derision
chanutim: the act of embalming
macheluyim: sickness
merukim: anointing, cleansing
tsammim: snare, perdition
shekulim: childlessness
shimurim: observance, celebration
teunim: toil, labor
shenhabim: ivory
geulim: release, redemption
chaim: life, refreshment
kippurim: expiation, atonement

These words all have a plural spelling even though the meaning is singular! The inherent intensity of many of the preceding terms can be easily seen in the meaning. This is why Hebrew scholarship recognizes them as "intensive plural nouns." As with *Elohim*, the words of this list have the masculine plural ending *im*; and as with *Elohim*, the connotation is singular.

The most comprehensive Hebrew-English lexicon that Christian scholarship has produced therefore explains that the plural form *Elohim* is simply the "plural intensive"[10] with a singular force. In similar fashion, the highly respected *Bible Dictionary* by Dr. William Smith calls it "the plural of majesty."[11]

Jewish scholarship points out that "*Elohim* is a plural form which is often used in Hebrew to denote plenitude of might."[12]

Plenitude of might! *Elohim* can express "plenitude of might" because of the very nature of the word itself. *Elohim* is the plural spelling of *Elo'ah*, but *El* is the abbreviated singular form—and thus the root word. Basically, *El* signifies "strength," "power," "might"; therefore, in agreement with the scholarship of both Jewish and Christian linguists, a Christian scholar has stated that the term *Elohim* means "the fullness of divine strength, the sum of powers displayed by God."[13]

Thus when the Hebrew writers referred to God in the Old Testament as *El*, *Elo'ah*, or *Elohim* more than two thousand times, those inspired writers were thinking of Him as one "Mighty God."

The God of the Bible is the One who *created* the heavens and the earth out of nothingness. The God of Abraham is the One who guides and controls the course

of humanity. This God upholds the laws of the universe—
thus *sustaining* the order of His creation. *Elohim*—
Mighty God—is an appropriate appellation for the God of
the Bible.

Pagan Trinities?

Whenever the authors of the Old Testament books
used the term *Elohim* to refer to the God of Israel, they
consistently used a singular verb. In Genesis 1:1 Elohim
is the One doing the creating, with the Hebrew verb for
"create" in the singular. In other words, the verb has a singular pronoun as a suffix, meaning *He* created.

On the other hand, whenever the writers of the Old
Testament discussed the many gods and goddesses of
neighboring lands, they consistently used a *plural* verb in
writing about the *elohim*, the gods of the nations. For
then they were writing about polytheism.

What is of particular interest is that the Hebrew Old
Testament also uses the term in reference to *one specific*
pagan deity. For some time now, certain authors have
claimed that the use of *Elohim* shows that the God of the
Bible is a trinity of three persons. Is this accurate? If the
Elohim of Israel is a trinity of three persons, what about
the *elohim* of the nations?

Judges 11:24 calls the pagan deity Chemosh by the
term *elohim*, "a god." Judges 8:33 refers to Baal-berith,
who also is called *elohim*. Judges 16:23 designates the
famous god of the Philistines, Dagon, as *elohim*. Baal-
zebub was a god of Ekron, and II Kings 1:2-3 calls him
elohim. Nisroch, a god of Assyria, is referred to as *elohim* in II Kings 19:37.

In I Kings 11:5 the writer records that "Solomon went

after Ashtoreth, the goddess of the Zidonians." This example is worthy of special note because the term "Ashtoreth" has the suffix -*eth*, the regular Hebrew ending for a *singular feminine* noun. And yet this goddess is called none other than *elohim—a masculine plural* noun in spelling!

Here is our question: Were these pagan gods trinities? Chemosh was an *elohim*, but was he a trinity of three persons? Dagon was an *elohim*; was he a trinity? The goddess Ashtoreth was an *elohim*; was she a deity of three persons? Each pagan deity was known individually as an *elohim*, but it surely was not considered to be a trinity of three divine persons.

Yahweh Himself Is Elohim

The Elohim of Israel identified Himself as possessing a special name. No one today can be absolutely certain of that name's exact pronunciation since the written Hebrew did not use vowels in script. Vowel sounds existed only in the spoken language, and it was many centuries later when Jewish scholars added makeshift vowels to the Hebrew Bible. Even then, they made no attempt to come up with the vowels of God's own name, for it was (and still is) the devout Jew's belief that to pronounce God's name might mean taking His name in vain.

We can perhaps reach an approximate rendering if we pronounce the Hebrew *YHWH* as Yahweh. In the Old Testament the name *Yahweh* is found more than six thousand times, and it carries a special connotation. The very name in the Hebrew language signifies *existence*. Consequently, it could very likely be a reference to God as "the Self-Existent One" or possibly "the Eternal," as

Moffatt rendered in his translation.

Because the term *Yahweh* is close to the Hebrew, in this book we have chosen to use this word for *YHWH*, although we have retained *Jehovah* and LṯRD in direct quotations from other authors. Whichever English term we use to represent the name of God in the Hebrew language, we should remember that we cannot be absolutely certain of the exact pronunciation of *YHWH*.

If Yahweh is the God of the Old Testament, then it must follow that Yahweh Himself is Elohim. That is precisely the point of this section of our study. As God revealed Himself to His people, He did so by introducing Himself as Yahweh, the Elohim of Israel.

When Yahweh appeared to Abraham as recorded in Genesis 17, He described Himself in these words: "I am the Almighty God [*El*]; walk before Me and be perfect" (Genesis 17:1).

As Yahweh continued His dialogue with the patriarch, He promised him: "I will establish My covenant between Me and you and your descendants after you . . . to be God [*Elohim*] to you and to your descendants after you. . . . I will be their God [*Elohim*] (Genesis 17:7-8).

We observe two important points from the preceding quotation: (1) Yahweh introduces Himself as *El*: "I am the Almighty God" (verse 1). (2) Then He identifies Himself as *Elohim*: "*I* [not "we"] will be their Elohim" (verse 8).

Several years later Yahweh appeared to Abraham's son, Isaac, and He announced: "*I* am the Elohim of Abraham your father" (Genesis 26:24).

Isaac's son, Jacob, likewise had an encounter with Yahweh, hearing His voice. That voice said: "I am Yahweh the Elohim of Abraham your father and the Elohim of Isaac" (Genesis 28:13).

Several hundred years afterward, Yahweh God told Moses: "I am Yahweh your Elohim" (Exodus 16:12).

As He thundered forth the Ten Commandments to the Hebrew nation, Yahweh reiterated: "I am Yahweh your Elohim" (Exodus 20:2).

God continued to emphasize the unity of His being to the Israelites time and again: "I am Yahweh your Elohim" (Leviticus 23:22; 24:22; Numbers 10:10; 15:41).

In this regard, the Book of Exodus describes an extraordinary vision of Yahweh; the scene is Mount Sinai: "Then Moses and Aaron, Nadab and Abihu, and seventy of the elders of Israel went up. And they saw the Elohim of Israel; and under *His* feet [not "their feet"] as it were a paved work of a sapphire stone, like the very heaven for clearness" (Exodus 24:9-10).

The prophets of Israel thereafter, from Moses to Malachi, constantly proclaimed that Yahweh Himself is the only true Elohim. From Isaiah we read: "Thus says Yahweh, the King of Israel and its redeemer, Yahweh of Hosts: I am the First, and I am the Last. Beside *Me* there is no Elohim" (Isaiah 44:6).

Jeremiah expressed the same sentiment: "But Yahweh is the true Elohim; *He* is the living Elohim and the eternal King" (Jeremiah 10:10).

Throughout the Book of Ezekiel, Yahweh consistently declared the very oneness of His nature. Here, as God spoke to His people through Ezekiel, He utilized the singular pronoun "I" literally *hundreds* of times in the Hebrew narrative. It is never "we"; it is always "I." And this same consistency is found from Genesis to Malachi.

"For Yahweh, *He* is Elohim; and there is no other beside Him" (Deuteronomy 4:35).

There Is One El

If the term *Elohim* would imply a plurality of persons in the Godhead, then that Godhead would be composed of more than one El—since *El* is the abbreviated singular form of *Elohim*. But the Scriptures show conclusively that there is but one El, Yahweh Himself.

King David praised Yahweh by acknowledging that "the El of Israel . . . gives power and strength to His people" (Psalm 68:35).

Several passages in Isaiah shine forth with the glory of El, the Mighty God of Israel. Through this prophet, Yahweh proclaimed:

- *"Remember the former things of old; for I am El, and there is no other"* (Isaiah 46:9).
- *"Look unto Me and be saved; . . . for I am El, and there is no other"* (Isaiah 45:22).
- *"I am He. Before Me no El was formed; nor will there be any after Me"* (Isaiah 43:10).

Clearly, the God of the Hebrew Scriptures is one Mighty God—one El—not two or three.

Adonai Is Yahweh

Adonai is another Hebrew word that the Old Testament uses for God. The singular term is *adon*, and it means "lord, master." The plural form, *Adonai*, is the majestic title for God, and it is regularly translated as "Lord."

In order to distinguish between the Hebrew *YHWH* and

Adonai in the Old Testament, some English versions translate *YHWH* as "LORD" or "GOD" (with all capitals) and *Adonai* as "Lord." Although *Adonai* in the Hebrew has the personal pronoun "my" as a suffix, the term is customarily translated as "Lord," instead of "my Lord."

A study of the Hebrew Old Testament confirms that *Adonai* (like *Elohim*) is an intensive plural noun—and also a plural-of-majesty noun—which is to be translated as a singular noun. The meaning of the term itself indicates that it is an exalted title for God as our Lord, and the following passages of Scripture show this.

In Genesis 18 the Lord God and two angels appeared to Abraham in a theophany, a physical manifestation as a man. Both before and after the Lord's dialogue with Abraham, God is identified as Yahweh (verses 22 and 33). During their dialogue over the fate of Sodom, Abraham called Yahweh "Adonai" (verses 27, 30-32).

Psalm 8 is a second passage which shows that Adonai is Yahweh. Here, David praised his God by using the plural form of *Adon*, putting it with *Yahweh* in the very same verse. And he did it in both verse 1 and verse 9: "O LORD, our Lord, how excellent is Your name in all the earth!" (Psalm 8:1, 9, NKJV).

Another verse which confirms that Yahweh Himself is Adonai is Psalm 109:21. Here again, David used both terms in the same verse as he cried out: "But You, O GOD [*Yahweh*] the Lord [*Adonai*], deal with me for Your name's sake; because Your mercy is good, deliver me" (Psalm 109:21, NKJV).

It is striking that David referred to the Lord by beginning the verse with the *singular* pronoun for "You" (*Atah* in the Hebrew). And in addition, the very presence of the personal pronoun here indicates an emphasis of "You Yourself." In fact, because of (1) the singular pronoun for "You," (2) several *other* singular pronoun suffixes, (3) singular verbs, and (4) the singular name *Yahweh*—all referring to *Adonai*—it is obvious that the writer understood *Adonai* as a singular noun as well.

Psalm 16 is still another enlightening passage which demonstrates that *Adonai* is a singular title for God. David called his Lord God *El* in Psalm 16:1, while in verse 2 he referred to Him as both *Yahweh* and *Adonai*. The singular terms *El* and *Yahweh* in this text prove that King David considered *Adonai* to be his one Lord, not Lords.

The Bible even applies the plural form of *adon* to a singular *man* on different occasions. For example, I Chronicles 12:19 uses the plural spelling of *adon* to refer to King Saul. Here, the plural form is used for a human "lord" or "master" who is king of Israel. (See also I Samuel 29:4.) Obviously, it is a plural of majesty.

Another example in which the plural spelling of *adon* refers to a man is I Samuel 29:8, where David called Achish, king of Gath: "my lord [*adonai*] the king." Again we clearly have a plural of majesty.

Psalm 68:17-20 is a particularly illuminating passage of Scripture. Here, David called his Lord God by the following: *Elohim* (verses 17-18), *El*—the singular form of *Elohim* (verses 19-20, twice in verse 20), *Adonai* (verses 17, 19-20), *Yahweh* (verse 20), and *Yah*—the abbreviated form of *Yahweh* (verse 18). In short, these verses identify *Elohim* and *Adonai* with the three singular nouns *El*, *Yah*, and *Yahweh*!

Furthermore, what makes this passage especially significant is that the apostle Paul in Ephesians 4:8 quoted

Psalm 68:18, applying it to Jesus Christ and His ascension into the heavens following His resurrection from the dead. In the inspired words of the apostle from Tarsus, "He Himself who descended is also the *One* who ascended far above all the heavens, that He might fill all things" (Ephesians 4:10, NKJV).

Thus, according to Paul in Ephesians 4:7-10, Jesus Himself is the One whom Psalm 68:17-20 identifies as Adonai, Elohim, El, Yahweh, and Yah!

If we were to go no further, we have already seen that the Scriptures glorify and honor Jesus as our Lord God in the highest language. According to Psalm 68 and Ephesians 4 alone, Jesus *is* the God of the Old Testament, as well as the God of the New Testament. And the Word of God reveals to us more concerning this great truth—much more—which the following chapters will show.

Three Honest Men

As we close this portion of our study, it might be well for us to contemplate three honest men. Two of the men lived in the sixteenth century—John Calvin and Michael Servetus of Villanova. Servetus died at the stake south of Geneva, Switzerland, on October 27, 1553. His crime? He was condemned to death for religious heresy. Because of his knowledge of the Hebrew Scriptures and the New Testament, Servetus had refused to worship a God of three persons. His honesty cost him his physical life.

Although a court of law passed Servetus's death sentence, John Calvin was the man primarily responsible for his death, for Calvin was the principal accuser and chief prosecutor in the trial. Unlike Servetus, he firmly believed in a God of three persons; and it was Calvin's excessive zeal in this regard that led to Servetus's death. And yet, even though John Calvin believed in a trinity of three persons, throughout his life he consistently *denied* that the Hebrew Old Testament supported the doctrine!

And he was correct. For if the Hebrew Bible has one overriding claim, it is the unique claim that God has identified Himself as one mighty Spirit-Being. It is ironic that some today would turn to the Old Testament to try to prove, of all things, a God of three persons. It was because of his honesty that Calvin never resorted to a misinterpretation of *Elohim* to try to justify *his* belief. For he knew Hebrew, and He knew the Hebrew Scriptures.

The third honest man to contemplate is Dr. William Smith, a respected scholar of more recent times. It took honesty and moral courage for Dr. Smith to freely acknowledge what some clergymen apparently do not *yet* realize: "The plural form of *Elohim* has given rise to much discussion. The fanciful idea that it referred to the trinity of persons in the Godhead hardly finds now a supporter among scholars."[14]

Conclusion

Plural forms for *God* in the Old Testament cannot teach a trinity because there is no consistency or pattern in their use that would indicate such a doctrine. On the contrary, the use of plural nouns is not limited to the true God. Therefore, they are not special terms that uniquely reveal a plurality of persons in the Godhead.

In fact, the Bible uses *Elohim* not only for the Hebrew God but also for other gods. In this regard, it uses *elohim* for both singular and plural pagan deities. In addition, it even uses *elohim* as a singular noun for human beings!

If *Elohim* shows a plurality of divine persons in a trinity, it is strange that the inspired writers used singular, not plural, pronouns for *Elohim* when referring to the God of Israel.

Besides *Elohim*, the singular forms *Elo'ah* and *El* are also used for the God of the Old Testament—another indication that *Elohim* is not a unique noun for the trinity. If *Elohim* pointed to a plurality of divine persons, then the Bible would not teach that the living God is one El, as it does in passages of Scripture like Isaiah 43:10; 45:22; and 46:9. These texts specifically show that there is only one El, not three Els in a trinity.

In short, *Elohim* is an intensive plural form that is used as a singular noun. As noted earlier, Hebrew has many intensive plural nouns in the Old Testament that are used as singular nouns.

Adonai, "my Lord" (and found with other pronoun suffixes), is another plural form that is used as a singular noun for *God*. Like *elohim*, the term *adonai* is not limited to the God of Israel. Thus *adonai* cannot be a unique title for the trinity, because it is used as a singular noun for *other* lords, including human kings.

In addition, the Hebrew writers referred to the Lord God by using *both* the singular and plural forms of *Adon*. A look at Psalm 110 alone proves that the singular and plural forms are equivalent. A comparison of Psalm 110:1 and Psalm 110:5 reveals that King David considered the singular form of "my Lord" (*Adoni*) in verse 1 to be equal to the plural form (*Adonai*) in verse 5. And in this short psalm the Lord *is* the Lord God.

As intensive plural nouns, both *Elohim* and *Adonai*

are used with the *singular* name *Yahweh* and its abbreviated form *Yah*. And when used for the God of the Israelites, *Elohim* and *Adonai* appear with singular verbs. All of this, of course, shows that these plural forms are considered as singular proper nouns.

The plural forms *Elohim* and *Adonai* are not only intensive plural nouns, but they are also undoubtedly plurals of majesty. The plural participle of the verb *bara* for "the Creator" in Ecclesiastes 12:1 is another intensive plural form that is a plural of majesty since it too refers to the true God who rules His creation. The plural participle of *bara* in Ecclesiastes 12:1 does not even *imply* a trinity of persons because it is not consistently found as a plural participle for God in the Old Testament. In Isaiah 40:28 "the Creator" is a translation of the *singular* participle of the verb *bara*. In this passage Isaiah also referred to his Creator by using the same singular pronouns that are repeatedly used for the one true God throughout the Old Testament.

In conclusion, it is not logical to assume that Abraham, King David, and the Hebrew prophets were all wrong in their firm belief in the oneness of God's nature. The Hebrew heritage of strict monotheism and one personal God is consistently and strongly affirmed throughout the Old Testament; and the inspired, original Hebrew language demonstrates it. Not only do the Hebrew Scriptures teach the oneness of God's nature and being, but the Greek New Testament also reveals this great truth to us, as the following chapters will show.

Chapter 2

Jesus: Yahweh-Savior

In his book *Christ: The Theme of the Bible* Professor Norman Geisler (who happens to believe in a trinity of three persons) made an astonishing claim for Jesus. In his own words: "*Jesus of the New Testament is the Jehovah of the Old Testament* [emphasis his]. . . . Jesus is Jehovah, that is, the God of the Old Testament."[1] This is the kind of statement that we hear scholars make from time to time—whether they be trinitarian or not. Why Bible scholars refer to Jesus as "the God of the Old Testament" is the subject of this chapter. One enlightening verse of Scripture in this regard comes from the Book of Philippians, penned by the apostle Paul:

"*That at the name of Jesus every knee should bow,*

of those in heaven, and of those on earth, and of those under the earth, and that every tongue should confess that Jesus Christ is Lord, to the glory of God the Father" (Philippians 2:10-11, NKJV).

The apostle made a remarkable application in testifying that at the name of *Jesus* every knee will bow and every tongue confess, for in so doing, Paul claimed for Jesus exactly what Isaiah had claimed for Yahweh! Yahweh was speaking (Isaiah 45:21) when He declared through this Old Testament prophet:

"Look to Me, and be saved, all you ends of the earth! For I am God and there is no other. I have sworn by Myself . . . that to Me every knee shall bow, every tongue shall take an oath. He shall say, 'Surely in the LORD *I have righteousness and strength'" (Isaiah 45:22-24, NKJV).*

"To me," proclaimed Yahweh, "every knee shall bow, every tongue shall take an oath." Commenting on the two related passages above, Professor Geisler added: "Jesus is Jehovah and some day everyone will confess it."[2]

Other verses of Scripture drive home the same point. Because Moses chose to be identified with God's people, he considered "abuse suffered for the *Christ* to be greater wealth than the treasures of Egypt, for he looked to the reward. By faith he left Egypt, not being afraid of the anger of the king. For he endured as seeing the *One* who is invisible" (Hebrews 11:26-27).

Likewise, the apostle Paul reminded the Christians of his day that the ancient Israelites were punished because they had "tested *Christ*" in the wilderness, and he warned his brethren not to make the same mistake. (See I Corinthians 10:9.)[3]

In the Old Testament Yahweh was the spiritual husband of Israel.[4] The New Testament reveals *Jesus* to be the spiritual husband of the church, the spiritual successor to Israel.[5]

That misunderstood prophet, John the Baptist, gave us further evidence of the identity of Jesus. Many thought that John himself was the Messiah, but he answered that he was not. "Then who are you?" they asked. He replied: "I am the voice of one crying in the wilderness, 'Make straight the way of the Lord,' as the prophet Isaiah said" (John 1:23).

John eventually learned that "the Lord" for whom he was preparing the way was none other than Jesus of Nazareth, for John was the forerunner of *Jesus*. When he quoted from Isaiah, however, John referred to Yahweh Himself! Here is his reference from the Book of Isaiah: "A voice is crying: In the wilderness prepare the way of *Yahweh*. Make straight in the desert a highway for our *God*" (Isaiah 40:3).

John the Baptist did not misunderstand Isaiah's prophecy when he identified the Messiah as Yahweh. In addition to the Gospel of John, by inspiration Matthew, Mark, and Luke all made the same identification in their books. (See Matthew 3:1-3; Mark 1:1-8; Luke 1:76; 3:2-6.)

The Old Testament Book of Malachi also expresses this identification. Here, Yahweh Himself is the One speaking:

"Behold, I send My messenger, and he will prepare the way before Me" (Malachi 3:1, NKJV).

Because the Gospel of Mark quotes the first portion of Malachi 3:1 immediately before it quotes Isaiah 40:3, the context shows that it associates "the messenger" in Malachi with Isaiah 40:3. Before Mark quotes the two verses of Scripture, it refers to them as "prophecies" (plural) that found their fulfillment in John the Baptist. After it quotes Malachi 3:1 and Isaiah 40:3, it then describes John the Baptist's ministry, showing that he is the one who prepared the way for the Lord.

Malachi's prophecy appears to have a dual sense. Although Mark explains that the messenger in the first part of Malachi 3:1 is John the Baptist, quoting only the *first* part of that verse, the context of Malachi 3 indicates that "the Messenger of the covenant" in the *second* part of Malachi 3:1 is the Messiah Himself. The subsequent verses also confirm that the Messiah is being discussed.

Prophecy in the Old Testament often has a dual sense, and this appears to be the case with Malachi 3:1 and Mark 1:2. The New King James Version correctly recognizes this duality in Malachi 3:1 by translating the first "messenger" with a small "m" and the "he" after it with a small "h," while the "Messenger" of the covenant and the "He" referring to Him have a capital "M" and "H" since the verse identifies *Him* as "the Lord."

In Malachi 3:1 the LORD was speaking. This was Yahweh speaking. And Yahweh claimed here that the time would come when a *messenger* would appear; "and that messenger," said Yahweh, "will prepare the way before *Me*." The messenger came, and the Messiah followed—in the person of Jesus. (By "person," we refer to Jesus' physical Sonship; please note the comments in the preface regarding the use of "person" in this book.)

When the rulers of the people rejected that One and had Him crucified, another amazing prophecy from the Book of Zechariah was fulfilled. Again, Yahweh spoke through His prophet: "And I will pour on the house of David and on the inhabitants of Jerusalem the Spirit of grace and supplication; then they will look on Me whom they have pierced; they will mourn for Him as one mourns for his only son, and grieve for Him as one grieves for a firstborn" (Zechariah 12:10, NKJV).

Although some of the English translations say, "They will look on *Him* whom they have pierced," the original Hebrew has Yahweh Himself predicting, "They will look on *Me* whom they have pierced."

In the Zechariah prophecy the Hebrew word for "pierce" is *dakar*, the linguistic source of the English word "dagger," according to at least one English etymological dictionary. In any case, Semitic scholars agree that the Hebrew word definitely means "pierce." This is an amazing prophecy because it reveals several specific aspects of the Messiah's sacrificial death, stating that (1) Yahweh Himself (2) would be pierced (3) by His own people (4) at Jerusalem (5) so that the Lord Himself could later pour out the Spirit of grace and supplication (6) on a people who will mourn for Him as an *only* son (7) who is a firstborn son!

This one Old Testament verse alone establishes that Yahweh Himself would later perform the role as a son in becoming the Messiah. And many other Old Testament and New Testament passages give the same revelation.

It is interesting that Old Testament prophecy predicted that the Messiah would be "pierced," particularly since the ancient Israelites carried out the death penalty through *stoning*, not crucifixion. In looking back about two thousand years, we can appreciate that the Book of Zechariah looked ahead in anticipating that both Jews and Gentiles would be involved in the piercing of that perfect sacrifice. It is well documented that the Romans, a great Gentile empire, perfected the "art" of public execution by crucifixion. And Old Testament prophecy predicted the crucifixion of the Messiah several hundred years before Rome appeared on the scene! In this regard, the New Testament reveals that the Jewish and Roman leaders conspired together to crucify Jesus, thus fulfilling the prophecy of Zechariah 12:10 that the Messiah's own people would "pierce" Him. (See Acts 2:23, 36.)

Some have speculated that Zechariah must have known of public execution by crucifixion and that it may have been commonly practiced before the Roman Empire and perhaps as early as the Persian Empire. However, historical evidence is lacking to support this speculation. In addition, other relevant Old Testament prophecies earlier than the Book of Zechariah foretold the crucifixion of the Messiah, long before even the Persian Empire.

Psalm 22 was written about 1000 B.C., and it contains several prophecies concerning the crucifixion of the Messiah. Verse 1, which introduces the psalm, is the very verse that Jesus quoted on the cross. Verses 1, 6-8, 16, and 18 contain specific prophecies that the Nazarene fulfilled in His death, and other verses in the psalm contain general prophecies that Christ fulfilled at the same time. Verse 16 says: "For dogs have surrounded Me; the assembly of the wicked has enclosed Me. They pierced My hands and My feet" (Psalm 22:16, NKJV).

The English versions have customarily translated the

final verb of the verse as "pierced"; however, some of the translations have unfortunate, misleading editorial comments about the verse. For example, the Revised Standard Version has a footnote to the verse that states: "Gk Syr Jerome: Heb *like a lion*." The translators of the RSV and some other modern versions have translated the verb as "pierced" because of ancient versions that were *translations* of the Hebrew (e.g., the Greek Septuagint and Jerome's Latin translation). Some modern versions' footnotes on Psalm 22:16 leave the *false* impression that either all or most of the Hebrew manuscripts have "like a lion" (RSV) or "like the lion" (NIV), and not "pierced" at all!

The scholars who wrote these notes believe that the Hebrew word in the verse means "lion." It is correct that the Hebrew term, *ka'ari, could* be understood as a noun ("the lion") after a prepositional prefix ("like"), but Hebrew syntax makes it improbable. Such a translation would leave the sentence without a verb, and the awkward sense of such a sentence is noticeable even in English.

The root word of *ka'ari* is *ka'ar*, and what the liberal scholars have not admitted in the modern versions' footnotes is that *ka'ar* is a very real Hebrew verb that the Hebrew lexicons define as "to pierce"! There is even a related verb with the same root, which is pronounced *kur* and has exactly the same meaning as *ka'ar*. In addition, other Hebrew words from the same root have either identical or similar meanings.

It is possible that David was making a pun with the term. Because lions do have sharp teeth and claws, they are capable of piercing hands and feet. Also, verses 13 and 21 mention a ferocious lion. If the writer had a pun in mind, Hebrew syntax indicates that the *primary* meaning is "to pierce" from the verb *ka'ar*, with "like the lion" as a possible secondary meaning. In any case, we should translate *ka'ar* as the verb "pierce" since the Hebrew is simple and straightforward here and since the parallel clauses (so common in Hebrew poetry) in verse 16 have verbs that are parallel to the verb *ka'ar*. On the other hand, if we understood the term as something other than a verb, then we disrupt the Hebrew parallelism in the verse, and the latter part of verse 16 becomes awkward. It is no wonder that the ancient versions have the verb "to pierce" in their languages. They were simply following the original Hebrew verb that the Hebrew manuscripts still preserve.

In summary, Psalm 22:16 is another remarkable prophecy of the Messiah's suffering and death on the cross, specifying that His "hands" and "feet" will be "pierced."

This psalm, the entire chapter, is commonly known as the "Psalm of the Cross" because of its numerous prophecies that Jesus fulfilled when He went to the cross. It may be more than a coincidence that this is the twenty-second psalm, since the twenty-second and final letter of the Hebrew alphabet is *tav*. The letter *tav* in paleographic Hebrew (the ancient script) is not only in the *shape* of a cross but also actually *means* "cross"! (For further discussion of *tav*, see the section "A Mark and a Name" in chapter 8.)

Besides Zechariah 12:10 and Psalm 22:16, Isaiah 53:5 is another verse of Scripture which predicts that the Messiah would be pierced. The Hebrew word *khalal* in verse 5, which is normally translated as "wounded," generally means "slain"—and specifically "pierced"! A related word, *khalil*, means "something hollowed out; a pipe; a lute." Some Semitic scholars believe that the English words "hollow" and "hole" come from the Hebrew root *khalal*. The New International Version and the New American Standard Version correctly translate *khalal* in Isaiah 53:5 as "pierced."

Like Psalm 22, Isaiah 53 is another majestic chapter that describes several aspects of the Messiah's suffering and crucifixion. And like Psalm 22, Isaiah 53 was written long before *either* the Roman Empire *or* the Persian Empire appeared on the scene. Therefore, we can be certain that the Messianic "piercing" prophecies in the Old Testament were not borrowed from the contemporary practice of a pagan nation, despite what some liberal scholars claim.

The Messiah was pierced and put to death as if He were a common criminal, thus fulfilling Isaiah 53 and other prophecies like it. But the bonds of death could not hold that One. In Paul's words: "There it is said, When He ascended on high, He led a host of captives; and He gave gifts to men. In saying, He ascended, what does it mean but that He had also descended into the lower parts of the earth? He who descended is He who also ascended far above all the heavens, that He might fill all things" (Ephesians 4:9-10).

The apostle here discussed the death, resurrection, and ascension of Jesus Christ, as we noted in chapter 1. But did he not realize that he was appropriating for Jesus another *Yahweh* passage from the Old Testament Scriptures? Indeed, Paul certainly knew, for he knew the Hebrew Scriptures well. Before his conversion, he had been taught from those Scriptures as a Pharisee "zealous after the law." And his teacher had been the famous Gamaliel, the most renowned Jewish teacher of that time. Thus when Paul wrote the foregoing passage, he naturally realized that he was quoting from the Book of Psalms, where David had praised Yahweh. We referred to this psalm in chapter 1 in our discussion of *Adonai*. Here is the complete passage from Psalms:

"The chariots of God are twenty thousand, even thousands of thousands; the Lord is among them as in Sinai, in the Holy Place. You have ascended on high, You have led captivity captive; You have received gifts among men, even from the rebellious, that the LORD God might dwell there. Blessed be the Lord, who daily loads us with benefits, the God of our salvation! Selah. Our God is the God of salvation; and to GOD the Lord belong escapes from death" (Psalm 68:17-20, NKJV).

As we discussed in Chapter 1, by identifying the risen Christ in Ephesians 4:8-10 with the God of Psalm 68:17-20, the Bible gives us a great revelation that Jesus Himself is Yahweh, Yah, Adonai, El, and Elohim. As the apostle Paul said, "He who descended is also the One who ascended far above all the heavens, that He might fill all things" (Ephesians 4:10, NKJV).

The Great "I Am"

We saw in the first chapter of this investigation that the most popular appellation for God in the Old Testament was the unique name *Yahweh*. Consequently, for the inspired writers of the New Testament to identify that name with Jesus is not something we can take lightly.

Dr. Harry Rimmer well stated that "this subject is too important to pass over quickly. What we are saying now is that Jehovah, the God of the Old Testament, is the same person as Jesus, the Savior of New Testament records."[6]

This subject is certainly "too important to pass over quickly." So let us now turn our attention to the Book of Exodus, where we find Moses experiencing a strange encounter with God at a burning bush. Moses was a mere shepherd at the time, but God had plans for this shepherd. So He appeared to him and identified Himself as Yahweh, the God of his fathers.

> *"And God said to Moses, 'I AM WHO I AM.' And He said, 'Thus you shall say to the children of Israel, "I AM has sent me to you."' Moreover God said to Moses, 'Thus you shall say to the children of Israel: "The LORD [Yahweh] God of your fathers . . . has sent me to you. This is My name forever"'" (Exodus 3:14-15, NKJV).*

Moses had just asked the Lord His name (Exodus 3:13), and in answering this question, God used "I AM" interchangeably with the name "Yahweh"—"the LORD." We saw earlier that the name "Yahweh" signifies in the Hebrew the idea of "self-derived and permanent existence."[7] The very basis of this name is derived from the Hebrew of "I Am." Why? A scholar answers that "we must connect the name *Jehovah* with the Hebrew substantive verb *to be*, with the inference that it expresses the essential, eternal unchangeable *being* of Jehovah."[8]

His name *identifies* Him to His people. The God of Israel is not a piece of wood or a stone. He is not an idol or an image carved out by the hands of humans. He is not dead. On the contrary, Yahweh makes Himself known as the self-existent, eternal One—the great I Am.

Do we fully appreciate what Jesus Christ claimed in the New Testament record when He referred to *Himself* as the I Am? From the eighth chapter of John, we hear the Christ declaring:

> *"'Your father Abraham rejoiced to see My day, and he saw it and was glad.' Then the Jews said to Him, 'You are not yet fifty years old, and have You seen Abraham?' Jesus said to them, 'Most assuredly, I say to you, before Abraham was, I AM.' Then they took up stones to throw at Him; but Jesus hid Himself and went out of the temple, going through the midst of them, and so passed by" (John 8:56-59, NKJV).*

Yahweh had appeared to Abraham on a number of occasions. Did Jesus claim that He Himself was the great I Am—the God of the Old Testament who had made Himself known to Abraham, Moses, and the prophets? Obviously, the Jews nearby who heard Jesus' statement took it in that light. They then made a vain attempt to stone to death the Nazarene for what they thought was blasphemy!

Besides the New King James Version, several other versions have also brought out the point of Jesus' words. The New Testament in Modern English by J. B. Phillips renders the "I Am" in all capital letters: "'I tell you in solemn truth,' returned Jesus, 'before there was an Abraham, I AM!'"

Likewise, the careful New American Standard Bible

and other English translations capitalize the "I Am," evidently because the scholars of these versions are aware that Jesus was specifically identifying Himself as the great I Am of the Hebrew Scriptures.

While a recent edition of the Revised Standard Version did not capitalize the phrase, the editors made an interesting comment in a footnote to John 8:58: "The *I am* is the divine name (Exodus 3:14), a claim to pre-existence and oneness with God (John 10:30-33)."[9]

For those who might question this line of thought, we should note that Jesus did *not* say, "Before Abraham was, I *was*." He said, "Before Abraham was, I *Am*." What else could it be other than the divine name? Indeed, this is why His Jewish hearers tried to stone Him to death. (See also John 18:5-8, where Jesus may have associated "I Am" with Himself again, since the clause "I am He" does not have "He" in the Greek. It is interesting that the Jewish guards were in shock in verse 6 when Jesus said, "I Am.")

What more can we say? Jesus said it all. By associating Himself with the "I Am," He directly made the claim to be Yahweh. It is indeed ironic that when He made the claim, misguided Jews began to pick up rocks in an attempt to stone to death the *Rock* of Israel!

The Rock

From earliest times the Israelites metaphorically looked to God as their "Rock"—their foundation. Moses declared to his people:

"I will proclaim the name of Yahweh. Ascribe greatness to our God. He is the Rock, and His work is

53

*perfect; for all His ways are justice. A God of faithful-
ness and without iniquity; just and right is He!"
(Deuteronomy 32:3-4).*

Again in the same chapter he chastised the Hebrew
nation: "You were unmindful of the *Rock* that begot you,
and you forgot the God who gave you birth"
(Deuteronomy 32:18).

Through Isaiah, Yahweh declared to the house of
Israel: "Fear not, nor be afraid. Have I not told you from
of old and declared it? And you are My witnesses. Is there
a God beside Me? There is no Rock beside Me. *I* know not
any" (Isaiah 44:8).

King David beautifully expressed the same thought:
"My soul waits for God alone; from Him comes my salvation. He *alone* is my Rock and my salvation" (Psalm
62:1-2).

Through the pen of His spokesmen the prophets, God
predicted that the time would come when He, the Rock of
Israel, would become a sanctuary for some but a Rock of
offense for others: "Regard Yahweh of hosts as holy; let
Him be your fear and your dread. And He will become a
sanctuary, but also a stone of stumbling and a rock of
offense to both houses of Israel" (Isaiah 8:13-14).

This amazing prophecy found its fulfillment in Jesus;
for it was *Christ*, as Yahweh, who became a rock of
offense to the unbelievers. Jesus Himself merely quoted
David and the Book of Psalms when He asked the inhabitants of Jerusalem:

*"Did you never read in the Scriptures: 'The stone
which the builders rejected has become the chief cor-*

nerstone. This was the LORD's [Yahweh's] doing, and it is marvelous in our eyes'? Therefore I say to you, the kingdom of God will be taken from you and given to a nation bearing the fruits of it. And whoever falls on this stone will be broken; but on whomever it falls, it will grind him to powder" (Matthew 21:42-44, NKJV). (See Psalm 118:22-23.)

The context of this passage indicates that the Jewish leaders of the day knew Jesus was discussing *their* rejection of Him as the Messiah.[10] Nevertheless His scathing indictment did not convince and convict them—because of stubborn wills and closed minds. The religious establishment of that age conspired and finally had the Christ put to death.

But by rising from the grave, Jesus proved to humanity that He was, in fact, the "Rock of Ages." Accordingly, His disciples began to shout this truth to the world. Peter proclaimed: "This is the 'stone which was rejected by you builders, which has become the chief cornerstone'" (Acts 4:11, NKJV). (See Psalm 118:22-23.)

Paul told his readers concerning Jesus: "As it is written: 'Behold I lay in Zion a stumbling stone and rock of offense, and whoever believes on Him will not be put to shame'" (Romans 9:33, NKJV). (See Isaiah 28:16.)

Humanity has invented various religions and many gods. Many have rejected the God of the Bible, but such rejection will bring consequences. Jesus, the Rock, is precious to those who believe in Him and seek His guidance for their lives, but He is a rock of offense to those who reject Him—whether they be Jews or Gentiles.

An apostle reminded Hebrew Christians in the first

century: "I want you to know, brethren, that our fathers were all under the cloud, and all passed through the sea. And all were baptized unto Moses in the cloud and in the sea. All ate the same spiritual food, and all drank the same spiritual drink. For they drank from the spiritual Rock that followed them. And that Rock was Christ" (I Corinthians 10:1-4).

In a comment on the foregoing passage, the Biblical scholar Leon Morris was certainly correct when he stated regarding the apostle Paul's intent in I Corinthians 10:1-4: "He refers to Christ. In doing so he transfers to the Lord the title, 'the Rock,' used in the Old Testament of Jehovah (Deuteronomy xxxii.15; Psalm xviii.2, etc.)."[11] Thus according to Paul, as Moses led the Israelites out of Egypt toward the Promised Land, Christ was there. Christ was that Rock—Yahweh Himself!

It behooves us to build our lives upon the foundation of *that* Rock. All else is simply sinking sand, which drifts away with the passing of time.

The Good Shepherd

Most of us are acquainted with the words of Psalm 23:

"The LORD is my Shepherd; I shall not want. He makes me to lie down in green pastures; He leads me beside the still waters" (Psalm 23:1-2, NKJV).

To the psalmist, Yahweh is the Shepherd, and we are His sheep. Several writers in the Old Testament depicted Yahweh as the Shepherd—the good Shepherd who cares for His sheep. It is no coincidence that the New Testament depicts Jesus as the good Shepherd. For in

Jesus Yahweh continues the role of a shepherd. The Christ announced:

- *"I am the good Shepherd. I know My own, and My own know me" (John 10:14).*
- *"I am the good Shepherd. The good Shepherd lays down His life for His sheep" (John 10:11).*

Yahweh, as Jesus, is the good Shepherd who *has* laid down His life for His sheep. *His* sheep know His voice and are known by Him. In a parable comparing human beings to sheep who become lost, Jesus said that there is great joy in heaven when only one lost sheep is found—when one human being repents and turns again to the Shepherd for guidance.[12] There is joy in heaven because He is the *good* Shepherd who cares for His sheep.

On a certain day when Jesus of Nazareth observed the multitudes before Him, "He was moved with compassion toward them, because they were as sheep not having a shepherd. And He began to teach them many things" (Mark 6:34).

Jesus also expressed this concern after His crucifixion and subsequent resurrection. At least three times the risen Christ instructed Peter: "Feed My sheep!" (John 21:15-17).

After Jesus' ascension into the heavens, the apostle Peter did just that, as one of the spiritual leaders of God's church in the first century. In obvious reference to the Christ, this apostle reminded fellow Christians: "For you were like sheep going astray, but have now returned to the Shepherd and Overseer of your souls" (I Peter 2:25, NKJV). Similarly, he wrote concerning the second coming of Jesus:

"And when the Chief Shepherd appears, you will receive the crown of glory that does not fade away" (I Peter 5:4, NKJV).

According to the Book of Hebrews, "our Lord Jesus" is the "great Shepherd of the sheep" (Hebrews 13:20).

Some people have the concept of an Old Testament God who was harsh, stern, and without mercy. But the Bible presents a Yahweh who possessed the attributes of grace and mercy—a compassionate Shepherd. The following passage is a metaphor not only of the power of God but also His gentleness: "See, the Sovereign LORD comes with power, and his arm rules for him. See, his reward is with him, and his recompense accompanies him. He tends his flock like a shepherd: he gathers the lambs in his arms and carries them close to his heart; he gently leads those that have young" (Isaiah 40:10-11, NIV).

The Bible plainly states: "And there will be one flock and one shepherd" (John 10:16, NKJV). One Shepherd! While David of old cried out, "Yahweh is my Shepherd," Jesus says to you and me: "*I* am the good Shepherd" (John 10:11, 14).

The Author of Life

A great edifice demands the existence of an architect to construct it. The existence of physical laws, such as gravity, demands a Lawgiver to create and sustain those laws. Life demands a Life-giver, since life only comes *from* life. The creation demands a Creator. And the evidence of the Creator is all around:

"For since the creation of the world His invisible attributes are clearly seen, being understood by the

things that are made, even His eternal power and Godhead, so that they are without excuse" (Romans 1:20, NKJV).

Paul warned that the atheists and the skeptics are *without* excuse. Madalyn Murray O'Hair? Without excuse. Robert Ingersoll? Without excuse. Voltaire? Without excuse. And Thomas Paine has not been the only skeptic who has cried out from his deathbed for his God to forgive him!

God Almighty challenges the atheists and the skeptics of our day by asking through Job of old, "Where were you when I laid the foundations of the earth? Tell Me, if you have understanding. Who determined its measurements? Surely you know! Or who stretched the line upon it? . . . Can you bind the cluster of the Pleiades, or loose the belt of Orion? Can you bring out Mazzaroth in its season? Or can you guide the Great Bear with its cubs? Do you know the ordinances of the heavens? Can you set their dominion over the earth?" (Job 38:4-5, 31-33, NKJV).

Two honest evolutionists who are scientists *have* replied to the above challenge—frankly speaking on behalf of their evolutionist contemporaries. They have admitted: "At the moment, we have to confess that our *ignorance* of the actual creation is more or less complete!"[13]

The ignorance of humans is "more or less complete" if they reject the record of the creation as found in Genesis. Their ignorance is more or less complete if they refuse to acknowledge the evidence of a Creator in that creation. Their ignorance is more or less complete if they choose to grasp a *theory* that has yet to be proved after thousands of years of the most intensive investigation and speculation. (Theories of evolution were expounded by the ancient philosophers!)

The Bible gives the ultimate answers that the various theories of evolution do not and cannot give. Christianity has the answers because it points us to the One who is not only a Creator but who is *interested* in His creation. In this regard, Dr. Carl Henry has pointed out: "Christianity says at the same time that Jesus Christ who is the Redeemer is also the Creator."[14]

Jesus the Creator? Why would this famous theologian make such a statement? When we turn to the Bible, we begin to find out.

According to the Gospel of John, God, as the Word, "became flesh and dwelt among us" in the person of Jesus of Nazareth. In John's words:

"In the beginning was the Word, and the Word was with God, and the Word was God. . . . All things were made through Him, and without Him nothing was made that was made. In Him was life" (John 1:1, 3-4, NKJV).

"All things," John stated, "were made through Him." Some other creator did not create this One, for He Himself brought *all* things into existence. Because this One is eternal, He was there "in the beginning" of the creation of all things.

The Gospel of John reveals that God Himself was the Word. According to John, God, as the Word, became personified in Jesus in order to communicate with us in a personal way as a human being:

"And the Word became flesh and dwelt among us, and we beheld His glory" (John 1:14, NKJV).

Just as our words represent us, the Word of God represents Him and cannot be separated from Him. Therefore, the Word (1) is "with" (Greek, *pros*: "toward, pertaining to") God and (2) *is* God (John 1:1-2).

The Book of Genesis immediately informs us that the Lord brought His creation into existence by using *words* (Genesis 1:1-31; 2:1-3). David said the same thing: "By the Word of *Yahweh* the heavens were made, and all their host at *His* command!" (Psalm 33:6). (See also Hebrews 11:3.)

This Creator put on flesh, and His creation refused to recognize Him for what He was. John testified: "He was in the world, and the world was made through Him. Yet the world did not know Him. And He came to His *own things* [literal Greek]; and His own people did not receive Him" (John 1:10-11).

The phrase "His *own* things" signifies ownership, as the scholars are aware. Jesus came to His *own* land, His *own* people, His *own* world—His *own* possessions! "Yet," John stated, "His own did not know Him." His own rejected Him. His own conspired against Him. His own put Him to death! By asking for the release of Barabbas and demanding the death of Jesus, "you people," said Peter, "disowned the Holy and Righteous One and asked that a murderer be released to you. You killed the author of life" (Acts 3:14-15, NIV; see also RSV).

Some translations have "the Prince of life," but the Greek is more correctly translated as "the Author of life." The Greek word in question is *archegos*, and the Greek

lexicons render it either as (1) "leader, ruler, prince" or
(2) "author, originator, pioneer, founder." However, the
lexicons normally give Acts 5:31 as the *only* New
Testament reference in which "prince, ruler, or leader" is
the "more likely" meaning. This is because the New
Testament customarily uses the related Greek word
archon for "ruler" or "prince" in the New Testament.

Actually, the context shows that the meaning of
archegos in Acts 3:15 is "Author." Let us notice the irony
of Peter's words. First of all, he contrasted Barabbas, a
murderer, with Jesus, the Author of life. Second, the murderer was spared and released, while the Author of life
was condemned and put to death. (Compare Acts 3:14-15
with Matthew 27:15-26.) Third, the name *Barabbas* literally means in Aramaic "the son of the father"—a human
father—in contrast to Jesus, the Son of God, the heavenly
Father. Fourth, the apostle Peter reminded his audience
that "the Author of life," who had been put to death, had
indeed risen *from* the dead. In this regard, it is important
to remember that even though the Man from Nazareth
was killed, dying on the cross for our sins, the eternal
Spirit that was in Jesus, "the Author of life," never did die.

Archegos is the word that Hebrews 2:10 uses when it
refers to Jesus as the "Author" of our salvation. (See NKJV
and NIV.) It also appears in Hebrews 12:2, which calls
Jesus "the Author" and Finisher of our faith. (See NKJV
and NIV.) The Author and Finisher of our faith (Hebrews
12:2) and the Author of our salvation (Hebrews 2:10) is
the same Author of *life* whom Peter discussed in Acts
3:15. It was as the Author of life that Jesus Himself had
earlier predicted, in speaking of His physical body:
"Destroy this temple, and in three days *I* will raise it up!"

(John 2:19, 21). As the Author of life, this One could not be bound by physical death, for God is an *eternal* Spirit.

Being both Lord and Spirit, Jesus Christ continues to hold together the universe by the very *power* of His Being:

"For in Him all things were created, in heaven and on earth, visible and invisible, whether thrones or dominions or principalities or authorities—all things were created through Him and for Him. He is before all things; and in Him all things hold together!" *(Colossians 1:16-17).*

This passage is discussing Jesus Christ, for the writer continued in the next verse: "He is the head of the body, the church. He is the beginning, the firstborn *from the dead*—that in all things He might have the preeminence!" (Colossians 1:18).

Jesus has the preeminence precisely because He is the Creator of all things. Even during His earthly ministry the Christ exhibited the characteristics of Yahweh, the Creator.

As Creator, Jesus supernaturally brought food into existence in order to feed several thousand people. As Creator, Christ displayed complete control over the forces of nature when He said, "Peace! Be still!" As Creator, He miraculously healed the sick and gave speech to the dumb, hearing to the deaf, and sight to the blind. As Creator, Jesus Christ commanded the dead Lazarus to come forth from a tomb—thus *re*-creating life from dead flesh! And as Creator, Jesus Himself rose from the grave as a "life-giving Spirit" (I Corinthians 15:45).

This One is our Creator, who has promised to create *eternal* life within the very beings of those who trust Him and obey Him. "Therefore, let those who suffer according to God's will do right and entrust their souls to a faithful Creator" (I Peter 4:19).

Jesus: Yahweh-Savior

Two statements from the Book of Isaiah declare to us that Yahweh considers Himself to be Savior, and He alone:

- *"I am Yahweh your God, the Holy One of Israel, your Savior" (Isaiah 43:3).*
- *"I, even I, am Yahweh; and beside Me there is no savior" (Isaiah 43:11).*

Through Hosea we have the same testimony from Yahweh: "There is no savior beside Me" (Hosea 13:4).

The days will come, according to the prophets, when the people will rejoice in Yahweh as their Savior. God predicted through Isaiah: "And in that day you will say: 'O LORD I will praise You; though You were angry with me, Your anger is turned away, and You comfort me. Behold, God is my salvation, I will trust and not be afraid; 'for YAH, the LORD, is my strength and my song; He also has become my salvation'" (Isaiah 12:1-2, NKJV).

Would the LORD God Himself of the Old Testament become our salvation? This is what was prophesied, and if we accept the claims of Jesus, we must acknowledge that in *Him* Yahweh has become our salvation. The writers of the New Testament referred to Jesus as Savior many times (Titus 2:13; I John 4:14, etc.). Concerning the virgin Mary and the Savior who was about to come into the world, an angel informed Joseph:

"She shall bring forth a Son. And you shall call His name Jesus, for He shall save His people from their sins" (Matthew 1:21).

This verse takes on significance when we recognize what that name means. The English word "Jesus" is actually from the Greek form of the Hebrew name "Joshua." The name "Joshua" means "Savior." Thus a reliable source informs us that in Matthew 1:21 "the Hebrew and Aramaic forms of *'Jesus'* and *'he will save'* are similar. The point could be suggested by translating, 'You shall call his name "Savior" because he will save.'"[15]

The careful translation of Charles B. Williams illustrates that in this verse the Greek verb is an "imperative future indicative." Therefore, Dr. Williams correctly rendered the clause: "You *must* name Him Jesus" (Matthew 1:21).

He must be named "Jesus"—"Savior"—simply because He, and only He, is the One who can save His people from their sins.

We should note, however, that the rendering of "Savior" only gives *part* of the Hebrew meaning. In the original Hebrew, "Joshua" literally means "Yahweh saves" or "Yahweh-Savior"![16] The first syllable of "Joshua" in the Hebrew is *Yah*, an abbreviated form of *Yahweh*, and *Yah* is the form in Isaiah 12:1-2, which we just quoted. The name *Yah*, as another form of *Yahweh*, was used many times in the Old Testament.[17] In the Psalms, King David was fond of using the word "praise" with "Yah" in the well-known exultation *Hallelujah*, which actually means "Praise the LORD"—"Praise Yah!"

It is no accident that the Hebrew term for "salvation" in Isaiah 12:1-2 and elsewhere in the Old Testament is very close in sound to the Hebrew pronunciation of "Jesus." This is because both the Hebrew noun for "salvation" (*yoshuah*) and the Hebrew name for "Jesus"— "Joshua" (*Yehoshua*)—are two forms of the same root word, which means "salvation, savior," as just noted concerning Matthew 1:21.

Because "Yah" is the prefix of the name "Jesus," we today, in praising Jesus as our Savior, can agree with Isaiah in singing: "For YAH, the LORD, is my strength and my song; He also has become my salvation!" (Isaiah 12:1-2, NKJV).

Since the name "Jesus" means in the Hebrew language "Yahweh-Savior," God has literally stamped upon the Messiah's name (1) His *own* name—*Yahweh*—and (2) His own title—*Savior*.

Thus His very name directly identifies Jesus as the God of the Old Testament Scriptures. The great I Am, the Rock, the Shepherd, the Creator—Yahweh Himself—has *become* our Savior; and the name "Jesus" affirms it: *Yahweh-Savior*.[18]

Chapter 3

Son of Man

What we have already studied has confirmed from the Biblical testimony that (1) Yahweh is one mighty Spirit-Being who rules this universe, and (2) approximately two thousand years ago this One clothed Himself in the humanity and person of Jesus of Nazareth.

The present chapter will establish from the Biblical record that (1) the Sonship of Jesus was to be temporary and (2) it involved the role of God (the Spirit) dwelling in the physical human form of the Nazarene.

We shall see that Jesus did not have a human father. Because He was conceived miraculously by the Holy Spirit of God, He was fully God. Because He was brought forth as a physical Son, He was also fully human. It is important to remember that because of the incarnation of

God—the Spirit of God dwelling in human flesh—Jesus had two completely different natures: divine and human.

In addition, it is important to remember that I Timothy 3:16 calls this incarnation of God the "mystery of godliness." Although the Bible says nothing about the mystery of a trinity or the mystery of the nature of the Godhead, this majestic verse of Scripture describes the mystery of godliness in reference to the time when "God was manifested in the flesh" and justified in the Spirit. I Timothy 3:16 shows that the mystery of godliness is concerned with the two natures of Jesus and what He did as the divine Messiah.

It is a mystery because we as human beings cannot absolutely comprehend how Jesus could have two natures that would make him both fully God and fully man. Although we cannot understand this mystery of God becoming a Son in order to die for our sins, we can firmly believe that it happened, and we can have a strong faith whose foundation is in the Word of God. The Nazarene proved that He was the Messiah by fulfilling hundreds of Old Testament prophecies in detail. Jesus Christ demonstrated both by His words and His actions that He was far more than mere mortal flesh.

The Bible calls Christ the "Son of God" and the "Son of Man." The first title emphasizes His complete deity while the second title emphasizes His complete humanity.

If Jesus was indeed God in the flesh, what does the New Testament mean when it speaks of Him as being "at the right hand of God"? This and other similar phrases appear in both the Old and New Testaments and are significant because they describe characteristics of the Sonship of God, which He created in the Nazarene.

At the Right Hand of God

Jesus Himself began to clarify the mystery of the "right hand" phrases when He asked the Pharisees to answer an intriguing question about the Messiah from the Psalms. Here is the account of this discussion according to the Gospel of Matthew:

> *"While the Pharisees were gathered together, Jesus asked them, saying, 'What do you think about the Christ? Whose Son is He?' They said to Him, 'The Son of David.' He said to them, 'How then does David in the Spirit call Him "Lord," saying: "The LORD said to my Lord, 'Sit at My right hand till I make Your enemies Your footstool'?" If David then calls Him "Lord," how is He his Son?'" (Matthew 22:41-45, NKJV).*

Because of their blindness, the Pharisees were not able to answer this penetrating question by Jesus of how David could call his descendant both his Son and his Lord. By having the inspired revelation of the New Testament, we today know that the Messiah was a Son because of His humanity and was Lord because of His deity. By quoting Psalm 110:1 in the above narrative, Jesus confirmed that this verse of Scripture is a prophecy about Himself as the Son. Because of this, it is important for us to go to Psalm 110 and see what David was prophesying about the Messiah throughout the psalm.

In verse 1 David began by saying, "The LORD said to my Lord." The first "LORD" (with all capital letters) is the Hebrew name for *Yahweh*. The second "Lord" is the English title for the Hebrew word *Adoni*, who is later called *Adonai* in verse 5. We saw earlier that David repeatedly identified Yahweh as Adonai. (See the section "Adonai Is Yahweh" in chapter 1, paying particular attention to the discussions of Psalm 16:1-2 and Psalm 68:17-20.)

Because King David explained throughout the Psalms that Yahweh Himself *is* Adonai, then we must obviously take Psalm 110 in a figurative sense. The Lord God spoke metaphorically to Himself in Psalm 110:1.

In His profound wisdom, God led David to use the Hebrew terms *Adoni* and *Adonai* in this psalm. As we saw in chapter 1, *Adonai* was not only an exalted title for God as "the Lord" in the Old Testament, but the term was also sometimes used for a *man* (e.g., I Samuel 29:8). In fact, *Adon, Adoni*, and *Adonai* were all exalted titles that were used for both God *and* man. It was appropriate for Yahweh (LORD) in Psalm 110 to refer to Himself as the coming physical Son by using the exalted titles *Adoni* and *Adonai* for "Lord" in verses 1 and 5, since the Messiah would be *both* God and man!

When David prophesied about the Messiah by writing, "The LORD said to my Lord, 'Sit at My right hand *until* I make Your enemies Your footstool,'" he specifically revealed that the Sonship of God in Jesus would be temporary. The apostle Paul revealed the same thing in I Corinthians 15:25, when he also used the word "until."

In Psalm 110 the metaphorical language of verse 1 continues in the following verses. Let us notice what verse 2 says regarding Adoni: "The LORD will send the rod of *Your* strength out of Zion." Even though the rod of strength will be sent from the LORD (Yahweh), it is actually the rod of Adoni's strength as well! Yahweh then "told" Adoni to rule in the midst of His enemies.

In verse 3 Adoni is told that His people will be "volunteers" (Christians?) in the day of His power. Adoni is then informed: "In the beauties of holiness, from the womb of the morning, You have the dew of Your *youth*" (Psalm 110:3).

In the figurative, symbolic language of this verse ("the womb of the morning"), there is another hint of the coming Sonship of the Lord. The Hebrew word for "youth" here is *yalduthekha*, and the root of this term is *yalad*, "to bring forth, to give birth." The verb *yalad* forms the Hebrew noun *yeled*, which means "child, son." Thus, besides *Adoni* and *Adonai*, here is another term in Psalm 110 that points ahead to the physical Sonship of the Lord in the Messiah!

In verse 4 Yahweh prophesied concerning Adoni (and Adonai): "The LORD has sworn and will not relent, 'You are a priest forever according to the order of Melchizedek'" (Psalm 110:4, NKJV).

The Book of Hebrews quotes this verse at different times to show that the risen Christ (Messiah) has become a glorified high priest after offering Himself as the perfect, sinless, human sacrifice on the cross for the sins of humanity.

Verse 5 states that "the Lord [*Adonai*] is at Your [Yahweh's] right hand," and yet the verse then says that Adonai is the One who shall "execute kings in the day of His wrath."

Verse 6 further discusses the role of Adonai as Lord and Judge of the earth, telling us that He "shall judge among the nations." This agrees with New Testament doctrine which teaches that Christ Himself will be our Judge (II Corinthians 5:10).

In summary, Psalm 110 reveals the following: (1)

Yahweh tells Adoni to sit at His right hand until He makes His enemies His footstool (verse 1). (2) Yahweh Himself will send out the rod of Adoni's strength (verse 2). (3) Adoni's people will be volunteers in the day of His power (verse 3). (4) Yahweh has sworn that Adoni will be a priest forever after the order of Melchizedek (verse 4). (5) Adoni is then identified to be Adonai; and although Adonai is at Yahweh's right hand, Adonai Himself will execute kings in the day of His wrath (verse 5). (6) Adonai Himself will be judge among the nations (verse 6).

We must read the dialogue of Yahweh and Adonai in this psalm in a metaphorical sense because David revealed elsewhere in the Psalms that Yahweh Himself is Adonai. Therefore, in Psalm 110 David anticipated the roles of God as Father (Yahweh) and Son (Adonai) when the Messiah would later come into the world. While David called Adonai "youth" in Psalm 110:3, Jesus called Him "Son"—in obvious reference to Himself. Jesus, of course, knew that Yahweh and Adonai were the same Lord because He Himself was that one Lord who had become a Son. Although Jesus' contemporary Jews also realized that there is one Lord, they could not understand how David could call his Lord his son unless or until they comprehended and accepted the incarnation of God in the Messiah as the Son of God and the Son of Man.

It is important to keep in mind that the words "Sit at My right hand" in Psalm 110:1 are figurative. This language focuses on the role of God as a Son.

At the Right Hand of Power

The "right hand" phrases are expressions of honor, power, and glory. "The right hand of God" means not simply God's right hand but basically His right side, including His right arm and hand. In the Hebrew, the word "hand," *yad*, is not present. The Hebrew term is *yamin* and means both "right side" and "prosperity."

It is a Hebrew concept that appears many times in the Old Testament, and frequently the word "arm," *zero'a*, appears in the same verse or the same context as *yamin*.

The following passages show beyond a shadow of a doubt that the "right hand" of the Lord is exalted, figurative terminology for the prosperity, glory, honor, and power of the Lord Himself. Many verses from the Psalms show that David was actually praising the Lord when he wrote of His right hand or arm. Psalm 17:7 says, "Show Your marvelous lovingkindness by Your right hand, O You who save those who trust in You."

Psalm 18:32 reminds us that it is God who "arms" us with strength and who makes our way perfect. Here, the word "arm" is used as a verb in the Hebrew, and it is associated with strength and power. We today have carried over the same concept in modern English. From the word "arm," we speak of arms, armed, firearms, armor, armory, and army in reference to strength, power, and might. Whenever a soldier today is said to be heavily armed, it does not mean that he literally has many human limbs or arms as part of his physical body. Everyone recognizes that the word "armed" and similar terms are to be taken in a metaphorical sense.

David once praised the Lord by saying: "You have also given me the shield of Your salvation; Your right hand has held me up, Your gentleness has made me great" (Psalm 18:35, NKJV). Here, the Lord's right hand is correlated with His own gentleness and His own salvation.

David realized that the Israelites did not conquer the land of Canaan by "their own arm." On the contrary, David acknowledged to the Lord, "It was *Your* right hand, *Your* arm, and the light of Your countenance because You favored them" (Psalm 44:3, NKJV).

When King David praised the Lord because His "right hand is full of righteousness" (Psalm 48:10), he naturally meant that the Lord Himself is full of righteousness.

In Psalm 89 the king of Israel glorified God by saying: "You have a mighty arm; strong is Your hand, and high is Your right hand. Righteousness and justice are the foundation of Your throne; mercy and truth go before Your face" (Psalm 89:13-14, NKJV). In this passage, the references to the Lord's mighty arm, His strong hand, and His high right hand were David's way of honoring the Lord Himself; he was not honoring a literal arm or a literal hand.

A few psalms later, the writer sang to Yahweh because "He has done marvelous things," adding: "His right hand and His holy arm have gained Him the victory. The Lord has made known His salvation" (Psalm 98:1-2, NKJV). Yahweh's "right hand" and "His holy arm" are, of course, figurative terms for God Himself; His "holy arm" refers to the holiness of the Lord.

Psalm 118 says: "The right hand of the Lord is exalted; the right hand of the Lord does valiantly" (Psalm 118:16, NKJV). This verse exalts the Lord. *He* does valiantly—not simply His right hand.

Later, when the writer stated that the Lord brought Israel out of Egypt "with a strong hand and with an outstretched arm," he praised both the Lord's strength and His compassion, adding that "*His* mercy endures forever" (Psalm 136:1-2).

Finally, David worshiped the Lord for His omnipotence and omnipresence when he freely acknowledged: "If I take the wings of the morning, and dwell in the uttermost parts of the sea, even there Your hand shall lead me, and Your right hand shall hold me" (Psalm 139:9-10, NKJV). Here, in beautiful, symbolic language, ancient Israel's king used the terms "hand" and "right hand" to represent both the almighty power and the tender, loving care of his Lord.

It is obvious that in *all* of the preceding verses of Scripture the psalmist used terminology in a figurative sense for the power and glory of the Lord God Himself.

Aside from the Book of Psalms, other Old Testament writers were also fond of using such terminology. The prophet Isaiah, in particular, gave us some specific, fascinating answers regarding the Messiah and "the right hand of God" phraseology.

Isaiah 40, like many other chapters in the book, is a prophecy of the coming Messiah. This is why the following verses are so significant: "Behold, the Lord GOD shall come with a strong hand, and His arm shall rule for Him; behold, His reward is with Him, and His work before Him. He will feed His flock like a shepherd; He will gather the lambs with His arm, and carry them in His bosom, and gently lead those who are with young" (Isaiah 40:10-11, NKJV).

In the phrase "a strong hand" of verse 10, "hand" is not in the Hebrew, although it is implied since "His arm" is present in both of the verses. As we pointed out earlier, the phrase "right hand" in the Old Testament is normally *yamin* and literally means "the right" or "the right side." Even though the Hebrew word *yad*, "hand," is usually not present, the English translators are not far from the original idea when they translate *yamin* as "right hand." However, we must remember that because *yamin* means "the right side," it is a concept that includes not only "the right hand" but also "the right *arm*." The point is that the Old Testament writers used symbolic language for the power of the Lord. While both the KJV and NKJV have "strong hand" in Isaiah 40:10, the NIV simply has the word "power."

The foregoing passage in Isaiah 40 is an amazing prophecy about both the power and the gentleness of the divine Messiah. Verse 10 identifies Him as "the Lord GOD," *Adonai Yahweh*. Just as David identified Adonai with Yahweh throughout the Psalms, Isaiah did the same thing here. Like Psalm 110, Isaiah 40:10 indicates the two roles of God in one divine Messiah—*Adonai* pointing to the flesh and *Yahweh* pointing to the Spirit of God that was in the flesh known as Jesus of Nazareth.

Let us notice Isaiah 40:10 a little more closely. Verse 10 discusses the power of the Messiah's salvation and His rule. He will come with a strong hand—with power; His *arm* shall rule for Him; His reward is with Him; and His "work" will go before Him.

Verse 11 speaks of the Messiah as a Shepherd. He will feed His flock like a Shepherd; He will gather the lambs with His *arm* and carry them in His bosom. He will gently lead the sheep that are with young. This prophetic language reminds us of Jesus, who is "the good Shepherd" and who "gives His life for the sheep" (John 10:11).

Only a few verses earlier in Isaiah 40 is verse 3, the well-known passage of Scripture that the Gospel writers quote as a prophecy that Jesus and John the Baptist fulfilled: "The voice of one crying in the wilderness: 'Prepare the way of the LORD; make straight in the desert a high-way for our God'" (Isaiah 40:3, NKJV).

We saw earlier that Matthew 3:1-3, Mark 1:1-8, Luke 3:2-6, and John 1:19-23 all testify that Isaiah 40:3 is a prophecy which found its fulfillment in John the Baptist (the one preparing the way for the Messiah) and Jesus (the Messiah). By associating Isaiah 40:3 with Jesus Christ, the Gospel writers revealed Jesus to be Yahweh Himself since Yahweh ("the LORD") is the subject of Isaiah 40:3. And two verses later, Isaiah says that "the glory of the LORD shall be revealed, and all flesh shall see it together" (Isaiah 40:5).

Before leaving Isaiah 40, may we take note of the "arm" of the Lord in both verses 10 and 11. A few chapters later, Isaiah returned to the subject of the coming Messiah, again associating Him with the arm of the Lord: "The LORD [Yahweh] has made bare His holy arm in the eyes of all the nations; and all the ends of the earth shall see the salvation of our God" (Isaiah 52:10, NKJV).

Luke quoted the last portion of this verse in Luke 3:6, giving it as a Messianic prophecy, together with Isaiah 40:3-4—which is another confirmation that Isaiah 52:10 is a prophecy that found its fulfillment in Jesus. Again, may we notice the prophet's emphasis on the arm of the Lord, calling it "His holy arm."

Then, only a few verses later Isaiah makes it very clear *who* this "holy arm" is! The very first verse of the well-known chapter 53 of Isaiah asks: "Who has believed our report? And to whom has *the arm of the LORD* been revealed? For He shall grow up before Him as a tender plant, and as a root out of dry ground" (Isaiah 53:1-2, NKJV).

All through Isaiah 53 are verses that the New Testament writers referred to in declaring that this chapter found its fulfillment in Jesus as the promised Messiah. John specifically quoted Isaiah 53:1 to show that "the arm of the LORD" was Jesus Himself (John 12:38). He added, "These things Isaiah said when he saw His glory and spoke of Him" (John 12:41).

In short, according to Isaiah 53:1 (and other verses in Isaiah) and the revelation of the New Testament, Jesus Christ is "the arm of the LORD"! Does this mean that Jesus was walking around as a literal arm? Of course not. We all know that it would be absurd to take this language as absolutely literal. We realize, as the Biblical writers and their contemporary readers realized, that the terminology is a beautiful, symbolic picture of the power and glory of our God. Jesus of Nazareth, as the arm of the Lord, was a personified, visible extension of an invisible God and His power and glory. The humanity of Jesus as the Son of Man was the arm of the Lord because He was the human expression of the invisible, eternal Spirit. As the New Testament puts it in more than one place, Jesus was the physical "*image* of the invisible God" (Colossians 1:15). (See also Hebrews 1:3.)

Just as Psalm 110 is an important verse of Scripture concerning the "right hand" passages in the New Testament, Isaiah 53:1 is another key verse in this regard. When the New Testament writers spoke of the Son—the risen, glorified Christ—returning to "the right hand" (Greek, "the right") of God, they simply meant "the arm of the Lord" was returning symbolically to where "the arm" belonged, since the *human* aspect of God's ministry was completed at the cross and the empty tomb.

Isaiah 53:10 had predicted that "the pleasure of the LORD shall prosper *in His hand*."

It is all symbolic language; however, it is language that portrays a real God in real history in a real Messiah named Jesus. The language is symbolic, but it depicts a real Lord and His glory.

Isaiah 53 focuses on the humanity of the Messiah who suffered as a righteous servant before dying on the cross. Because the ministry of the Messiah involved a God who became a human being as a Son, it is probably no coincidence that the Hebrew word for "arm" in Isaiah 53:1 (and other verses in Isaiah) has the same root letters as the Hebrew term for "seed"! The word for "arm" is *zeroa'* and is related to *zera'*, "seed, human descendant," which verse 10 mentions: "He shall see His seed [*zera'*], He shall prolong His days, and the pleasure of the LORD shall prosper in His hand" (Isaiah 53:10, NKJV).

The Hebrew Bible often indicates the relationship of words by using puns, particularly using words that are similar in spelling and sound.

Therefore, when Isaiah repeatedly associated the arm of the Lord with the coming Messiah, there is a definite hint in the very word "arm" (*zeroa'*) of the physical Sonship of God through His "seed" (*zera'*). As a consonantal language, Hebrew only has consonants in its alphabet; and both words have the same three consonants—no more and no less.

This Messianic promise of God's "seed" was first made in Genesis 3:15 (compare with Romans 16:20) and was repeated in later passages of Scripture (Genesis 22:18; Galatians 3:8, 16). In Galatians 3 Paul stated: "Now to Abraham and his Seed were the promises made.

He does not say, 'And to seeds,' as of many, but as of one, 'And to your Seed,' who is Christ" (Galatians 3:16, NKJV).

Let us briefly mention two more passages from Isaiah before turning to the New Testament Scriptures regarding "the right hand of God." Concerning the Lord, the prophet wrote: "He saw that there was no man and wondered that there was no intercessor; therefore His *own* arm brought salvation for Him; and His own righteousness, it sustained Him" (Isaiah 59:16, NKJV). As with previously quoted passages of Scriptures, this verse teaches that the Lord's arm represents the Lord Himself when He would bring salvation through "His own arm" in the human form of the Nazarene.

Benjamin, the son of Jacob, received his name for a reason. Benjamin was the youngest son of Jacob, and Joseph and Benjamin were the only sons that Jacob had by his beloved wife Rachel. She died while giving birth to Benjamin, and in her dying breath she gave Benjamin a name; but after Rachel's death, Jacob immediately changed his son's name to "Benjamin," *Ben-yamin*—"son of my right hand." Jacob did this because of the deep love that he had for both Rachel and his newborn son.

Therefore, the Jewish writers and readers of the New Testament in the first century knew that the phrase "right hand of God" was symbolic of power, honor, glory, and love. The resurrected Jesus received all of these things because of what He had accomplished as the Son of God.

The expression "right hand of God" is wrapped up in the Sonship of God and the glorification of the Son of God after His resurrection from the dead. Mark 16:19 states that after our Lord rose from the grave, "He was received up into heaven, and sat down at the right hand of God" [literal Greek, "out of the right things of God"]. The next verse explains that this same risen Lord was the God who *continued* to work with His apostles, confirming the word through miraculous signs (Mark 16:20).

The "right hand of God" phrases in the New Testament do not mention the Father. This is because the writers were not pointing out persons of a trinity. The Holy Spirit is not referred to either. This omission of both the Father and the Holy Spirit is strange indeed if God were trying to reveal three persons of a trinity in the New Testament. What the "right hand" passages do have are majestic references to divine titles like "God," "Power," and "Majesty."

If Jesus Christ is "at" the right hand "of" God in a literal sense, then He cannot be God Himself or even a part of God. This fact alone proves that we cannot take the phrase in the literal sense that trinitarians take it. Is Jesus God or not? Hundreds of verses throughout the Bible confirm that He is; the strongest language possible reveals Him to be deity.

We must take the phrase "right hand of God" in a figurative sense as an expression of honor, glory, power, and love for a risen, exalted Son. Sometimes in the New Testament passages, the "right hand" expression is in the plural—"out of the right things of God"—as in Mark 16:19. This construction reminds us of the Hebrew plural of majesty, which we discussed in chapter 1. King David once praised his Lord by writing, "At Your right hand are pleasures forevermore" (Psalm 16:11).

It is interesting that this verse comes from the same Psalm that Peter quoted when he referred to the risen Jesus as going to the right hand of God in Acts 2. In the first gospel sermon, Peter focused on the *humanity* (Sonship) of Jesus when he declared how God raised Him from the dead to be exalted to the right hand of God (verses 32-33). Besides the reference to Psalm 16, the apostle then specifically quoted Psalm 110:1 in Acts 2:34-35.

We saw earlier that Christ quoted Psalm 110:1 in order to show that (1) the verse is to be taken in a figurative sense and (2) it is a prophecy of the Sonship of God in the Messiah. (See Matthew 22:41-45.) In fact, the New Testament quotes Psalm 110:1 several times, and the inspired writers explained that it was a prophecy which foretold the temporary role of God as a Son. After quoting this verse, Peter went on to state that God "made" Jesus of Nazareth to be "both Lord and Christ" (Acts 2:36).

Peter and his Jewish hearers at Pentecost knew that the Yahweh who had "told" Adoni in Psalm 110:1 to sit at His right hand cannot be separated from Adoni in His nature or being. Peter emphasized the majesty of the Son when he stated that God "highly exalted" Jesus to His right hand to be Prince and Savior following His resurrection and ascension (Acts 5:31).

Ephesians 1:20-23 honors Christ in the highest terminology. As in all the other New Testament "right hand" texts, the focus is the glorification of the risen Son of Man. God has raised Him from the dead and seated Him at His right hand in the heavenly places (verse 20), where Jesus is "far above *all* principality and power and might and dominion and every name that is named, not only in this age but also in that which is to come" (verse 21). "All things" are put under Jesus' feet, and He is head over all things for the church (verse 22). Jesus Christ is the One who fills "all in all" (verse 23)!

The first chapter of Hebrews is also enlightening because of at least five significant points that it makes: (1) The Sonship began when Jesus came into the world. (2) The Son is both God (Elohim) and the LORD (Yahweh) Himself. (3) After He purged our sins by His sacrificial death, the risen, glorified Son sat down at the right hand of the Majesty on high. (4) The Son is at the right hand of Yahweh until a certain time. (5) Although the Son will no longer be at the right hand of God after His enemies are subdued, His kingdom, as the kingdom of God, will last forever. Let us examine Hebrews 1 in detail to consider each of these five points.

1. The Sonship of God began when Jesus came into the world. Verse 5 quotes Psalm 2:7, where Yahweh said, "You are My Son, today I have begotten You." As in Psalm 110:1, Yahweh used symbolic language to foretell His two roles of Father and Son, which He would portray when the Son was conceived and born. The last part of Hebrews 1:5 quotes II Samuel 7:14, as Yahweh continued: "I will be to Him a Father, and He shall be to Me a Son."

Concerning Hebrews 1:5, most English translations leave out two important Greek words—*eis*, which is used two times in the verse. *Eis* has different meanings in the Greek New Testament, depending on its context. One of these meanings is "as," according to the lexicon by Arndt and Gingrich, the standard lexicon for the Greek New Testament. *Eis* means "as" in Acts 10:4, where the NIV correctly translates it in the phrase "*as* a memorial offering." In Hebrews 1:5, *eis* is used before "Son" and before "Father." What makes this Greek term significant here is that it emphasizes the *roles* of God as Father and Son: "I will be to Him *as* a Father, and He will be to Me *as* a Son" (Hebrews 1:5). Hebrews 1:5-6 specifically tells us that the Son will be "conceived" and that the roles of Father and Son will begin when God "brings the firstborn into the world." This is an obvious reference to the birth of Jesus.

2. The Son is revealed to be God (Elohim) and the LORD (Yahweh) Himself. Verse 8 calls "the Son" *God*, quoting Psalm 45:6: "Your throne, O God, is forever and ever." Because the Hebrew word for God in Psalm 45:6 (and elsewhere in the Old Testament) is *Elohim*, Jesus Himself is identified as Elohim. Hebrews 1:10 then calls the Son *Yahweh*, quoting Psalm 102:25-27: "You, LORD [*Yahweh*] in the beginning laid the foundation of the earth, and the heavens are the work of Your hands." Thus, verse 10 not only reveals the Son to be Yahweh but also the Creator of all things.

Because the Son became God in the flesh, the angels were told to worship Him (verse 6). This is why Hebrews 1 begins with the revelation that in these last days "God . . . has spoken to us in a Son [literal Greek]" (verses 1-2).

3. After He purged our sins by His sacrificial death, the glorified, risen Son sat down at the right hand of the Majesty on high (verse 3). This verse is a magnificent exaltation of the Son: "The Son is the radiance of God's glory and the exact representation of his being, sustaining all things by his powerful word. After he had provided purification for sins, he sat down at the right hand of the Majesty in heaven" (Hebrews 1:3, NIV).

The NIV rendering of this verse is not a bad translation. However, a few changes are appropriate. First of all, the NIV does not capitalize the personal pronouns for

God and the Son, and the capitalization of all pronouns for God is justified. Second, the NIV rendering of "in heaven" is literally "on high" in the Greek and is actually in the plural. It is also helpful to keep in mind that all the English versions give a loose translation of the "right hand" passages when they say "at the right hand." "Hand" is not in the original languages of either the Old Testament or the New Testament. Also, in the New Testament the exact Greek differs in different passages. In Hebrews 1:3 the original is "in the right of the Majesty [a feminine noun] in the high places."

In addition, for some reason the NIV chose *not* to translate the middle voice of the verb "purged" or "purified." The KJV and NKJV both properly translate the middle voice here: "He had *by Himself* [literal Greek] purged our sins." By using the middle voice, the inspired writer emphasized that the Son, as God, did not have to depend on someone else to purify our sins. He did it Himself on the cross!

Verse 3 glorifies the Son by high, exalted language. Here is how four English versions translate the first part of Hebrews 1:3:

- *"The Son is the radiance of God's glory and the exact representation of his being, sustaining all things by his powerful word" (NIV).*
- *"He reflects the glory of God and bears the very stamp of his nature, upholding the universe by his word of power" (RSV).*
- *"Who being the brightness of His glory and the express image of His person, and upholding all things by the word of His power" (KJV and NKJV).*

All of the foregoing translations are accurate enough to bring out the glory of Christ that the writer intended. However, some comments are in order. The KJV and NKJV refer to "His person." The Greek word here, *hupostasis*, clearly means "nature" or "being," not "person" as we usually think of it. As we mentioned in the preface, it is better not to use the English word "person" in reference to deity since the word normally implies a human being. Certainly the verse shows that *hupostasis* refers to the eternal, immortal Spirit-Being known as God. The word *hupostasis* often appeared in the decrees of church councils and church creeds when the debates of the nature of God were raging. Even then, Christian scholars recognized that *hupostasis* means "nature" or "being."

According to the RSV, the Son "reflects" the glory of God. The English term "reflects" gives an inaccurate sense of the original word *apaugasma*. This word is a noun that means "radiance" or "effulgence." Hebrews 1:3 is the only place that this noun appears in the New Testament, and because it means "radiance," the Son is far more than a mere reflection of the glory of God. In fact, several passages in the New Testament show that Jesus *is* the glory of God (e.g., Acts 7:55-56; John 1:14; Revelation 21:23). Hebrews 1:3 says the same thing in explaining that the Son is "the *exact* representation of His being."

Some Greek scholars refer to an active and a passive sense of *apaugasma*, "radiance." In this regard, a respected Greek linguistic source states:

> The active meaning has the idea of emitting brightness and the meaning is that the shekinah glory

of God radiated from Him. The passive idea is not so much that of reflection, but rather the radiation through the source of the light. It is as the sun radiates its rays of light.[1]

Consequently, the KJV, NKJV, and NIV are accurate when they translate the word as "the brightness" or "the radiance" of God's glory.

4. The Son is at the right hand of Yahweh *until* a certain time. Hebrews 1:13 quotes Psalm 110:1, where Yahweh said to Adoni, "Sit at My right hand until I make Your enemies Your footstool." By quoting this verse, the writer of Hebrews confirmed what David and Jesus (Matthew 22:41-45) had earlier established—that Psalm 110:1 has figurative language regarding the Messianic roles of God as Father and Son. Because Yahweh and Adoni (as well as Adonai) is the same Being throughout the Psalms, these divine appellations for God signify a distinction in roles and manifestations, not in persons. It is interesting that throughout the first chapter of Hebrews the Father clearly speaks to the Son in a metaphorical sense—with verse 13 simply being the last verse of the chapter in which He does so.

When verse 13 quotes Psalm 110:1, the Greek literally says, "Sit *out of* My right things." As in verse 3, the terminology associates the risen, glorified Son with God in the closest terms. The Son is symbolically sitting "out of the right things" of God *until* His enemies are made His footstool. The definite indication is that the time will come when the Son will no longer be there.

5. Although the Son will no longer be at the right of God after His enemies are subdued, His kingdom, as the

kingdom of God, will last forever. Hebrews 1:8 has the Father telling the Son, "Your throne, O God, is forever and ever." After verse 8 identifies Jesus the Son as God, verses 11 and 12 state that He will always "remain" and that His years "will not fail." (See also Hebrews 13:8.)

Before leaving Hebrews 1, we should note that the Son normally *sits down* at the right hand of God in the "right hand" passages of the New Testament. Only in Acts 7 do we find the Son "standing" at the right of God. This language is possibly an expression of concern because of Stephen's imminent martyrdom. In Hebrews 1:3 the Son sat down at the right of the Majesty after He made purification for our sins. The clear implication is that the Son sat down to demonstrate that His work of redemption was *complete* at the cross.

In this regard, Hebrews 9:11-12 says: "But Christ came as High Priest of the good things to come, with the greater and more perfect tabernacle not made with hands, that is, not of this creation. Not with the blood of goats and calves, but with His own blood He entered the Most Holy Place *once and for all*, having obtained eternal redemption" (Hebrews 9:11-12, NKJV).

Our high priest, Jesus, is far different from other priests: "And every priest stands ministering daily and offering repeatedly the same sacrifices, which can never take away sins. But this Man, after He had offered one sacrifice for sins forever, *sat down* at the right hand of God, from that time waiting *till* His enemies are made His footstool. For by one offering He has perfected forever those who are being sanctified" (Hebrews 10:11-14, NKJV).

These passages of Scripture show that the "right hand" language portrays the Son as symbolically sitting down as high priest at the right hand of God—*only* for a temporary period of time, as Psalm 110:1 and I Corinthians 15:25 state. It is a beautiful, symbolic picture of a high priest who intercedes with God on behalf of our sins. "Now this is the main point of the things we are saying: We have such a High Priest who is seated at the right hand of the throne of the Majesty [feminine noun] in the heavens" (Hebrews 8:1, NKJV).

This symbolism of a high priest "*in* the right of the throne of the Majesty [literal Greek]" involves a priest who Himself became a perfect sacrifice as the Lamb of God. "For such a High Priest was fitting for us, who is holy, harmless, undefiled, separate from sinners, and has become higher than the heavens: who does not need daily, as these high priests, to offer up sacrifices, first for His own sins and then for the people's, for this He did *once and for all* when He offered up Himself" (Hebrews 7:26-27, NKJV).

In Acts 7, immediately before Stephen was stoned to death for being faithful to Jesus Christ, "he, being full of the Holy Spirit, gazed into heaven and saw the glory of God, *even* [*kai*] Jesus standing *out of* [*ek*] the *right things* [*deksion*] of God and said, 'Look! I see the heavens opened and the Son of Man standing out of the right things of God'" (Acts 7:55-56, literal Greek). In considering this text, we should ponder four points:

1. Being a mere man, Stephen could not have seen God as a Spirit-Being in His full majesty and holiness (I Timothy 6:16). He could not have seen Jesus as the immortal Spirit that He is (I Corinthians 15:45). But Acts 7:55 informs us that Stephen saw "the glory of God"— even Jesus. How?

2. Undoubtedly, Stephen saw a supernatural vision, for he saw "the Son of Man" standing out of the right of God. As pointed out earlier, the phrase "Son of Man" is a Messianic title which emphasizes the *humanity* that the Messiah possessed during His earthly pilgrimage. Even though Stephen could not have seen His Lord as an eternal Spirit, he did see Him as "the Son of Man." The "right hand" passages in the New Testament always focus on the Messianic role that Jesus had as the Son.

3. As we noted before, if Jesus, as deity, is literally at the right hand of God, then how could He be God? Many verses of Scriptures reveal that Jesus is deity. Therefore, He cannot *literally, physically* be at God's right hand, either in Acts 7 or in any other verse in the Bible.

4. As far as Stephen was concerned, Jesus Christ was *his* Lord and *his* God. Because of this, with his dying breath, Stephen called on His Lord God by crying out, "Lord Jesus, receive my spirit!" (Acts 7:59).

What we have discussed has demonstrated beyond a shadow of a doubt that the "right hand" passages of Scripture are figurative, symbolic expressions of honor, glory and power. In this regard, the Greek lexicons inform us that the phrase "at the right hand" is metaphorical language for "the power of God."[2]

We have already seen many verses of Scripture from the Old Testament which indicate that the phrase is an idiomatic expression for God's own power. In one passage, Moses exulted: "Your right hand, O Yahweh, has become glorious in power!" (Exodus 15:6).

Jesus of Nazareth once declared: "I cast out demons with the finger of God" (Luke 11:20, NKJV). We realize here that Jesus was not talking about a literal finger.

Instead, we must understand His terminology of "the finger of God," like "the right hand of God," in a figurative sense for the power of God.

Furthermore, it is interesting that the Bible does not only speak of the Son as being at the right hand of God. As we saw earlier, it sometimes says that He is at the right of "Majesty," which is a feminine abstract noun (Hebrews 1:3; 8:1). Jesus Himself predicted that the Son of Man would later be "at the right hand of Power" ("out of right things of the Power," in literal Greek). Like "Majesty," the term "Power" [*dunamis*] is another feminine abstract noun. "Jesus said to him, . . . Hereafter you will see the Son of Man seated out of the right things of the Power and coming on the clouds of heaven (Matthew 26:64, literal Greek).

Some may misunderstand today, but those who heard Jesus' words understood that He was making claims of deity, for when Christ spoke of later being "out of the right things of the Power," the high priest angrily accused Him of blasphemy (Matthew 26:65-66).

Therefore, when Stephen saw the Son of Man standing "out of the right things of God," he realized that the Son was glorified with the power of God. Because Acts 7:54-60 is such a significant passage for our discussion, let us summarize this enlightening text. It is an inspired account from early church history that explains how the first-century Christians understood the New Testament "right hand" terminology.

Acts 7:55 specifically notes that when Stephen saw "the glory of God," he saw "the Son of Man" standing at the right hand of God. The "right hand" passages were another way for the New Testament writers to show that

Jesus, the Son of Man, had been raised from the dead, exalted, glorified, and completely vindicated following His death on the cross.

Furthermore, if we take the phrase "right hand of God" and similar terminology literally, then we have the unsolvable problem of how Jesus, who is deity, can be God or even a part of God. He simply cannot *be* God if He is at the right hand *of* God.

And to the puzzlement of all trinitarians (and others who do not give Jesus credit for possessing full deity), the dying Stephen *prayed* to the "Lord Jesus," asking Him to receive his spirit (Acts 7:59). It is significant that he did not pray to some other person in the Godhead. Stephen prayed to the only Lord God he knew—"Lord Jesus." If anyone finds this to be strange behavior on Stephen's part, then he or she does not yet really comprehend who Jesus was and who He is. Stephen *knew* who Jesus was because he was full of the Holy Spirit (Acts 7:55). Stephen *knew* who Jesus was because the Lord had blessed him with this wonderful experience of supernaturally seeing the Son of Man and the glory of God. Stephen *knew* who Jesus was because he prayed to the Lord Jesus *as* his God.

Do we know who Jesus is? If we do, then let us follow Stephen's example and honor the Lord Jesus in the same way that he did, both in life and in death.

There are many expressions in the Bible that we must understand in a figurative sense. John 1:18 tells us that the only begotten Son "is in the bosom of the Father." The Book of Revelation describes Jesus as "a Lamb" that had been slain, "having seven horns and seven eyes" (Revelation 5:6). In the symbolism of Revelation 5, "the Lamb" came and took the scroll out of "the right hand" of the One who sat on the throne (Revelation 5:7). This figurative depiction of the Lamb taking the scroll out of the right hand of the One on the throne reminds us of the other "right hand" passages in the New Testament. The detailed symbolism of Revelation 5:1-14 describes Jesus as the perfect sacrifice, the Lamb of God. The Book of Revelation elsewhere reveals that the Lamb, Jesus, is none other than the Lord God Almighty Himself! (Revelation 7:15, 17; 15:3; 17:14).

According to the Book of Ephesians, just as the Son is at the right hand of God, so we are to be at the same place—of course, like the Son, in a figurative sense. As God raised Him from the dead and seated Him at His right hand in the heavenly places (Ephesians 1:20), He also "raised us up together, and made us sit together in the heavenly places in Christ Jesus" (Ephesians 2:6, NKJV)!

Therefore, Paul said: "If then you were raised *with* Christ, seek those things which are above, where Christ is, sitting at the right hand of God. Set your mind on things above, not on things on the earth. For you died, and your life is hidden *with Christ* in God" (Colossians 3:1-3, NKJV).

If Christ is literally sitting at the right hand of God "in the heavenly places," then we are also literally "sitting together in the heavenly places in Christ Jesus" (Ephesians 2:6). According to Ephesians 1:20; 2:6 and Colossians 3:1-3, we are sitting there with Christ. And just as we realize that we are there only in a metaphorical sense, Christ is also there in a metaphorical sense.

The Book of Hebrews depicts the perfect human sacrifice, our high priest, as being there to make intercession for us (Hebrews 8:1-6). And I Timothy 2:5 specifically informs us that the *only* Mediator between God and men is "the *Man* ["human being," literal Greek] Christ Jesus."

All the New Testament "right hand" passages emphasize the glorification of this perfect, human sacrifice who went to the cross as the Son of God and the Son of Man. This is why Stephen saw "the Son of Man" standing at the right hand of God. The "right hand" texts all exalt the climactic activity of the Incarnation and the wonderful work of salvation that God performed in the Son of Man.

An important passage of Scripture that is directly related to the "right hand" passages is I Corinthians 15:24, which states that in the end Christ will deliver or hand over the kingdom to God the Father. In this verse, like the "right hand" texts, we could take the statement literally or figuratively. If we take it literally, then we have the problem of two Lords and two Gods. On the other hand (pardon the figurative pun), there are compelling reasons why we should take it in a figurative sense: (1) the Old Testament passages, such as Psalm 110, that we discussed earlier, (2) the New Testament passages that we have already looked at, e.g., Acts 7:55-60, and (3) Ephesians 5:20-27, which is a parallel to I Corinthians 15:24.

As the context of I Corinthians 15:24 reveals, it speaks of Christ reigning *until* death is destroyed. Here are verses 20-26:

"But now Christ is risen from the dead, and has become the firstfruits of those who have fallen asleep. For since by man came death, by Man also came the resurrection of the dead. For as in Adam all die, even

so in Christ all shall be made alive. But each one in his own order: Christ the firstfruits, afterward those who are Christ's at His coming. Then comes the end when He delivers the kingdom to God the Father, when He puts an end to all rule and all authority and power. For He must reign till He has put all enemies under His feet. The last enemy that will be destroyed is death" (I Corinthians 15:20-26, NKJV).

This passage teaches the same thing that Psalm 110 teaches. Psalm 110:1 reveals the two roles of God as Father (Yahweh) and Son (Adoni) during the time when the Messiah is on the earth. Both Psalm 110:1 and I Corinthians 15:24-25 explain that the Messiah will reign *until* He puts an end to all rule and authority—*until* He has put all enemies under His feet.

The entire chapter of I Corinthians 15 emphasizes the *human* ministry of God which He performs as a Messiah who is a Son. In other words, the focus is the Sonship of God in Jesus. As we have seen in Psalm 110 and the "right hand" passages, the role of the Son as Mediator and Savior will remain in existence as long as there are human beings in this age who need forgiveness of their sins.

The New Testament symbolically pictures the risen Jesus as being at God's right hand as a mediator and high priest. Although Jesus is no longer a mortal human being on earth, He is figuratively at God's right hand *as* the Son of Man who earlier gave His human life for the *sins* of man.

I Corinthians 15 discusses the ministry of the Son throughout the chapter. Verses 21 and 22 state that since death came by a man (Adam), the resurrection from the dead also came by "a Man" (Christ). Therefore, when the Son "delivers" the kingdom to God the Father, this is obviously a symbolic picture of the future when the Sonship of God will come to an end (verses 24-28). At that time, there will no longer be a need for a mediator and forgiveness of sins. This is because, by that time, death itself will already have been destroyed (verse 26).

We know that when Jesus delivers His kingdom to the Father (verse 24), this cannot literally mean that Christ will stop reigning as King. Although Jesus will stop reigning as a Son, He will continue to reign as the Lord God. Many passages of Scriptures tell us explicitly that the kingdom of Jesus will never end and that our Lord Jesus Christ will *never* relinquish His kingdom to another (Isaiah 9:6-7; Luke 1:31-33; II Peter 1:11).

In addition to all that we have already presented, one verse proves conclusively that we must take I Corinthians 15:24 in a figurative sense. The apostle Paul wrote that verse also. It is in Ephesians 5, and it reveals that when Christ "delivers" the kingdom to the Father, He will actually deliver the kingdom to Himself! In discussing the end time, Paul wrote that Christ loved the church and gave Himself for it (verse 25) that He might sanctify it (verse 26):

"That He might present it to Himself a glorious church, not having spot or wrinkle or any such thing, but that it should be holy and without blemish" (Ephesians 5:27, NKJV).

By allowing the Bible to interpret itself through a comparison of two parallel passages of Scriptures, we understand the meaning. Ephesians 5:27 proves that we are to understand I Corinthians 15:24 metaphorically and not literally.

We find another key to understanding I Corinthians 15:24 in the passage itself. I Corinthians 15:28 says that "the Son" is subjected so that God may be "all in all." Other verses of Scripture by Paul make it clear that Jesus Himself, as God, is the One who is "all in all" (Ephesians 1:23; 4:10; Colossians 3:11; I Corinthians 8:6).

Of course, what all of this illustrates is that the apostle in I Corinthians 15 was not writing of two divine persons in a literal sense. Rather, he was writing of the Sonship of Jesus, which will be subjected so that God may be all in all. Many times in the New Testament "the Son" is spoken of in terms of the Sonship. Oscar Cullmann agrees, for in his comment on I Corinthians 15:28, he noted:

> Here lies the key to all New Testament Christology. *It is only meaningful to speak of the Son in view of God's revelatory action, not in view of his being* [emphasis his]. But precisely for this reason, Father and Son are really one in this activity. Now we can say of the "Son of God" what we said earlier of the Logos [the Word]: he is God as God reveals himself in redemptive action. The whole New Testament speaks of the redemptive action. Therefore the kingdom in which we live now, before the end, is the "kingdom of the Son" (Colossians 1:13).[3]

Although it is the kingdom of God, it is also now known as the *Son's* kingdom. In this age we can receive the very Spirit of *God*,[4] yet it is also called "the Spirit of

His Son"[5] (as well as "the Spirit of Christ"[6]). Therefore, we should thoughtfully reflect upon Dr. Cullmann's following quote, for in it he presented the Biblical viewpoint: "The distinction between the Father and the Son has significance only from the point of view of *Heilsgeschichte* [German, "salvation history"]."[7]

In future ages, there will be no need for the Son's "redemptive action"; there will be no need for the *Sonship* of God. In the new heavens and the new earth—after we are completely reconciled to our Creator—there will be no need for our God to live and die again as a Son on our behalf. At that time, the role of God as "Son" is to be subjected—"that God may be all in all."

However, *until* humanity is reconciled to the Creator in the new heavens and the new earth, humans will need a "mediator" between themselves and their God:

"For there is one God and one Mediator between God and men, the Man *Christ Jesus" (I Timothy 2:5, NKJV).*

This plain verse is another important key in comprehending the Biblical concept of the Sonship of Jesus. The Greek word for "man" in the above verse is *anthropos*, and it literally means "a human being." (It is the very term from which English has derived *anthropology*, "the study of humans.")

According to the above verse of Scripture, the *only* "mediator" that we have is the human being, Jesus of Nazareth—the time when God robed Himself with flesh as a Son and walked among us "full of grace and truth."[8] "This," says the apostle, "is our only mediator"! And the remainder of our present chapter will confirm that this mediator is: (1) a Son who received all power, (2) a Son who was over His own house, and (3) a begotten Son— not an eternal Son.

All Power

Daniel 7 contains an enlightening prophecy about power and authority. It speaks of "the Ancient of Days" (verses 9-10) and "One like the Son of Man" (verses 13-14). This prophecy appears to foretell the two roles of God as Father and Son in the Messianic age.

Even as Psalm 110:1 prophesies of the risen, glorified Son who is symbolically at the right hand of Yahweh, Daniel 7 speaks of "One like the Son of Man" who is brought to the Ancient of Days (verse 13). In Psalm 110:1, Adoni is to rule until His enemies are made His footstool; in Daniel 7:14, the Son of Man receives dominion, glory, and a kingdom.

Some have suggested that the phrase "Son of Man" likely represents the glorified church, instead of the risen Christ in particular. One reason is that the Hebrew does not have the definite article in the title "Son of Man." A literal translation of the phrase is "*a* Son of Man" (Daniel 7:13). Another reason is that the passage promises that the saints will "receive the kingdom" (Daniel 7:18, 22, 27) and that they will rule with Christ in His kingdom (I Corinthians 6:1-3; Revelation 2:26-27; 20:4, 6).

If the Son of Man in Daniel 7 is representative of the church in general, it is a wonderful promise for Christians to appreciate. However, the prophecy may have a dual sense, referring to the church in general and to Christ in particular. Or it may be even more specific than this, referring only to Jesus Christ as the King of kings. In any case, there is much that speaks for including Jesus in the interpretation.

Revelation 1 may actually be a parallel of Daniel 7. Like Daniel 7:13, Revelation 1:13 speaks of "One like the Son of Man." Revelation 1 unquestionably describes Jesus, and the reference to the Son of Man in Revelation 1:13, as in Daniel 7:13, does not have the definite article. In other words, the phrases in Daniel and Revelation are identical in the original languages: "One like *a* Son of Man."

Divine titles in the Bible, like divine names, often do not have the definite article because the definite idea is implicit in the name or the title itself. There are other references to "the Son" in both Testaments that do not have the article, even though the definite idea is intended. If the phrase applies to Jesus, "One *like* a Son of Man" indicates a Messiah who is like a man—emphasizing His human nature. Therefore, it may be significant that the "Son of Man" phrases in Daniel 7 and Revelation 1 are identical, especially since the Revelation passage definitely refers to Jesus.

What is interesting is that Revelation 1 not only describes Jesus, but it also uses descriptive language that is similar to Daniel 7's descriptions of *both* the Son of Man and the Ancient of Days.

Let us first notice the similarities between "One like a Son of Man" in Daniel 7 and Jesus, who is specifically called "One like a Son of Man," in Revelation 1:

1. The Son of Man is brought to the Ancient of Days (Daniel 7:13). Jesus is the firstborn from the dead (Revelation 1:5).

2. The Son of Man comes with the clouds of heaven (Daniel 7:13). Jesus Christ is coming again with clouds (Revelation 1:7).

3. The Son of Man receives an eternal dominion (Daniel 7:14). Jesus is the ruler over the kings of the earth (Revelation 1:5; 17:14) in an eternal dominion (Revelation 1:6; 5:12-14).

Next, let us notice the striking similarities between "the Ancient of Days" in Daniel 7 and the Son of Man in Revelation 1 and throughout the Book of Revelation:

1. The Ancient of Days is a title that indicates an eternal Being (Daniel 7:9). Jesus is called the Alpha and the Omega, the Beginning and the End, the First and the Last, and the One who is and who was and who is to come (Revelation 1:8, 11). (See also Micah 5:2.)

2. The Ancient of Days is the only One who sits on a throne after all other thrones are destroyed (Daniel 7:9; the inspired Aramaic word for "Ancient" also means "stately," "regal"). The Son of Man is "the Almighty" (Revelation 1:8), and He *rules* after conquering death (Revelation 1:5).

3. The hair on the head of the Ancient of Days is like pure wool (Daniel 7:9). The Son of Man's head and hair is white like wool (Revelation 1:14).

4. The Ancient of Days' throne is like a fiery flame and a burning fire. A fiery stream goes forth from before Him (Daniel 7:9-10). The Son of Man's feet are like fine brass as if refined in a furnace (Revelation 1:15).

5. Judgment is set before the Ancient of Days, and the books are opened (Daniel 7:10). Out of the mouth of the Son of Man went a sharp two-edged sword (Revelation 1:16). The Word of God is associated with a two-edged

sword in Hebrews 4:12-13, which states that our Judge will use it to judge us. (See also II Corinthians 5:10; Revelation 19:11-15.)

6. A thousand thousands ministered to the Ancient of Days; ten thousand times ten thousand ministered to Him (Daniel 7:10). Around the throne of the Lamb (the Son of Man) were many angels, the living creatures, and the elders; and the number of them was ten thousand times ten thousand and thousands of thousands (Revelation 5:9-11). "He who is on the throne, *even*" [*kai*] the symbolic Lamb (verse 13), is worshiped as one God. They worship "Him," not them (verse 14).

The Book of Revelation itself consistently confirms the two roles of God as Father and Son. Jesus sometimes speaks as a Son (and the Lamb) when He refers to God as His Father (Revelation 1:1, 5). At other times, Jesus reveals *Himself* to be the Almighty (Revelation 1:8), the Alpha and the Omega, the First and the Last (Revelation 1:11, 17), and even God Himself in the role of our Father (Revelation 21:6-7).

In summary, whether "One like the Son of Man" in Daniel 7 is Jesus in particular, or the church in general, or both, one thing is certain: Jesus, "the One like the Son of Man" in Revelation 1, is Himself "the Ancient of Days" in Daniel 7—yet another confirmation that the Father and Son are two roles of one Spirit-Being!

As we mentioned earlier, Jesus is not simply at the right hand of power, but He Himself *possesses* power—all power. The New Testament depicts a Christ with real power precisely because it is in Jesus that we can see the power of God. There were those who could see that Jesus of Nazareth was different—that He had the answers. But did they realize *why* He had the answers? On one occasion a young ruler ran up to the Nazarene and asked Him: "'Good Teacher, what shall I do that I may inherit eternal life?' So Jesus said to him, 'Why do you call Me good? No one is good but One, that is, God'" (Mark 10:17-18, NKJV). (Both the KJV and NKJV translate the Greek correctly by rendering the Greek term *heis* as "One.")

Was Christ chastising the young man because he had called Him good? Or was Jesus saying, in effect, "When you call Me *good*, do you know what you are acknowledging? Do you actually realize who I am?" In the words of John Stott:

> "Why do you call me good?" He asked the rich young ruler. "No one is good but God alone." "Exactly," he should have replied. "It is not that You are better than other men, nor even that You are the best of men, but that You are good—good with the goodness of God."[9]

It hardly seems logical that Jesus would rebuke the young man for calling Him good; Christ Himself claimed that He was good! "I am the good Shepherd," said He on more than one occasion.[10]

If Jesus was the good Shepherd, if He was good, then He had power that others do not possess—the *power* to be good. Unlike us, Jesus Christ never lied; He never entertained an evil thought; He never committed a sin of any kind. For He is good—capable of leading others always toward the good. Naturally, Jesus was aware that He radiated the very goodness of God, for He went on to command the young ruler: "Follow Me!" (Mark 10:21). If

Jesus Himself was not good, if He was *not* God "who alone is good," then what authority did He have to tell the young man to follow *Him*?

Only when we begin to take John at his word that God "became flesh"[11] can we begin to understand the power and the authority of Jesus Christ.

Certain scribes and Pharisees plotted in their minds against Jesus, but the *power* that He had at His disposal enabled Him to read their minds—to look into the very depths of their hearts: "He *knew* their thoughts" (Luke 6:8).

When His disciples possessed a wrong attitude in their hearts, "Jesus *perceived* the thoughts of their hearts" (Luke 9:47).

At a Passover feast in Jerusalem, many believed in His name when they saw the signs He did. "But Jesus did not trust Himself to them, because He *knew* all men. And He did not need anyone to bear witness of man, for He *knew* what was in man" (John 2:23-25).

This is no ordinary power. This is power that no ordinary man can possess. And this extraordinary power that Christ exhibited carried with it authority as well—the right to use that power.

Jesus had the *authority* to say to a repentant woman, "Your sins are forgiven" (Luke 7:48).

The Christ had the *authority* to announce to a paralyzed man: "My son, your sins are forgiven" (Mark 2:5).

Some today may question such authority—the authority to forgive sin. When Jesus uttered that very claim, people in *that* day began to question His right to make such a claim. So Jesus Christ demonstrated His authority by miraculously *healing* a forgiven one before the eyes of all. Here is the account of such an incident:

"But some of the scribes were sitting there and reasoning in their hearts. 'Why does this Man speak blasphemies like this? Who can forgive sins but God alone?' And immediately, when Jesus perceived in His spirit that they reasoned thus within themselves, He said to them, 'Why do you reason about these things in your hearts? Which is easier, to say to the paralytic, "Your sins are forgiven you," or to say, "Arise, take up your bed and walk"? But that you may know that the Son of Man has power on earth to forgive sins'—He said to the paralytic, 'I say to you, arise, take up your bed, and go your way to your house.' And immediately he arose, took up the bed, and went out in the presence of them all, so that all were amazed and glorified God, saying, 'We never saw anything like this!'" (Mark 2:6-12, NKJV).

That is real power. On another occasion, a desperate woman tested the power of the Messiah by merely touching His garments, with the trust that she would be healed of a terrible affliction. As a result of her faith, she was healed—immediately. And at that very moment, "Jesus perceived that *power* had gone forth from Him" (Mark 5:30).

The King James Version renders "power" here as "virtue," for "virtue" is merely an old English term for "power." And "power" is certainly the correct translation of the Greek word *dunamis*, from which we obtain "dynamo" and "dynamic."

Power had gone out of Jesus to heal that woman because He *was* dynamic—because He was virtually a living dynamo who possessed an endless supply of power!

His power did not "run out"; His power was not limited to the healing of one or a few, for on still another occasion, "the whole multitude sought to touch Him. For *power* went forth from Him and healed them all" (Luke 6:19).

The power of the living Christ was not limited to the healing of the physical body; His power enabled Him to recall dead flesh back to the living at a mere beckoning: "Lazarus, come forth!" (John 11:43).

In similar manner, when the power of Jesus supernaturally raised a dead man at Nain, the multitudes were moved to cry out: "*God* has visited His people" (Luke 7:16).

And this power of Jesus was not merely limited to bringing *others* back to life. Predicted the Nazarene in speaking of His own body: "Destroy this temple, and in three days I will raise it up" (John 2:19). "I ["I Myself," Greek] lay down My life that I may take it again. No one takes it from Me, but I ["I Myself," Greek] lay it down of Myself. I ["I Myself," Greek] have power to lay it down, and I ["I Myself," Greek] have power to take it again" (John 10:17-18, NKJV). It is significant that Jesus repeatedly used the emphatic pronoun "I Myself"; He *Himself* has the power to raise up His own life!

Can we catch the significance of the above claim? We can if we realize that *God* is "the One who raises the dead" (II Corinthians 1:9). For Jesus said, "*I* will raise it up. . . . *I* have power to take it again."

This One who walked out of the tomb two thousand years ago tells us: "I am the resurrection and the life" (John 11:25). He is still saying: "Most assuredly, I say to you, the hour is coming, and now is, when the dead will hear the voice of the Son of God; and those who hear will live" (John 5:25, NKJV).

May we hear the voice of Jesus at the last day to rise and live, for that One has the *power* to impart within us eternal life. Following His own resurrection, the glorified Christ declared that He possessed "all authority . . . in heaven and on earth" (Matthew 28:18, NKJV).

The word translated as "power" in John 10:18 (above) is translated as "authority" in Matthew 28:18 (NKJV) and in Ephesians 1:21 (below). The Greek word is *exousia*, and according to the lexicons, it means any or all of the following: "authority, might, power, all power." That is power—infinite power. The apostle to the Gentiles summed it up well when he wrote that Jesus is *"far* above all rule and authority and power and dominion, and above every name that is named—not only in this age, but also in that which is to come" (Ephesians 1:21).

A Son over His Own House

It must have been a shocking scene when the Carpenter began to throw out of the Temple the corrupt moneychangers who had been exploiting the helpless masses in God's house. "He would not allow *anyone* to carry anything through the temple" (Mark 11:16). In so doing, the Son of Man was certainly acting as if He was in *His* house. William Barclay suggested:

> In the action of the cleansing of the Temple the mind of Jesus is clearly revealed to us. . . . He did not cleanse the Temple like some church officebearer or official attacking some abuse or cleaning up some evil and improper situation. He cleansed the Temple *as if it belonged to him* [emphasis his], as if it were his own personal house and dwelling-place. . . . He does

not act like a man dealing with some abuse; he acts like God sweeping the evil from his own house.[12]

If Jesus "acted like God," He also spoke like God when He claimed, making reference to Himself: "But I say to you that in this place there is One greater than the temple" (Matthew 12:6, NKJV). The people received various forms of testimony to that effect—His miracles, His teachings, and even His perfect life.

In addition to these things, a supernatural voice at times gave *verbal* testimony to the people. On one occasion, John the Baptist testified of Christ, "I did not know Him, but He who sent me to baptize with water said to me, 'Upon whom you see the Spirit descending, and remaining on Him, this is He who baptizes with the Holy Spirit.' And I have seen and testified that this is the Son of God" (John 1:33-34, NKJV).

God informed John that the Spirit would descend upon the Messiah. When Jesus was baptized by John, a voice from heaven indicated to the Baptist that "the dove" that was descending was actually the Spirit of God. The voice declared: "This is My beloved Son, in whom I am well pleased" (Matthew 3:17, NKJV).

It is helpful to see this verse of Scripture translated literally, since the English versions have not done so thus far. While it is obvious that the voice from heaven was an expression of divine approval, it was particularly a declaration that God Himself was *in* Jesus of Nazareth. Here is the verse translated accurately:

"This is My Son, the Beloved, within whom I was well pleased" *(Matthew 3:17, literal Greek).*

Again, on the Mount of Transfiguration that voice spoke out on behalf of the Nazarene:

"This is My Son, the Beloved, within whom I was well pleased" *(Matthew 17:5, literal Greek).*

In virtually all the Gospel parallels describing these two occurrences, the records utilize the Greek aorist tense: "*was* well pleased." They never utilize the regular present tense: "am well pleased." Quite frankly, whether the English translations fully portray it or not, God was saying: "In the Son *I* was well pleased to dwell."

And this is precisely what the apostle Paul claimed:

"For in *Him all the fullness of God* was well pleased to dwell" *(Colossians 1:19).*

This illuminating verse has the identical Greek verb that is found in the foregoing references from the Gospels. Furthermore, the verb is found in the same aorist tense—"was" well pleased!

Other verses of Scripture also indicate that God was here in His own house—as a Son.

The prophets and messengers of God were sent "from" God. For example, "There was a man sent from God, whose name was John" (John 1:6). Of course, this does not mean that John was with God before his mission; it does mean that God raised him up and sent him on His behalf. But unlike John and the other prophets, Jesus of Nazareth was not only sent *from* God, for the Bible also uses another Greek preposition with regard to Jesus. Whenever the New Testament records speak of the sending forth of Christ, they repeatedly state that He was sent "*out of*" God (*ek* or *ex*, "out of," John 13:3; 16:27-30).

The words of Nicodemus indicate that he may not have fully comprehended the mission of Jesus, for he told the One from Nazareth: "Rabbi, we know that you have come *from* God as a teacher. For no one can do these signs that You do unless God is *with* him" (John 3:2). Nicodemus recognized that Jesus had come "from" God, but he did not acknowledge that He came *out of* God—as the writers of the New Testament declared. The Jewish teacher recognized that God was "with" Christ, but he did not acknowledge that the Father Himself was *in* the Son—as Jesus Himself testified. Whereas God was merely "with" His prophets, He was "in" Jesus Christ (John 14:10-11).

From Romans 8 is an important, remarkable verse whose full meaning has been obscured by the English translations:

> "*For what the law could not do in that it was weak through the flesh, God did by sending His own Son in the likeness of sinful flesh, on account of sin: He condemned sin in the flesh*" (Romans 8:3, NKJV).

The preceding translation is a fairly acceptable rendering of the Greek. However, we should note that the English phrase "His own Son" can be misleading, for the Greek actually says that God sent "the Son of Himself." In other words, God sent *Himself* as a Son!

The Greek word for "Himself" is *heautou*. On rare occasions *heautou* (or a form of it) apparently has the idea of "own." However, the basic meaning is reflexive, "himself." The context of Romans 8:3 indicates that this is the meaning here.

If Paul meant that God sent His "own" Son, then it is strange that he did *not* employ the normal Greek word (*idios*) to express that thought. Conversely, if the apostle did not mean that God had sent the Son *"of Himself,"* it is also strange that he utilized the very Greek term (*heautou*) that normally and basically has *that* meaning. The word that the versions have rendered as "His own" in Romans 8:3 is the same word they have correctly translated as "Himself" in Ephesians 5:27, which says that Jesus will present the church to "Himself." (The same term is also correctly translated in II Corinthians 5:19 and Titus 2:14.)

Therefore, according to the inspired Greek of the apostle Paul:

"For what the law could not do in that it was weak through the flesh, God did by sending the Son of Himself in the likeness of sinful flesh on account of sin: He condemned sin in the flesh" (Romans 8:3, literal Greek).

It is not surprising that Dr. Alfred Marshall placed the above rendering in his well-known Greek-English interlinear New Testament, for it is exactly what the Greek means.

For those who do not know Greek and do not have a Greek-English interlinear, there is the benefit of the *context* of Romans 8:3 itself. That context gives the answers for these important questions: (1) Who is the subject of the verse? The answer is "God." (2) How did God "condemn sin"? The answer is "in the flesh"! And how *could*

God have condemned sin in the flesh unless He *had* become a Son of Himself in the person of Jesus? Christ's own words make the same point:

- *"He who believes in Me, believes not in Me but in Him who sent me" (John 12:44, NKJV).*
- *"And he who sees Me sees Him who sent Me" (John 12:45, NKJV).*
- *"If you had known Me, you would have known My Father also" (John 14:7, NKJV).*
- *"He who has seen Me has seen the Father" (John 14:9, NKJV).*
- *"He who hates Me hates My Father also" (John 15:23, NKJV).*

Frankly, these statements by Jesus do not appear to be sane statements unless God *had* sent Himself into the world in the person of the Nazarene. The conclusive verse of Scripture in this regard declares:

"God was in Christ, reconciling the world to Himself" (II Corinthians 5:19).

Here, *heautou* ("Himself") is in the singular dative case.

We must emphasize that this verse and other verses of Scripture do not merely say that God was "with" Christ. God Himself was *in* Jesus Christ.

For this reason, at the end of the era, Jesus will not present the church to another. He will simply present the church to Himself: "Husbands, love your wives, even as Christ also loved the church, and gave Himself for it—

that He might sanctify and cleanse it with the washing of water by the Word, that He might present to *Himself* a glorious church" (Ephesians 5:25-27).

Another related, majestic verse of Scripture declares that we are "awaiting our blessed hope, the appearing of the glory of our great God and Savior Jesus Christ, who *gave Himself* for us—to redeem us from iniquity and to purify *for* Himself a people of His own who are zealous for good deeds" (Titus 2:13-14). (See Exodus 19:5; Deuteronomy 14:2.)

When we remember that "our great God gave *Himself,*" then John 3:16 and similar verses of Scripture take on real significance: "For God so loved the world, that He *gave* His only begotten Son, that whoever believes in Him should not perish but have everlasting life" (John 3:16, NKJV).

The man Moses was certainly a great prophet, but even he does not really compare with this One in whom we can find eternal life:

"Therefore, holy brethren, partakers of the heavenly calling, consider the Apostle and High Priest of our confession, Christ Jesus, who was faithful to Him who appointed Him, as Moses also was faithful in all His house. For this One has been counted worthy of more glory than Moses, inasmuch as He who built the house has more honor than the house. For every house is built by someone, but He who built all things is God. And Moses indeed was faithful in all His house as a servant, for a testimony of those things which would be spoken afterward, but Christ as a Son over His own house, whose house we are if we hold fast the confidence and

the rejoicing of the hope firm to the end" (Hebrews 3:1-6, NKJV).

This amazing passage contrasts Moses and Jesus. Verse 3 makes a significant point with the word translated "appointed." The original Greek word is *poieo*, and its basic meaning is "to make." The noun from this verb is *poiema*, meaning "what is made, creation." The noun appears only two times in the New Testament: in Romans 1:20 (concerning what is made in God's physical creation) and in Ephesians 2:10 (concerning what is made in God's spiritual creation). Hebrews 3 thus states vividly that "Christ Jesus" (verse 1) "was made" (verse 2) to be "a Son over His own house" (verse 6).

Let us notice the greatness of this One when we compare Him to Moses:

1. Moses was a part of God's house (verse 3). Jesus *built* the house (verse 3). Indeed, *God* built the house (verse 4).

2. Moses was faithful as a servant in the Lord's house (verse 5). Jesus was faithful as One who had been *made* (verse 2) an apostle, high priest and Son (verses 1, 6). Jesus was a Son over His *own* house (verse 6).

What is His house? The church, the world, even the universe. This passage specifically refers to Jesus' spiritual creation—the church. But we have observed that the Bible also describes this One as the Creator of all things. Thus, *His* house must include both His physical creation and His spiritual creation. According to the Scriptures, Jesus is over it all—even as a Son. This is so simply because "God wanted all of himself to be in his Son" (Colossians 1:19, Living Bible)!

Eternal Son or Begotten Son?

In chapter 2 we learned that Zechariah 12:10 anticipated the Sonship of Yahweh in the physical form of Jesus
Christ. According to this verse, the Messiah was to be a
"firstborn Son." The concept of the "only begotten Son" is
also implied in the Hebrew word *yachid*, which is normally translated in Zechariah as "the only Son" or a similar phrase. The word actually has a dual meaning of (1)
"the *only* One" and (2) "the *forsaken* One"! It is well documented in the pages of the New Testament that the
Nazarene was not only rejected and forsaken by His own
Jewish people but even by His own apostles shortly
before His crucifixion.

Besides Zechariah 12:10, another Old Testament
prophecy that foretold the incarnation of God as a Son is
in the Book of Psalms. From the writings of King David
we have this interesting disclosure:

*"I will tell of the decree of Yahweh. He said to me, 'You
are My Son; today I have begotten you'"* (Psalm 2:7).

Like so many statements in the Psalms, the foregoing
is a Messianic prophecy that would find its fulfillment in
the lineage of David. Paul applied this verse of Scripture to
the resurrection of Christ in Acts 13:33. Elsewhere, Jesus
was considered as "begotten" when He rose from the
grave, for Revelation 1:5 calls Jesus Christ "the firstborn
[or "first-begotten"] from the dead"—a definite reference
to His resurrection.

However, when the New Testament writers spoke of
the "begotten" Son, they typically referred to the coming
of the Messiah into the world. For example, Hebrews 1:5

quotes Psalm 2:7 to establish two significant points: (1) A Son was begotten. (2) He was begotten on a certain day. Here, the writer had in mind the *birth* of the Messiah, for he said in the next verse, "When He brings the first-begotten into the world, He says, 'Let all God's angels worship Him'" (Hebrews 1:6). But what is particularly interesting in Psalm 2:7 is that the Son was to be begotten and that He was to be begotten on a certain *day*.

Although some religious authors have depicted Christ as an "eternal" Son, nowhere does the Bible ever call Jesus an "eternal Son." Actually, the Biblical concept of a begotten Son does not permit the possibility of an eternal Son, for the two concepts are an obvious contradiction in terms. As far as the Bible is concerned, Jesus Christ was a begotten Son—"the only begotten Son." If we are to be consistent, we must decide whether to believe in an eternal Son or an only begotten Son.

Fortunately, the New Testament has a great deal to say about the Sonship of Jesus. As we just saw, Christ, as a Son over His own house, was "made" (Hebrews 3:2, 6, literal Greek). An illuminating verse of Scripture in this regard is in Romans:

"Concerning his Son Jesus Christ our Lord, which was made of the seed of David according to the flesh" (Romans 1:3, KJV).

Here, we see that the Son was "made" from the lineage of David. Whereas in Hebrews 3:2 the Greek verb for "made" is *poieo,* in Romans 1:3 the Greek verb is *ginomai.* The KJV correctly translates this verb as "made," for it is the very verb that also occurs in John 1:3

and Hebrews 11:3—two verses of Scripture that deal with the creation of all things. And in these two latter verses, the English versions customarily translate *ginomai* as "made" (KJV, NKJV, RSV, NIV, etc.). The verb has the same meaning in Romans 1:3 regarding the making of the Sonship of Jesus!

Another related verse is in Galatians:

"But when the fulness of the time was come, God sent forth his Son, made *of a woman,* made *under the law" (Galatians 4:4, KJV).*[13]

In Galatians 4:4 the KJV is again correct in translating the Greek verb as "made" both times, for it is *ginomai*, the same verb that appears in Romans 1:3, John 1:3, and Hebrews 11:3!

Although the Son was "made" from a woman and "made" under the law, here was no ordinary son. For the Gospels declare that this Son was born of a virgin:

- *"Now the birth of Jesus Christ took place in this way. When His mother had been betrothed to Joseph, before they came together, she was found to be with child* of the Holy Spirit" *(Matthew 1:18).*
- *"When Joseph learned of Mary's pregnancy, an angel of God appeared to him and said: 'Do not fear to take Mary as your wife, for that which is begotten in her is out of [literal Greek] the Holy Spirit'" (Matthew 1:20).*

According to this Biblical record, the Son was begotten when the Holy Spirit overshadowed the virgin with the divine presence. Furthermore, according to these references, the only Father that the Son had was the Holy Spirit of God Himself. From Luke's account, we find that an angel told Mary:

"The Holy Spirit shall come upon you. And the power of the Most High shall overshadow you. Therefore, that Holy Thing which will be born of you shall be called the Son of God" (Luke 1:35).

We should emphasize that, according to Luke, this One "shall" be called the Son of God when He is born— *not before* His birth. The same angel said concerning the Messiah: "He shall be great. And He *shall* be called the Son of the Most High" (Luke 1:32).

Whether this One was to be known as the Son of "God" or the Son of the "Most High," the Biblical concept of the Sonship of Jesus centers upon His supernatural physical birth. In the words of a perceptive scholar: "Matthew and Luke try by means of the *infancy* narratives to explain Jesus' Sonship, and to lift the veil from the question of 'how the Father begets the Son.'"[14]

How does the Bible explain the Sonship of Jesus Christ? From the "infancy narratives" of Matthew 1 and Luke 1! But unfortunately, the church councils and the theologians of later centuries were not willing to accept the Biblical explanation of how Jesus became a Son: "With their completely philosophical approach the later Christological speculations tried to explain this 'how' in a different way."[15]

According to John 1:18, "the only begotten Son" has made God known.[16] It is evident in the context of this verse that John had one thing in mind—the coming of a divine Messiah into the world as a human being—for he stated only four verses earlier that the Word "became flesh" as "the only begotten One of the Father" (John 1:14). John 1:1 had already stated that this Word was God Himself. Thus John 1, like Matthew 1 and Luke 1, directly associates the only "begotten" Son with the physical birth of Jesus Christ.

The Bible sometimes calls others "sons of God," but John 1:14, 18 and John 3:16 specifically identify Jesus of Nazareth as "the only begotten Son" because only He was begotten or conceived by the Holy Spirit of God (Matthew 1:20; Luke 1:35). Of all human beings, with the exception of Adam and Eve, only Jesus had no human father. Jesus alone is both fully God and fully human—a Messiah with a divine nature (His Spirit) and a physical nature (His flesh). Jesus alone is the divine Word who became flesh.

The New Testament does not refer to Jesus only as the Son "of God," for we have already seen that the angel called Him the Son "of the Most High." In addition, the Messiah is the "Son of David" and the "Son of Man"—these two latter expressions *especially* indicating that the Sonship of Jesus rests upon the *humanity* of the divine One. In fact, the New Testament calls Christ the "Son of Man" many more times than "Son of God." The title "Son of Man" was "a Hebraistic expression of a somewhat frequent type, indicating *a human being with all the characteristics of a human being*, . . . (a Messianic title especially favoured by our Lord for this very reason)."[17]

As the "Son of Man" He was a man—a human being—but He was also deity in the flesh (John 1:1, 14; II Corinthians 5:19; Titus 2:13-14; Hebrews 1:6, 8). Again, the

Biblical concept of the Sonship of Jesus revolves around the temporal humanity, the physical incarnation, of a divine Savior.

From the Book of Hebrews we learn that Christ as the Son was "being made perfect." "Although He was a Son, He learned obedience through what He suffered. And *being made perfect*, He became the source of eternal salvation to all who obey Him" (Hebrews 5:8-9; see also 7:28). The Son was "being made perfect" in the earthly pilgrimage of Jesus.

In the Son, God was speaking. This is precisely what the writer of Hebrews claimed: "In many and various ways God spoke of old to our fathers by the prophets. But in these last days He has spoken to us in a Son [literal Greek]" (Hebrews 1:1-2).

The eternal God is still speaking to us in a Son. May we listen to His words.

We stated earlier that if Jesus is a begotten Son then He cannot be an eternal Son. However, even though the Bible does not speak of Him as an eternal Son, the One who became flesh—who became a Son—*is eternal*. He is eternal—but as God, not as a Son.

Jesus Himself said: "For as the Father has life in Himself, so He *has given* the Son to have life in Himself" (John 5:26). If the Father "has given" the Son to have "life in Himself," then there was a time when the Son did not have that life! Of course, Jesus had life as Lord and God, but not as a Son. The One who was to become the Messiah had "origin from of old, *from days of eternity*" [literal Hebrew] (Micah 5:2).

The giving of life to the Son is the work of *Yahweh*—the great I Am that Jesus identified Himself as being.

Yahweh, the eternal Father, is the Mighty God who was willing to *become* a Son—which is exactly what Isaiah prophesied would happen seven hundred years before the Nazarene was born:

> *"For to us a child is* born; *to us a son is given. . . . And His name will be called Wonderful, Counselor, Mighty God, Eternal Father, Prince of Peace" (Isaiah 9:6).*

In this majestic verse, the Hebrew word for "child" is in the masculine gender, and it literally means "one who is brought forth in birth"—having the same root letters as the Hebrew verb for "born." Therefore, we easily recognize that Isaiah 9:6 has at least three words which point to the physical Sonship of the coming, divine Messiah: "child," "born," and "Son." In addition, a fourth word declares that God would become a Son—"Prince" (Hebrew, *sar*, from which the English word "sir" is derived, according to some scholars). A prince is a royal son of a king, which Jesus truly was when He came into the world as "the Prince of Peace."

Only when we comprehend the Biblical teaching of the Sonship of Jesus can we understand how the *"child"* could also be our *"Mighty God"*—and how the *"Son,"* the *"Prince of Peace,"* could also be our *"Eternal Father"*!

Chapter 4

Eternal Father

The Christian writer Theodore Pitcairn once asked an intriguing question:

> If a man were not sure whether his father was one person or three, and he was uninterested in finding out or considering the matter, could it be said that the man loved his father? If a man were in such a predicament, would it not affect his life—his point of view? Would it not disturb him profoundly?[1]

If we are not sure whether our God is one eternal Father—or more—how can we expect to worship Him in spirit and in truth?

"God is a Spirit, and those who worship Him must

worship in spirit and truth" (John 4:24, NKJV).

But some say we should leave the Godhead question alone—and let the theologians take care of it. Unfortunately, in too many cases the theologians are not "taking care of it." Too often the theologians point us toward philosophical speculation, completely ignoring the Bible, the Word of God. Too often when the theologians point us *to* the Bible, they point us only to a few verses of Scripture, and those taken out of context, thus *distorting* the Biblical view of God. In his enthusiasm, an evangelist once wrote:

> But there are three persons in the Godhead. . . . In Ephesians 4:4-6 inspiration declared there is "one Spirit," "one Lord," and "one God." Now, how many does that make? Add them up. "One Spirit," "one Lord," and "one God"—one, two three! How simple![2]

No, it is not quite that simple, for the foregoing comment designates the "one God" as only one of three persons in the Godhead—in other words, the author claimed that there are two other persons within the Godhead *besides* the "one God"! But if the "one God" is the first person in the Godhead, then any other persons could not *be* God—and thus could not even *be* in the Godhead.

This is a classic example of a "slip of the pen," for it illustrates the mentality (conscious or unconscious) that many professing Christians people seem to have. They claim to believe in the full deity of Jesus, but the only *God* they speak and write about is (to them) the first person in the Godhead. As a result, they often speak of "Jesus and

God" as two distinct persons when they evidently *mean* "Jesus and the *Father."*

May we not forget the Father. The Bible teaches us that there is "one God—the Father" (I Corinthians 8:6). According to the Scriptures, He is the *"Eternal Father"* who has become our Savior *as* Jesus Christ (Isaiah 9:6). May we not forget *Him.*

The New Testament Salutations

Several New Testament Epistles have a common salutation or greeting, and almost all of these greetings are in letters written by the apostle Paul. All of Paul's salutations are either identical or very similar in wording.[3]

For a long time, many people have assumed that these New Testament greetings show a distinction of persons in the Godhead. Perhaps, this is partly because of trinitarian presuppositions that some have concerning the nature of God, and perhaps it is partly because of the excessive commas and the second preposition "from" that are found in a translation (but not in the Greek text). The following is an example of a salutation according to the KJV:

"Grace be unto you, and peace, from God our Father, and from the Lord Jesus Christ" (I Corinthians 1:3, KJV).

There are several reasons why the greetings do not show either a distinction of divine persons or the doctrine of the trinity.[4] Actually, what we have already studied has confirmed from the Scriptures that God is one eternal Spirit-Being who cannot be separated into persons. This and the following chapters will provide even more

Biblical evidence that will substantiate this great truth still further.

As far as the salutations are concerned, it is significant that virtually all of Paul's greetings leave out any reference at all to the Holy Spirit. If the Christian God consists of three persons known as the Father, the Son, and the Holy Spirit, it would certainly be natural for the New Testament salutations to consistently include the Holy Spirit. And yet the Holy Spirit is conspicuously absent.

It is also interesting that the New Testament greetings do not have the title "Son" or "Son of God." This terminology was always present in the *post*-biblical trinitarian creeds of Catholic church history. However, like "Holy Spirit," the title "Son" or "Son of God" is missing in the salutations.

As we reflect on the greetings, it is important to understand that the Epistles were written to Jewish and Gentile Christians who believed in and worshiped *one God* who is *one Lord*. If we keep this in mind, then we can appreciate why the readers were consistently greeted with the words: "Grace and peace from God our Father and the Lord Jesus Christ."

Both the Jewish and Gentile believers surely appreciated the complete greeting since every word in the salutation has significance. The Jewish brethren would certainly have related to the writer's reference to "God our Father." Even before they had put their faith in the Lord Jesus Christ, they had worshiped God as their heavenly Father.

In addition, the title "Lord" would have had significance to them because they had always worshiped God their Father *as* Lord. The Greek term for "Lord," *Kurios*, in the greetings (and the rest of the New Testament) is the same word used in the Septuagint, the popular Greek translation of the Old Testament. The Jews knew that in the Old Testament *Kurios* was the Greek translation of the Hebrew words *Yahweh* and *Adonai* (and its related titles) for the Lord of the Old Testament. Therefore, they would not have distinguished "the Lord" Jesus Christ from Yahweh, the Lord of the Old Testament.

The Hebrew Christians of the New Testament world would also have appreciated the title "Christ," as a Greek translation of the Hebrew title "Messiah." The coming of a Messiah into the world was an important concept throughout the Old Testament. Those early saints knew that just as "Messiah" (from the Hebrew *Mashiach*) means "the Anointed One," the title "Christ" (from the Greek *Christos*) means the same thing.

In addition, the early Jewish Christians recognized that "Jesus" (*Yesous*) was the Greek form of the Hebrew name "Joshua" (*Yehoshua*), which means "Yahweh-Savior" or "Yahweh Is Salvation." Therefore, they would not have distinguished "Jesus" in the salutations from Yahweh.

Finally, while every Jew of that day used the word "peace" (*shalom*) in every greeting, "grace" and "peace" were Old Testament terms that were becoming important New Testament concepts associated with the Lord Jesus Christ.

There is also much in the salutations that the *Gentile* Christians would have appreciated. Many of these Gentiles had been followers of Judaism (either as "proselytes" or as "God-fearers") and were worshipers of the true God even before they had been "baptized into Christ" (Galatians 3:27). Therefore, they, like their Jewish brethren, had already worshiped God as "the Father," who was also their "Lord."

Some of these Gentiles had already known about the Old Testament prophecies of the coming Messiah even before they accepted Jesus Christ as their Savior. Many of the Gentile brethren had only a pagan background, but even they would have related to the Greek title *Kurios*— "Lord." This is because throughout the Greek and Roman Gentile world *Kurios* was a divine title for the pagan deities. Now, as Christians, these Gentiles realized that *their* "Lord," Jesus Christ, was the only true Lord who existed.

"Grace" was a common greeting among Greek-speaking Gentiles, but like their Jewish brethren, these Gentile believers were learning that both "grace" and "peace" were significant Christian concepts.

Whether Jewish or Gentile, the early Christians believed that God was one eternal Spirit (I Corinthians 12:11, 13; Ephesians 4:4). And the phrase "God our Father" in every salutation points to the immortal Spirit-Being and His role of Creator, Father, and Sustainer of all life. His role of Father and Creator was first proclaimed throughout the Old Testament (Malachi 2:10) and was declared again throughout the New Testament (I Corinthians 8:6; Ephesians 4:6).

The phrase "Lord Jesus Christ" points to the role and manifestation of God as a *Son* who had become flesh in the form of the Nazarene (John 1:1, 14). Messianic prophecies had predicted in the Old Testament that God Himself would come into the world in order to become its Savior (Micah 5:2; Zechariah 12:10).

Numerous New Testament passages confirm that

those prophecies were fulfilled when Yahweh, the Lord of the Old Testament, became a Son as Jesus of Nazareth (Isaiah 9:6; Luke 1:31, 35). And many verses in the New Testament identify Jesus Christ as both Lord and God (John 20:26-29; Jude 4). All of this absolutely proves that in the New Testament greetings (or anywhere else in the New Testament), we cannot identify "God our Father" as a different person from "the Lord Jesus Christ." The two phrases do emphasize two important roles and manifestations of one God.

As we have already seen, the title "Lord Jesus Christ" is a majestic title. It is significant that "Lord," "Jesus," and "Christ" are all terms that point to an *earthly* ministry of *God*. The name "Jesus" (Yahweh-Savior) indicates that Yahweh came into the world to save. This was the name given to the Messiah when He was *born*, after being supernaturally conceived in the virgin Mary by the Holy Spirit of God (Matthew 1:18-25; Luke 1:30-35).

As already noted, "Christ" or "Messiah" means "the Anointed One" who was to come into the world to be its Savior (I Timothy 1:15). In the Old Testament, prophets, priests, and kings were all anointed with olive oil, but Christ, "the anointed One," was anointed with the Holy Spirit (Isaiah 61:1; Luke 4:18) at the beginning of the Incarnation. Even more so than John the Baptist, He was "filled with the Holy Spirit, even from His mother's womb" (Luke 1:15). And this anointing was confirmed at His baptism (Matthew 3:16-17).

The early Christians knew what God had done in the Nazarene, and the Epistles themselves, including the salutations, reinforce the great truth of the Incarnation and visitation of God.

The New Testament writers were strict monotheists, and the Bible emphasizes monotheism from Genesis to Revelation. Because both writer and reader alike understood that the Epistles' greetings referred to *two* important roles of God (*not* three persons of a trinity), the Holy Spirit is not even mentioned. Of course, the salutations properly honor the Godhead by the terms they use because (1) "God our Father" *is* a holy, immortal Spirit who (2) clothed Himself with flesh *as* a Son, "the Lord Jesus Christ."

Naturally, the greetings were not confusing to the Christians of New Testament times as they seem to be to some people today. This is because they were written and read several hundred years before the doctrine of the trinity had evolved in the Roman Catholic Church. The terminology and doctrines of the trinity did not become established until the fourth century—long after the New Testament was completed.

Today, there is a long-standing traditional heritage of interpreting certain passages such as the New Testament salutations from a trinitarian point of view. Even though a careful examination of the context (as well as other passages of Scripture) does not support such an interpretation, it is still difficult for some believers to throw off the shackles and bonds of religious traditionalism. Because all of us are creatures of habit, tradition often dies hard. It is natural for many believers to feel a sense of security in traditional beliefs and a familiar religious heritage. However, Jesus warned us that religious traditions that are not built upon His Word are foundations of sand. Therefore, He urged us to build upon *His* words in order to have a foundation of solid rock (Matthew 7:24-29).

Jesus said that if we abide in His Word, we are "truly" His disciples (John 8:31). Then we will know the truth, and the truth will make us free (John 8:32).

The general context of the salutations themselves shows that the writers emphasized two different manifestations of God, and all these New Testament greetings focus on the two roles of God as Father and Son. When one reads the remarks immediately after the salutations, it is obvious that the writer, in the context of the greetings, was praising and glorifying what God has done in Jesus as a Son. (See Romans 1:1-7, note verses 3 and 4; I Corinthians 1:1-9, note verses 2, 4, 9; Galatians 1:1-5, note verse 4; Ephesians 1:1-8, note verses 3, 5, 6-7.)

Whenever we go to a passage of Scripture, it is always helpful to examine it prayerfully and carefully in its immediate context. We should ask what the passage itself is saying. It is also important to study other passages of Scripture that are related to the text in question. Concerning the divine terminology in the salutations, what does the Bible say elsewhere about "God," "the Father," "Lord," "Jesus," and "Christ"? In this regard, the Word of God explains itself in a wonderful and profound way again and again. The Bible is its own best commentary, and the more we know the Scriptures, the more we will understand God's beautiful truths. The Lord has promised us that we will be richly blessed if we will study His Word honestly and cherish it in our hearts (Psalm 119).

I Corinthians 8 is one passage of Scripture among many that explain the terminology in the greetings. Here, we read:

"Therefore concerning the eating of things offered

*to idols, we know that an idol is nothing in the world,
and that there is no other God but one. For even if
there are so-called gods, whether in heaven or on
earth (as there are many gods and many lords), yet
for us there is only one God, the Father, of whom are
all things, and we for Him; and one Lord Jesus Christ,
through whom are all things, and through whom we
live" (I Corinthians 8:4-6, NKJV).*

When Paul stated in verse 5 that "there are many gods
and many lords," both he and his readers knew that in the
pagan Gentile world the term "lords" was simply another
word for "gods." Both terms referred to the deities of the
Gentiles. Likewise, in verse 6 when the apostle used the
terms "God" and "Lord," both the writer and his first-century readers recognized that these terms always referred
to the same Spirit-Being who created and rules the universe. For they knew well Deuteronomy 6:4, which states,
"The LORD our God, the LORD is one."

As mentioned earlier, the New Testament Jewish and
Gentile Christians knew that the term "Lord" in the
Scriptures was equivalent to "God." In I Corinthians 8
Paul said that there is *"no other God but one"* (verse 4)
and that *"there is only one God, the Father"* (verse 6).
However, he also declared that there is only *"one Lord"*
and that He is Jesus Christ (verse 6). In making these
comments, the inspired writer spoke of two roles or functions of the same wonderful Lord God.

I Corinthians 8:4-6 demonstrates that the salutations
also honor two roles of one Lord God when they consistently refer to "God our Father" and "the Lord Jesus
Christ." Jude is another inspired New Testament writer

who proved conclusively that we cannot separate our Lord God into two distinct persons as "God" and "Lord," when he stated categorically that "the *only* Lord God" who exists is "*our* Lord Jesus Christ"! (Jude 4).

The Salutations and Commas

When scholars go to the Greek manuscripts, they find that there are no punctuation marks in the ancient texts. Consequently, all forms of punctuation, including commas, must be added in translation—and should be added according to the context and the meaning that the inspired authors intended.

In addition, as startling as it might be to some, the inspired Greek text of the salutations does not have "from" before the phrase "the Lord Jesus Christ." It is noteworthy that this is the case in all thirteen of the apostle Paul's epistles that have the greetings. A proper rendering of the inspired Greek would be:

"Grace to you and peace from God our Father and the Lord Jesus Christ" (I Corinthians 1:3, NKJV and RSV; see also NIV).

It is now common for the English versions only to have one "from," in accordance with the Greek, and it is before "God," as the preceding translation of I Corinthians 1:3 shows. Perhaps many people have been confused because the King James Version adds a second "from" before "our Lord Jesus Christ" in the greetings. However, even in this case, the *KJV* adds the extra "from" in only five of Paul's epistles (I and II Corinthians, Galatians, Ephesians, and Philippians), while it faithfully leaves out the extra preposition in Paul's eight other epistles (Romans, Colossians, I and II Thessalonians, I and II Timothy, Titus, and Philemon). So the King James Version itself does translate the salutations correctly in most cases. And in the epistles that have the second "from," the KJV places it in italics to indicate that it is not in the Greek.

In this regard, it is indeed curious that the New International Version has translated Romans 1:7 by adding the extra "from," while it translates Paul's twelve other salutations correctly by omitting the second preposition! Unfortunately, unlike the KJV, the NIV does not have the additional preposition in italics, thus leaving the wrong impression that it belongs in the text. In any case, the Greek is explicit that only one preposition belongs in the salutations, since a second "from" does not appear in any ancient Greek manuscripts. Most English versions now correctly translate the salutations accordingly.

Because the ancient Greek text did not have any punctuation, it is left for us to decide from the context whether or not commas should be added. It is not unusual to find no commas in the salutations when one reads the modern English translations. And this is a sound rendering of the Greek both from a linguistic and a theological perspective.

If a comma is to be added at all, it should be placed after "God" or after "Lord," while omitting "the" before "Lord." Although the Greek definite article is lacking before "Lord" in the salutations, the definite idea is intrinsically present since "Lord Jesus Christ" is a proper name. Also, "the" is not needed in the English to bring out the definite sense if "our" is associated with both "Father" *and* "Lord," as it appears to be in the Greek.

A natural translation according to Greek syntax would be ". . . God, our Father and Lord Jesus Christ," especially since Paul placed the possessive pronoun "our" after "Father" and not before it! Because we consistently find "our" *between* "Father" and "Lord Jesus Christ" in the Greek, Paul *very likely* had in mind, "God, our Father and Lord Jesus Christ." An additional comma after "Lord" gives the same meaning. Therefore, if any English commas are to be added, the sense of the Greek is still the same whether the phrase is "God, our Father and Lord Jesus Christ" or "God, our Father and Lord, Jesus Christ." Either English rendering properly associates "Father" with "Lord," as Paul did when he repeatedly placed the one possessive pronoun "our" *between* these two divine titles.[5]

In any event, the salutations definitely do not suggest that grace and peace come *from* one and then *from* another. As a matter of fact, there is a crucial Greek word in all of the salutations that sheds even more light on this important discussion.

The Truth about *Kai*

The common word for "and" in the Greek New Testament is *kai*. However, *kai* is also the usual term for "even" or "that is."[6] Therefore, it very well may be significant that the New Testament greetings have *kai* between "Father" and "Lord Jesus Christ." This means that a possible English translation would be: "Grace to you and peace from God our Father, *even* [*kai*] the Lord Jesus Christ" (I Corinthians 1:3).[7]

Although this translation may seem strange to some, the probability of its accuracy is high, particularly in light of parallel passages like Jude 4, where the context proves that we are to understand *kai* as "even" or "that is." In the Jude passage it is a *certainty* that the correct translation is: "the only Lord God, even [*kai*] our Lord Jesus Christ"!

So we can accurately and faithfully translate the salutations in Paul's epistles from Greek into English in a number of ways—all of which significantly bring out the oneness of our God. The important thing to appreciate is that the original language of the greetings, like so many New Testament passages, emphasizes two roles of one Lord God and certainly not three persons of a trinity.

The apostle John placed a salutation in his second epistle that is slightly different from Paul's greetings. John once wrote to fellow Christians:

"Grace, mercy, and peace will be with you from God the Father and from the Lord Jesus Christ, the Son of the Father, in truth and love" (II John 3, NKJV).

Whereas Paul used the proposition *apo* for "from" in his greetings, John used the preposition *para* in this verse. Both *apo* and *para* have the same general meaning of "from." However, *apo* also emphasizes the idea of *agency*—"by." Thus Paul apparently said in his salutations that "grace and peace" not only come from God but also *by* Him. And of course, this agency is *specifically* by "our Lord Jesus Christ"—as Paul repeatedly stated in his greetings. As pointed out earlier, it is significant that *apo* ("from, by") always appears only one time in each of his salutations, another indication that the divine titles refer to one Spirit-Being who is our Father and Lord.

In II John 3, it may be significant that John employed

para as a preposition two times in this salutation. *Para* not only means "from," but it emphasizes the *source* of something. Therefore, John apparently said that just as "grace, mercy and peace" come *from* "God the Father" (as the ultimate Source), these blessings also come *from* "the Lord Jesus Christ, the Son of the Father" (as that same ultimate Source). This explanation is credible, not only because of the meaning of *para*, but also because John, like Paul, used *kai* ("and" or "even") between the divine titles in II John 3.

Of course, John did not try to make a distinction of two divine persons by using two prepositions. Otherwise, Paul, who wrote a much more literary Greek than John, easily could have done the same thing if he wanted to make that point—and he never did so. The apostle John, like the apostle Paul, knew that we cannot separate "God" from "the Lord," since He is one Lord God. And John, like Paul, did not refer to the Holy Spirit at all in his salutations. Why? Because neither author was referring to divine persons of a trinity.

As we might expect, in II John 3 the use of two prepositions with *kai* and two proper names of one God does not indicate two divine persons. In His wisdom God has made it plain for anyone who can read the English versions. (Greek scholarship is not necessary.) John himself demonstrated this truth both in the context of II John 3 and in another salutation that he wrote in the Book of Revelation. Before we look at the greeting in Revelation, it is most enlightening to examine the context of the salutation in II John itself.

What is interesting is that II John 3 makes note of "the Son of the Father," a phrase that clearly focuses on the two roles of God as Father and Son. This salutation actually restates the same concept of God's two roles in a divine Messiahship that appear in Paul's greetings.

In addition, John confirmed here (as he did many times elsewhere in the New Testament) that we cannot distinguish God the Father as a different person from the Lord Jesus Christ. Here is why. Immediately after John's salutation, he spoke of receiving a commandment "from the Father" (II John 4). Then, in the very next verse "the disciple whom Jesus loved" gave a startling revelation when he explained that the commandment he received from the Father "from the beginning" was that "we love one another" (verse 5). This is the very commandment that *Jesus Christ* gave to John and the other apostles, as John recorded in John 13:34! Thus according to the author of the salutation in II John 3, Jesus Himself was the Father who gave the commandment.

Furthermore, the apostle went on to state that we should have "the doctrine of Christ," the truth that Jesus came in the flesh (verses 7-9). In the profound grammar of the inspired Greek, we can understand the genitive case "of Christ" in the phrase "the doctrine of Christ" either as a subjective genitive or an objective genitive. If the case is an objective genitive, then the doctrine of Christ is a doctrine *about* Christ. If it is a subjective genitive, then it is a doctrine *from* Christ. New Testament teaching shows that the doctrine of Christ is *both* a doctrine about Christ and from Christ. The doctrine of Christ is the gospel of Christ—the "good news" of Christ—and it is a gospel that is both *from* Him as deity (God the Father) and *about* Him as flesh (the Son of Man).

Because the doctrine of Christ is a doctrine about

Christ, the Son, it is a message of what God the Father did *in* Him in order to offer us forgiveness of sin, redemption, and eternal life. (See John 7:16-17; I Corinthians 15:1-4; II Corinthians 5:17-19.) Because the doctrine of Christ is also a doctrine from Christ, the Lord, it is a message from Him as deity. He spoke with divine authority. (See Matthew 7:24-29, 28:17-20; Jude 3-4; Revelation 22:12-16.) The Greek word in the phrase "His teaching" in Matthew 7:28 is the same word that John used in II John 9 in the phrase "the doctrine of Christ." So the doctrine of Christ is a doctrine we must not trifle with, since it is a divine, Biblical doctrine that is both from and about our Lord and Savior Jesus Christ. John stressed the seriousness of engaging in fellowship with those who reject the doctrine of Christ when he wrote: "If anyone comes to you and does not bring this doctrine, do not receive him into your house nor greet him; for he who greets him shares in his evil deeds" (II John 10-11, NKJV).

John's association of Jesus with the Father in verse 5 continued in the following verses, including verse 9, where he wrote: "Whoever transgresses and does not abide in the doctrine of Christ does not have God. He who abides in the doctrine of Christ has both the Father and the Son" (II John 9, NKJV).

This clear verse and the ones before it all teach that if we have the doctrine of Christ, we do not have to worry that we are neglecting the Father. If we have the doctrine of Christ, we have *both* the Father *and* the Son. In other words, according to the doctrine of Christ, when we believe in the Son, we believe in the Father at the same time. And this is exactly what Jesus Himself taught in John 12:44 and other passages of Scriptures!

John taught the same wonderful truth with the same clarity in his *first* epistle as well: "Whoever denies the Son does not have the Father either; he who acknowledges the Son *has the Father also*" (I John 2:23, NKJV).

Therefore, in studying the salutation and the following verses in II John, as well as other related passages, we see that the apostle's use of two prepositions certainly does not signify two divine persons in the Godhead. On the contrary, John identified Jesus with the Father in the most revealing language. According to this inspired writer, we simply cannot distinguish the Son from the Father except in manifestations and roles.

We pointed out earlier that John has another salutation with more than one preposition. In the Book of Revelation he wrote:

"John, to the seven churches which are in Asia; Grace to you and peace from Him who is and who was and who is to come, and from the seven Spirits who are above His throne, and from Jesus Christ, the faithful witness, the firstborn from the dead, and the ruler over the kings of the earth. To Him who loved us and washed us from our sins in His own blood" *(Revelation 1:4-5, NKJV).*

This greeting uses "from" (*apo*) at three places in the Greek that are relevant to our discussion: before "Him" (verse 4), before "the seven Spirits" (verse 4), and before "Jesus Christ" (verse 5). The trinitarian approach would be to count the number of times "from" appears in the salutation. According to this reckoning, by including the seven Spirits, there would be nine divine persons in the Godhead!

Another aspect of the trinitarian approach would be to count the number of times "and" (*kai*) appears in the salutation at relevant places. But according to *this* reckoning, there would be, not nine, but as many as twelve divine persons in the Godhead!

This is the approach that trinitarians take with the *other* salutations in the New Testament. Here in Revelation 1:4-5 we have observed that this approach (1) contradicts itself and (2) leaves us with far more than three persons in the Godhead. Thus the trinitarian approach can calculate only *two* divine persons in the Godhead in all of the other New Testament salutations, while in Revelation the same trinitarian approach would calculate the contradictory numbers of *nine* and *twelve* divine persons in the Godhead.

Of course, the trinitarian approach is not the correct approach to take, and the contradictory trinitarian conclusions are not the correct conclusions to reach. It is a matter of using common sense and of understanding the terminology. In short, it is a matter of allowing the Bible, the Word of God, to explain *itself*.

Who are the seven Spirits in Revelation 1:4? Revelation 4:5 refers to the seven Spirits of God as "seven lamps of fire burning before the throne." Then, Revelation 5:6 further reveals that the seven Spirits are "seven eyes" of the Lamb, and they are sent out into all the earth. In other words, the seven Spirits belong to the Lamb, and the Lamb is Jesus Christ (John 1:29; Revelation 5:1-14).

Apparently, the seven Spirits symbolize the one eternal Spirit of God, since seven in the Scriptures is a symbolic number for completion, totality, and perfection. In any case, the seven Spirits of Revelation 1:4 belong to Jesus Christ, according to Revelation 5:6. And it is indeed noteworthy that all of the other divine terms in verses 4 and 5 belong to Jesus as well. Immediately after the mention of the seven Spirits, verse 5 specifically notes "Jesus Christ" by name, with particular emphasis on what He did as a Son—as a Man—for "His God and Father" (Verse 5). The *role* of "the Son of Man" is the focus here, as reference is to "Him who loved us and washed us from our sins in His own blood" (verse 5).

In verse 5 of the salutation there is the phrase "from Him who is and [*kai*] who was and [*kai*] who is to come." It becomes clear who this One is when we translate the present participle in the latter part of the phrase more precisely as any of the following:

- "the coming One"
- "the One coming"
- "He who is coming"
- "who is coming"

In fact, this present participle, "the coming One," is the same Greek word used as a present-tense finite verb only two verses later:

"Behold, He is coming *with clouds, and every eye will see Him, and they also who pierced Him. And all the tribes of the earth will mourn because of Him. Even so, Amen" (Revelation 1:7, NKJV).*

Verse 8 further describes Jesus, "the coming One" (verse 4 and 7), where John quoted Him directly:

"'I Myself [literal Greek] am the Alpha and the Omega, the Beginning and the End,' says the Lord, 'who is and who was and who is the coming One [literal Greek], the Almighty'" (Revelation 1:8).

In summary, the salutation of Revelation 1:4-5 (not including verse 6-8) has the preposition *apo* ("from") three times and *kai* ("and" or "even") five times before titles and functions of God. It is significant that all of these divine references are to Jesus. In the immediate context of the greeting, "the One who is and who was and who is coming" in verse 4 describes Himself again with these words in verse 8. Furthermore, He whom verse 5 identifies as Jesus Christ is the same One who gives Himself the exalted, divine titles in verse 8.

In addition, Jesus Christ, as the Alpha and Omega, the Beginning and the End, who is and who was and who is coming (verse 8), is also "the Lord God Almighty" (Revelation 4:8; 11:17; 15:3-4).

In conclusion, it is revealing to look at both the salutations of II John and Revelation 1 in light of the context. As a matter of fact, it is interesting to study the first chapters of *all* the epistles in which we find the New Testament greetings. The context of these passages focuses on the Lord Jesus and His manifestation as the Nazarene—both before and after His resurrection. Indeed, as we read through not only the first chapters of the Epistles but the entire Epistles, we notice an emphasis on the Lord Jesus Christ; they glorify Him in the highest terms. The salutations are simply an introduction to a continual exaltation and praise for Jesus because of what *God the Father* has done *in* Him as a Son (II Corinthians 5:19).

The greetings customarily begin with "grace and peace." Both grace and peace are constantly associated with *Jesus* throughout the Epistles and very often in the writers' farewell messages. Grace comes from the Lord Jesus Christ (Galatians 6:18; Ephesians 6:24; Philippians 4:23; II Peter 3:18, etc). Peace also comes directly from Jesus (Ephesians 2:14-18; II Thessalonians 3:16, 18; I Peter 5:14, etc.).

The salutations are actually *Christocentric*, Christ-centered, to use a theological term. Besides grace and peace introducing the greetings (and the Epistles), the salutations almost always end with the divine name "Lord Jesus Christ." Observant Bible readers realize that, indeed, the entire New Testament is Christ-centered from beginning to end. For example, the phrase "in Christ," or similar terminology, appears in the short Book of Ephesians more than thirty times. Likewise, in the first chapter alone of the Book of Philippians Paul referred to "Jesus" or "Christ" no less than eighteen times, and this does not include the other references that Paul made to Jesus through the use of "Lord" and personal pronouns.

The first book of the New Testament begins: "The book of the genealogy of Jesus Christ" (Matthew 1:1). The last book of the New Testament closes: "The grace of our Lord Jesus be with you all" (Revelation 22:21). And everything between Matthew 1:1 and Revelation 22:21 focuses on Jesus the Son and the grace that God has given us in Christ (John 1:16). Consequently, it is not surprising that many English Bibles title the New Testament as "The New Testament of our Lord and Savior Jesus Christ."

Another important passage of Scripture that uses *kai*

with "Christ," "God," and "the Father" is in the second chapter of Colossians:

"For I want you to know what a great conflict I have for you and those in Laodicea, and for as many as have not seen my face in the flesh, that their hearts may be encouraged, being knit together in love, and attaining to all riches of the full assurance of understanding, to the knowledge of the mystery of God, both of the Father and of Christ, in whom are hidden all the treasures of wisdom and knowledge" (Colossians 2:1-3, NKJV).

In this remarkable passage, the apostle has informed us through the exactness of the original, inspired language that all the treasures of wisdom and knowledge are hidden in Christ. Before we consider this point in detail, a comment is appropriate concerning the use of *kai*. In the phrase "both of the Father and of Christ" (NKJV), the two words "both" and "and" are *kai* and *kai*. The two *kais* may mean "both . . . and," but they may also be translated as "even . . . even." In any event, the context shows that the writer discussed two modes and manifestations of one God, not two persons of a trinity. As in the salutations and so many other passages of Scripture that emphasize two important roles of God, the Holy Spirit is not even mentioned.

Regarding Colossians 2:1-3, let us consider these four points:

1. Following the phrase "of God, both of the Father and of Christ" the writer used the words "in whom." In the Greek, the "whom" is a *singular* relative pronoun. In the

precision of the inspired language, it is significant that the singular "whom" points back not only to "Christ" but also to "the Father," as well as to "God." This means that the terms "Christ," "the Father," and "God" all refer to *one* Spirit-Being, not two or three.

2. There is no doubt that we must associate the phrase "in whom" with Christ since He is mentioned immediately before it.

3. If we are to connect the singular pronoun "whom" with Christ, then Paul asserted that Jesus Christ Himself possesses "all the treasures of wisdom and knowledge."

4. Finally, if Christ Himself possesses *all* the treasures of wisdom and knowledge, then this does not leave any wisdom and knowledge for either God or the Father unless "Christ," "the Father," and "God" are one and the same.

Some have noted that there is a variant ancient reading in the passage which leaves out the words "both the Father and." The variant reads: ". . . the knowledge of God's mystery, of Christ" (Colossians 2:2, RSV; see also NIV).

According to Oscar Cullmann, "A majority of investigators consider this reading to be original, especially since the following relative clause (verse 3) ["in whom are hidden all the treasures of wisdom and knowledge"] . . . ascribes to Christ what otherwise is said to be true of God."[8] We should note that *whichever* reading one accepts, the apostle Paul "ascribes to Christ what otherwise is said to be true of God."

Both the King James Version and the New King James Version have the longer reading (*kai* the Father *kai*) in verse 2, following the text of the Byzantine family of manuscripts. As we have already pointed out regarding other passages of Scriptures in this study, the Byzantine text, in our judgment, represents the correct reading because of the consistency and reliability of these numerous manuscripts. And the longer reading of Colossians 2:3 identifies Christ with both "God" and "the Father" by very specific language.

It is important to remember that both readings have "God" and "Christ" in the text, with "Christ" immediately preceding the singular relative pronoun phrase "in whom." As we saw earlier, this *does* mean that Jesus is the One who has all the treasures of wisdom and knowledge. It is also important to realize that in this passage of Scripture, like so many others about Jesus throughout the New Testament, the reference point of "Christ" in Colossians 2:2-3 is His *Sonship*. Whenever "God" and "Christ" are mentioned in the same context—as in Colossians 2:2-3, the salutations, and the "right hand" passages—there *is* a distinction between God and Christ. That distinction is of two roles of one Lord as God the Father and Jesus Christ the Son. It is not logical to see a distinction of two divine persons of a trinity in these passages. As in the salutations, the Holy Spirit is almost never mentioned whenever the discussion is about "God" and "Christ" (or similar titles).

Very often, "God" is used with "the Father," as in Colossians 2:2-3 and the salutations. And even when "God" is without the title of "the Father," the *concept* of Him as our Creator and Father is normally present, because the Scriptures identify Him in those terms. And just as a reference to "God" or "God the Father" points to His role of Creator and eternal Father, a reference to the Nazarene as "Jesus," "Christ," "Jesus Christ," "our Lord

Jesus Christ," "the Son of God," "the Son of Man," "the Son," or related terminology points to the role that God has played as a Son cloaked in humanity on this earth. The name "Jesus" and His Messianic titles were given to the Messiah when He came into the world as the Son of Man. This divine Messiah was "the Lord" when He was born (Luke 2:11). Therefore, whenever there is a reference "God" and "Christ," no careful reader of the Bible believes that Christ Himself is *not* God. The consistent message of the New Testament Scriptures confirms that verses about "God" and "Christ" (and equivalent terms) refer to two divine roles and modes of one Lord God: (1) the Father (as an eternal Spirit) and (2) the Son (as a Messiah born in Bethlehem).

In addition to Christ's very real humanity, the Bible does reveal that He was also definitely deity—the Spirit of the eternal God dwelling in temporal flesh (John 1:1, 14; Colossians 1:19, 2:9; I Timothy 3:16, etc.). Paul's exalted language for Christ in Colossians 2:2-3 appears in many related passages, some of which are in this very epistle. In Colossians 1:19 we read that in Jesus "all the fullness" was pleased to dwell. Similarly, in Colossians 2:9 we read that in Christ "dwells all the fullness of the Godhead bodily." Because of this, we are "complete in Him, who is the head of *all* principality and power" (Colossians 2:10). These passages of Scripture reveal that God the Father Himself was pleased to dwell in Jesus. (See also John 14:10.)

Children of the Light

In a world of spiritual darkness the Hebrew prophets turned to Yahweh for light. They considered *Him* to be their "Light." Micah exclaimed: "When I sit in darkness, Yahweh will be a *Light* to me!" (Micah 7:8). David cried out: "The LORD is my light and my salvation; whom shall I fear?" (Psalm 27:1, NKJV). When Yahweh put on the mantle of human flesh in the person of Jesus, John explained:

"The true Light that enlightens every man was coming into the world" (John 1:9).

But many in the world have rejected the guidance of that Light, and they have done so for a reason:

"This is the judgment, that the Light has come into the world; and men loved darkness rather than the Light because their deeds were evil. For everyone who does evil hates the Light and does not come to the Light, lest his deeds should be exposed. But he who does what is true comes to the Light, that it might be clearly seen that his deeds have been done in God" (John 3:19-21).

Do humans really have any excuse if they turn their back on this Light? If we reject this Light, is it not because our deeds are evil? For when this light shines forth, He exposes us for what we are; and He tells us to repent and come out of darkness: "The land of Zebulun and the land of Naphtali . . . Galilee of the Gentiles—the people who sat in darkness have seen a great Light. And for those who sat in the region and shadow of death, Light has dawned. From that time, Jesus began to preach, saying, Repent" (Matthew 4:15-17).

If we turn away from this Light, we turn away from

God Himself. The apostle John related: "This is the message we have heard from Him and proclaim to you, that God is Light and in *Him* is no darkness at all" (I John 1:5).

John had personally encountered the Light of God, for he had observed that Light in the life of Jesus. And the Nazarene had in fact claimed: "I am the *Light* of the world" (John 8:12).

When the Light came into the world, those who were willing to *come* to the Light could experience a genuine guidance by that Light: "The darkness is passing away, and the true Light is already shining. . . . He who loves his brother *abides* in the Light; and in Him there is no cause for stumbling" (I John 2:8, 10).

Toward the end of His earthly ministry, Jesus told people:

> *"A little while longer the light is with you. Walk while you have the light, lest darkness overtake you; he who walks in darkness does not know where he is going. While you have the light, believe in the light, that you may become sons of light" (John 12:35-36, NKJV).*

The New Testament sometimes refers to believers in Jesus as "sons" in the kingdom, whether they are men or women. Whether we are male or female, we all shall inherit the eternal kingdom of God as if we were a "son." A son in the ancient world either received the entire inheritance or a much greater inheritance than a daughter. Also, a son in Biblical times had much greater status and honor than a woman. The Christian promise is that, as a child of God, every believer will receive the inheritance of a son. There are no double standards in the kingdom of God.

The "sons of light" are sons of a particular Light. The definite article "the" occurs before "Light" no less than four times in John 12:35-36. In this passage, Jesus encouraged us to "believe in *the* Light." Therefore, "sons of light" should be translated as "sons of *the* Light" because the context confirms that Jesus spoke about one Light in particular—Himself, "the Light of the world" (John 8:12).

The Greek grammarians Dana and Mantey have reminded us that it is not necessary for the definite article to be present for a noun to be definite. Quoting the Greek scholar A. T. Robertson, they noted: "Whenever the article occurs the object is certainly definite. When it is not used the object may or may not be."[9] These scholars then stated: "The genitive case [as in "sons *of* light"] also tends to make a word definite. At such times, even if the article is not used, the object is already distinctly indicated."[10] In the language of Greek scholarship, "Sometimes with a noun which the context proves to be definite the article is not used. This places stress on the qualitative aspect of a noun [e.g., stressing the quality of the Light as light]."[11]

In John 12:35-36 the context proves that "the Light" is definite by the use of the definite article before "light" on four different occasions. Because the immediate context establishes that "sons of light" should be translated as "sons of *the* Light," Jesus Himself encouraged us to become *His* sons—*His* children—since He is the Light of the world (John 8:12).

On another occasion, Jesus contrasted the sons of

this world with "sons of *the* Light [literal Greek]" (Luke 16:8). Although most English versions have not translated the Greek definite article before "Light" in Luke 16:8, the Gospel of Luke quotes Jesus as using the article while having Himself in mind as that Light. Greek grammarians know that the presence of the definite article in Greek always has significance. Because the New Testament reveals Jesus to be "the Light," the use of the definite article here cannot be misunderstood. In Luke 16:8 Jesus Christ referred to His disciples, "sons of the Light," as *His* sons!

A few years later the apostle Paul reminded his brethren in Christ: "You are all sons of the light" (I Thessalonians 5:5, NIV). The New International Version is justified to translate "Light" as "*the* Light" since the context shows that the apostle Paul was discussing the Lord Jesus Christ in I Thessalonians 4:13-5:10. So *Jesus* is the Light that Paul referred to in I Thessalonians 5:5. Also, as noted earlier, the definite sense is commonly found in the genitive case without the Greek article. Jesus *is* "the" Light in I Thessalonians 5:5, as He is in the foregoing passages.

If Jesus Christ is the Light of the world (John 8:12) and if His disciples are "sons of the Light" (Luke 16:8; John 12:35-36; I Thessalonians 5:5), then this not only means that His disciples are His children but also that Jesus is their Father.

The Book of James identifies the Lord as "the Lord Jesus Christ" (James 1:1; 2:1), and it refers to Him as both the Lord of the Old Testament (James 5:11) and of the New Testament, the Lord of the second coming (James 5:7-8). James 1:17 calls our Lord "the Father of lights," and He has this title because it was by His own

will that He "gave birth to us" (verse 18, literal Greek).
We will discuss James 1:17-18 in greater detail a little
later in this chapter when we compare it with the new
birth of I John 2:29. If the Lord Jesus of the Book of
James gave birth to us as the Father of lights, then we are
His children and He is our Father.

The Father of lights does not change; He neither fal-
ters nor wavers. As long as we abide in *this* Light, we
shall be guided by an eternal Light. The apostle admonished Christians in Ephesus:

"For you were once darkness, but now you are light
in the Lord. Walk as children *of light. . . . But all things
that are exposed are made manifest by* the light, *for
whatever makes manifest is light. Therefore, He says:
'Awake, you who sleep, arise from the dead, and* Christ
will give you light'" (Ephesians 5:8, 13-14, NKJV).

Like John 12:35-36 and I Thessalonians 5:5, we
should translate this passage with an English definite article: "children of the Light." We observed earlier that
Jesus' words in Luke 16:8 do have the Greek definite article in the phrase "sons of the Light." The presence of the
Greek definite article in Luke 16:8 shows that Jesus
spoke as our heavenly Father. And Luke 16:8 indicates
that the *other* related passages that we have noted should
be translated with an English definite article as well.

Another reason why we can be certain that the sense
is definite in all of these passages is that the context shows
Jesus to be the one and only true Light who can enlighten
the world (John 1:4-9). In Ephesians 5 "Light" has the
definite article before it in verse 13, although (as in Luke

16:8) the English versions have generally not translated the article. The context informs us that we are "light in the Lord" (verse 8) and that Christ Himself is the One who gives us light (verse 14). This shows that Jesus is the Light to whom Paul guided us in Ephesians 5. So Jesus Christ is the One whom verse 13 refers to as "*the* Light."

Because the definite sense is obvious in the passage, it is only logical to translate "children of Light" as "children of the Light," especially since definite nouns are often found without the article in the genitive case whenever the immediate verses confirm that the noun is a definite noun. Our Lord and Savior Jesus Christ, the Light of the world, still desires to give us light, to make us "children of the Light"—to make us *His* children.

One God—The Father

While people may have their own various concepts of God, the New Testament writers testify:

"Yet for us there is only one God, the Father, of whom are all things" (I Corinthians 8:6, NKJV).

The God of the Bible is the very One within whom we live and move and have our being. This God is the:

"One God and Father of all, who is above all, and through all, and in you all" (Ephesians 4:6, NKJV).

Four verses later the writer revealed that this "one God and Father" who is "above all" and "through all" and "in all" is none other than our Lord Jesus Christ! For *He* is the One who was crucified and "descended" and who also "ascended far above all the heavens that *He* might fill all things" (Ephesians 4:10; compare with I Corinthians 8:6).

In his second letter to the Thessalonian brethren, Paul offered a prayer to this God on behalf of his readers:

"Now may our Lord Jesus Christ Himself, and our God and Father, who has loved us and given us everlasting consolation and good hope by grace, comfort your hearts and establish you in every good word and work" (II Thessalonians 2:16-17, NKJV).

Both the King James Version and the New King James Version translate this passage as well as any of the other English versions. However up to now, none of the major English translations has translated this passage exactly as it appears in the original, inspired language. Since Greek is a very precise and exact tongue, all verbs are either singular or plural. Because the verbs in this long sentence are all in the *singular*, the writer demonstrates that "our Lord Jesus Christ Himself" and "our God and Father" are one and the same! In view of this, the "and" [*kai*] between the two phrases "our Lord Jesus Christ Himself" and "our God and Father" should definitely be translated as "even" or something equivalent. In the Greek a singular subject must agree in number with the singular verbs. Here is how the passage should be translated:

"Now may our Lord Jesus Christ Himself, even [kai] our God and Father, the One who loved us, and [kai, or "even"] the One who gave us eternal comfort and good hope in grace, may He comfort your hearts

and may He *establish you in every good word and work"* (II Thessalonians 2:16-17, literal Greek).

In this passage of encouragement the apostle Paul identified Jesus Himself as the Father in no uncertain language. And he did so by using four verbals—two participles and two finite verbs. We emphasize that it is significant that *all four verbals* are in the singular in the inspired Greek text. Therefore, we must translate the two singular participles as "the *One* who loved" and "the *One* who gave." In like manner, both of the two finite verbs have singular pronoun suffixes, and we must translated them as "may *He* comfort" and "may *He* establish."

It is interesting that the KJV and NKJV use "hath" and "has" to bring out the singular idea of the participles (but not the finite verbs). The KJV translates the first two verbals as *"hath loved* us, and *hath given* us." The NKJV says *"has loved* us and *given* us," with "has" probably going with both verbals. In any event, the singular sense is very clear in the Greek.

Because a singular subject must agree in person and number with the four singular verbals, we should translate Paul's subject in the sentence as "our Lord Jesus Christ Himself, even our God and Father." By using the divine titles not only with *kai* but also with four singular verbals, the apostle Paul made it unmistakably clear that our Lord Jesus Christ is also our God and Father.

We find a similar example in which Paul directly referred to Jesus as his heavenly Father:

"Now may our God and Father Himself, and our

Lord Jesus Christ, direct our way to you" (I Thessalonians 3:11, NKJV).

Here is the verse according to the original Greek:

"Now may our God and Father Himself, even [kai] our Lord Jesus Christ—may He direct our way to you" (I Thessalonians 3:11, literal Greek).

As in the previous reference, the inspired writer used a singular verbal, and here he placed it with the phrase "our God and Father Himself, even our Lord Jesus Christ." In this instance, the finite verb "direct" has the singular pronoun suffix—thus requiring us to render it as "may *He* direct"!

We cannot *confess* the Son without confessing the Father. We cannot *deny* the Son without denying the Father: "No one who denies the Son has the Father. He who confesses the Son has the Father also" (I John 2:23).

We realize that it may seem strange for some to think of our Lord Jesus Christ as also our heavenly Father. However, as far as the Bible is concerned, we cannot distinguish Jesus from the Father except in modes, manifestations, or roles of one God. If Jesus is both Lord and God, then He is certainly our heavenly Father. In writing of the second coming of our Lord Jesus Christ, the apostle John exhorted:

"And now, little children, abide in Him, so that when He appears we may have confidence and not shrink from Him at His coming. If you know that He is righteous, you may be sure that every one who does

right is born of Him" *(I John 2:28-29).*

"Born of Him"! We need to let these inspired words sink deep into our minds and hearts. For John was writing of Jesus here and of *His* second coming. If we are born of Jesus, then we are *His* children. And if we are His children, then He is our Father. This is exactly what John *called* the Christ in the next two verses:

"See what love the Father *has given us, that we should be called children of God; and so we are. The reason why the world does not know us is that it did not know* Him! *Beloved, we are God's children now. It does not yet appear what we shall be, but we know that when He appears we shall be like Him; for we shall see Him as He is" (I John 3:1-2).*

This passage is a continuation of the preceding verses, so it is still discussing the second coming of Jesus. In verse 1, John specifically identified the "Him" that the world "*did not know*" as "the Father."

A comparison of I John 2:28-3:1 with James 1:17-18 proves conclusively that Jesus is "the Father of lights" in the Book of James. In I John the subject is Jesus: (1) He is the One who is "coming" again. (The Greek word is *parousia*, which the New Testament consistently uses for the second coming of Christ.) (2) He is "the Father." (3) He is the One whom the world "did not know." (4) We "are born" of Him. If Jesus Christ is the Father whom the world did not know *and* who is coming again, He is also, according to this passage, the One of whom we are born.

James 1 says "the Father of lights" is the One who

"brought us forth" by His own will. The One who brought us forth in James must be the same majestic One of whom we are born in I John. Therefore, we learn that, in a wonderful way, the epistles of James and I John substantiate one another in their revelation that our Lord Jesus Christ is the Father who brings us forth as His children in order to give us an eternal inheritance.

Jesus Himself had personally promised His disciples:

"I will not leave you orphans; I will come to you" *(John 14:18, NKJV).*

It is perplexing why some of the English versions have rendered the Greek word as "desolate" or "comfortless," for it unquestionably means *"orphans."* The Greek word here is *orphanous,* the very term from which the English word "orphan" comes. At any rate, we can appreciate that several of the English translations *have* rendered the Greek as "orphans," including the New King James Version, New International Version, New American Standard Bible, and Amplified Bible.

When Jesus Christ promised His disciples in John 14:18, "I will not leave you as *orphans*; I will come to you," He was, in effect, promising: "*I* will be your Father; *I* will come to you." Today, Jesus still wishes to come to us and to bring us forth as His spiritual children. He still wishes to become our Father.

"The Father Is in Me"

The prophets of old considered Yahweh to be their Father in a spiritual sense: "A Father of the fatherless, a defender of widows, is God in His holy habitation" (Psalm

68:5, NKJV). The people of Israel did not always recognize God as their Father, but the Lord's true prophets acknowledged it: "But now, O Yahweh, You are our Father" (Isaiah 64:8; see also Deuteronomy 14:1).

Jesus personally made many statements about the Father, and some of these come in the form of commandments. According to the Christ, we should not call any human being our father in a spiritual sense. This is because we should have only one spiritual Father—the heavenly Father, who is God. "Do not call anyone on earth your father; for One is your Father, He who is in heaven" (Matthew 23:9, NKJV).

It is interesting that this verse occurs in the middle of two verses that exalt the Christ (Messiah) in the same way that it exalts the Father. It is impossible to overlook the profound parallel that Jesus was making. First, He commanded His disciples not to be called "Rabbi," "for *One* is your Teacher, the Christ" (Matthew 23:8). Second, Jesus stated, "Do not call anyone on earth your father, for *One* is your Father, He who is in heaven" (verse 9). And third, He told His disciples not to be called teachers, "for *One* is your Teacher, the Christ" (verse 10)!

"Rabbi" is an Aramaic word that means "my teacher," or more literally, "my great one." Jesus warned the disciples not to accept the adoration of people by being called "Rabbi"—"my Great One," simply because we should have only one "Teacher," the Christ. In verse 8 the *second* word means not only "teacher" but also "leader" and "master." (It is not *didaskalos*, the term normally used for "teacher"—although some ancient texts disagree with the Byzantine manuscripts by having *didaskalos*.) Of course, the implication by Jesus in this verse is that we are not to be called "Rabbi" because there is only *one* Great One, the Christ, who is our only Teacher, Leader, and Master.

Next, Jesus warned His disciples not to call anyone on earth their Father (in a spiritual sense), because there is only one Father, He who is in heaven (verse 9). A problem existed in that day (as it does today) of some people adoring religious leaders by the use of "Father" in a spiritual sense.

Finally, in verse 10 Jesus reiterated that His disciples are not to be called "teachers," because "One" is our Teacher, the Christ. In this verse both words—"teachers" and "Teacher"—are identical to the term that Jesus used in verse 8, *kathegetes*, which is a lofty title meaning "teacher, leader, and master."

By exalting "the Christ" (the Messiah) on earth in the same context and in a parallel manner in which He exalted the "Father" in heaven, Jesus exalted one God of two manifestations (heavenly and earthly) and two roles (Father and Son). It is striking how Jesus emphasized the oneness of God by making reference to the one earthly Messiah immediately *before* and immediately *after* making reference to the one heavenly Father: "one . . . Teacher" (verse 8), "one . . . Father" (verse 9), "one . . . Teacher" (verse 10).

The apostle Paul also referred to the physical manifestation of a Messiah who has appeared as the representation of the eternal Spirit-Being. In the words of Paul, Jesus is "the *image* of the *invisible God*" (Colossians 1:15)!

Before leaving Matthew 23:8-10, one more comment is appropriate concerning Jesus' command not to call anyone on earth our Father in a religious sense. Many professing Christians disobey this explicit command when they look to *men* as spiritual fathers. Some clergymen willingly allow others to revere them as "Father." The very term "pope"—a title that comes from the ancient Latin and Greek languages—means "papa, father."

As lofty as the title of "Father" is, it is not surprising that some rebellious people from the Jewish nation attempted to stone Jesus to death after He announced:

"I and the Father are one" (John 10:30).

The people standing around Jesus understood that He made reference to Himself as deity—to be one with the Father, and not only in the sense of purpose. In the words of one commentator:

> The claims of Christ are sometimes misunderstood by modern man, but they were not so misconstrued by His contemporaries. When Jesus said to the strict monotheistic Jews of His day, "I and the Father are one" (John 10:30), they took up stones to kill Him, because, said they, "You, being a man, make yourself God" (verse 33).[12]

The Messiah has challenged: "I have come in My Father's name and you do not receive Me. If *another* comes in his own name, him you will receive!" (John 5:43). Is this not another way of saying that He, Jesus, came in *His* own name—the Father's name? This is the natural conclusion to draw.

Because the Nazarene identified Himself so often with

the Father, it was only natural that He would speak to His followers as "little children": "Little children, yet a little while I am with you" (John 13:33). (See also Mark 10:24.)

It was only natural for Jesus to refer to adults that He healed as "son" or "daughter" (Matthew 9:2, 22; Mark 2:5; 5:34). The thirty-year-old Nazarene could do so as the eternal Creator God and heavenly Father.

It was only natural that Jesus would also say: "He who hates *Me* hates My Father also" (John 15:23). We cannot really separate the Father from the Son in view of such a declaration. And other statements come from Jesus with just as much clarity: "He who *believes* in Me, believes not in Me but in Him who sent Me. . . . He who *sees* Me sees Him who sent Me" (John 12:44-45, NKJV).

At one time, Christ promised that the Father would later send the Holy Spirit to His disciples (John 14:26). On another occasion, Jesus promised that He *Himself* was the One who would send the Spirit! (John 16:7). He emphasized this point by using the Greek personal pronoun *ego*, "I Myself," in John 16:7 (according to the dependable Byzantine family of manuscripts, which the KJV and NKJV correctly follow).

Some of Jesus' statements concerning the Father might have been confusing to His disciples, but He later clarified to them that He had, at times, spoken of the Father in proverbs. Then He promised them that He *would* speak to them plainly of the Father (John 16:25). And there is much in the Gospels and the rest of the New Testament that does reveal Jesus' oneness with the Father.

In the previous chapter we observed that God was not simply with Jesus; He was *in* the Son. In this regard, we gave attention to Paul's statement that "God was in Christ, reconciling the world to Himself" (II Corinthians 5:19). In addition to this revelation by Paul, we also have Jesus' testimony in which He told His disciples plainly of the Father:

- *"If I am not doing the works of My Father, then do not believe Me. But if I do them, even though you do not believe Me, believe the works,* that you may know and understand *that the Father is in Me and I am in the Father" (John 10:37-38).*
- *"Now the Son of Man is glorified, and* in *Him God is glorified" (John 13:31).*
- *"And whatever you ask in My name, that I will do, that the Father may be glorified* in *the Son" (John 14:13, NKJV).*
- *"If you ask anything in My name, I Myself [literal Greek] will do it" (John 14:14).*

The Christians of the first century understood the ramifications of Jesus' claims. One New Testament writer later encouraged fellow Christians: "Thus be imitators of *God* as beloved children" (Ephesians 5:1).

"But Paul," one might ask, "how can we imitate God, who is an invisible Spirit?" Paul gave us his reply in the very next verse: "Walk in love as *Christ* loved us and gave Himself up for us" (Ephesians 5:2).

We can imitate God "as beloved children" if we turn to Jesus of the New Testament and imitate Him! For in Jesus we can see what the Father was doing *in* the Son. In Jesus we can see the Father's love in the Son.

By paying the supreme sacrifice in both life and

death, Jesus taught us a great deal about love. And the Messiah also had much to *say* about love. He, in fact, emphasized that His disciples should "love one another" (John 13:34-35).

One of those disciples who had personally heard Jesus Christ give this charge later wrote to other saints that he had actually received the commandment from "the Father." To the apostle John, Jesus Himself was the Father (II John 4-5), for this apostle had learned that the Father was *in* Jesus Christ.

Perhaps we can do nothing better than to close this chapter of our study by referring to one of the most direct claims of His oneness with the Father that Jesus personally made. These are the Messiah's own words as He spoke to His apostles:

> *"'If you had known Me, you would have known My Father also. Hereafter you know Him and have seen Him.' Philip said to Him, 'Lord, show us the Father, and we shall be satisfied.' Jesus said to him, 'Have I been with you so long, and yet you do not know Me, Philip? He who has seen me has seen the Father. How can you say, Show us the Father?'" (John 14:7-9).*

These remarks of our Lord Himself are certainly clear enough. And the following comment by Dr. Harry Rimmer expands well the point that Jesus made:

> Every reader is familiar with the fourteenth chapter of John, and the bewilderment of the disciple over the strange teaching of Jesus. It was for that reason that Philip presented his sincere request and received

a definite reply. Read again John 14:8-9:

"Philip said unto him, Lord, show us the Father, and it sufficeth us. Jesus saith unto him, have I been so long time with you, and dost thou not know me, Philip? He that hath seen me hath seen the Father; how sayest thou, Show us the Father?"

An honest reader cannot escape the intended conclusion. When Jesus said, "He that hath seen me hath seen the Father," he certainly avowed His deity in the strongest words that man could use.

Go back and read that paragraph again and then consider this illustration: Suppose I should say to a company or congregation who had been listening to me lecture from night to night, "Would you like to have the President of the United States address you tomorrow night?" They would undoubtedly reply with enthusiasm, "We would. . . ." What do you suppose would happen if I were to answer them in these words: "What, have I been speaking to you all these times and you know me not? He that hath seen me hath seen the President of the United States. How sayest thou then, 'Show us the President?'"

What do you suppose the congregation would reply? Probably some deacon would rise and say, "You people hold him and I'll phone for the wagon!"

I recently had the great pleasure of shaking hands with Napoleon Bonaparte. At the same time I had the added joy of meeting Alexander the Great and the Duke of Wellington. In shaking hands with these notables, I had to reach through iron bars, and I noticed that they had mattresses on the walls as well as on the beds! Sad as was the mental lapse of these poor mortals, I have never met anyone either inside an asylum or wandering at large, who was so crazy he thought he was God! But here is a man who said to His most intimate followers, "You don't need to ask to see the heavenly Father. Look at Me and you see Him."[13]

Chapter 5

The Holy Spirit

What about I John 5:7?

Because I John 5:7 is sometimes used as a proof-text with regard to the Godhead question, it is perhaps appropriate at this point to present a definitive statement concerning this verse. It reads, according to the King James Version:

"For there are three that bear record in heaven, the Father, the Word, and the Holy Ghost: and these three are one."

It is illuminating to understand how I John 5:7 found its way into the King James Version. Except for the NKJV, the verse is not found in the other major English translations.

And this is understandable since the verse does not have the support of the Greek manuscripts.

In their translation of 1611 the scholars of the King James Version used essentially the Greek text that the Catholic Erasmus had published in the previous century. When Erasmus published the first edition of his Greek text of the New Testament, he was met with severe criticism; and that criticism dealt with our verse in question.

The following is a summary of the story as related by a well-known scholar. His remarks are particularly worthy of our attention, not only because he is as a leading scholar in textual criticism but also because he himself is a trinitarian. Here is Professor Bruce Metzger's comment:

> Among the criticisms leveled at Erasmus one of the most serious appeared to be the charge of Stunica . . . that his text lacked part of the final chapter of I John, namely the Trinitarian statement concerning "the Father, the Word, and the Holy Ghost: and these three are one. And there are three that bear witness in earth" (I John 5:7-8). Erasmus replied that he had not found any Greek manuscript containing these words, though he had in the meanwhile examined several others besides those on which he relied when first preparing his text. In an unguarded moment Erasmus promised that he would insert the Comma Johanneum, as it is called, in future editions if a single Greek manuscript could be found that contained the passage. At length such a copy was found—or was made to order! As it now appears, the Greek manuscript had probably been written in Oxford about 1520 by a Franciscan friar named Froy (or Roy), who

took the disputed words from the Latin Vulgate. Erasmus stood by his promise and inserted the passage in his third edition (1522), but he indicates in a lengthy footnote his suspicions that the manuscript had been prepared expressly in order to confute him.

Among the thousands of Greek manuscripts of the New Testament examined since the time of Erasmus, only three are known to contain this spurious passage. They are Greg. 88, a twelfth-century manuscript which has the *Comma* written in the margin in a seventeenth-century hand; Tisch. w 110, which is a sixteenth-century copy of the Complutensian Polyglot Greek text; and Greg. 629, dating from the fifteenth or . . . from the latter half of the sixteenth century. . . . The passage does not appear in manuscripts of the Latin Vulgate before A.D. 800. . . . Modern Roman Catholic scholars . . . recognize that the words do not belong in the Greek Testament; for example, the four bilingual editions of the Vogels edited by Bover, Merk, Nolli, and Vogels include the words as part of the Vulgate text . . . but reject them from the Greek text that faces the Latin on the opposite page.[1]

The foregoing comment illustrates the honesty that the scholars display as they voice their suspicion about I John 5:7. Although the added words appear in later copies of the Latin Vulgate, they do *not* appear in any of the thousands of the ancient Greek manuscripts of the New Testament text. (And we should remember that the New Testament was originally written by inspiration in the *Greek* language, not the Latin language.)

Consequently, it is small wonder that both Protestant

and Catholic scholars unanimously agree that we should not consider I John 5:7 to be part of the original Greek text. Although many of these scholars are trinitarian, they are all in agreement with a fellow advocate of the trinity who has frankly acknowledged: "The manuscript evidence of I John 5:7 is insufficient. . . . This text should *not* be used."[2]

Both the King James Version and the New King James Version have included I John 5:7 in the text, apparently out of respect for tradition more than anything else, since manuscript evidence for the added verse is lacking. Usually, these two English translations wisely follow the Byzantine family of Greek manuscripts, but for some reason they chose not to do so for I John 5:7. As a matter of fact, because the verse does not appear in *either* the Byzantine manuscripts *or* in any of the other ancient Greek manuscripts, none of the other major English versions has the questionable words: "There are three who bear witness in heaven: the Father, the Word, and the Holy Spirit; and these three are one." And of course, because of the total lack of manuscript evidence, modern editions of the accepted Greek texts do not have the spurious verse either.

It is significant that the truth of Biblical doctrines in general, and the oneness of God teaching in particular, has been consistently taught and preserved in the manuscript evidence for both the Hebrew Old Testament and the Greek New Testament. And in this regard, it is interesting that the added words in I John actually do not conflict with the oneness of God doctrine that is taught from Genesis to Revelation since the passage itself states that "these three are one."

It is revealing to consider I John 5:7 according to its context. Here are verses 5-9:

> *"Who is he who overcomes the world, but he who believes that Jesus is the Son of God? This is He who came by water and blood—Jesus Christ; not only by water, but by water and blood. And it is the Spirit who bears witness, because the Spirit is truth. For there are three who bear witness [in heaven: the Father, the Word, and the Holy Spirit; and these three are one. And there are three that bear witness on earth:] the Spirit, the water, and the blood; and these three agree as one. If we received the witness of men, the witness of God is greater; for this is the witness of God which He has testified of His Son" (I John 5:5-9, NKJV).*

We have added brackets to point out the words in question that are absent from the ancient Greek manuscripts. Even though they are actually part of *two* verses, 7 and 8, verse 7 is usually discussed since this is the verse that contains most of the added words. Also, it is the words in verse 7 that are sometimes cited to support the doctrine of the trinity.

Without the doubtful words of verses 7 and 8, the passage flows smoothly. Even though this fact is obvious, it is of supreme importance to remember. Throughout the entire chapter, the writer explained how vital it is to believe that Jesus Christ is the Son of God, referring to the incarnation of God in Jesus. In regard to this, John declared that God has not left us without witness; the three witnesses that God has given us are the Spirit, the water, and the blood. Furthermore, "these three agree as one" (verse 8). The original text in verse 8 is a smooth and natural continuation of the discussion of these three witnesses in verse 6 and the first part of verse 7.

The interpolation of "the Father, the Word, and the Holy Spirit" in verse 7 is an obvious distraction that does not fit the context of the passage. Throughout his discussion, John was concerned with witnesses of the Incarnation—i.e., those which testify that Jesus is the Son of God. And when he identified "the Spirit," "the water," and "the blood," John referred to Jesus' Sonship in the flesh.

Let us notice how these three witnesses testify of Jesus in the Scriptures. Long before Jesus was born as the Son of God, "the Spirit of Christ *testified*" in the prophets "beforehand the sufferings of Christ and the glories that would follow" (I Peter 1:10-11).

Shortly before Jesus was miraculously conceived in the virgin Mary, the angel Gabriel appeared to her to tell her that "the Holy Spirit" would come upon her and that "the power of the Highest" would overshadow her (Luke 1:35). Not long after this announcement, Elizabeth, the future mother of John the Baptist, "was *filled* with the Holy Spirit" and praised Mary since she was about to become "the mother" of her "Lord" (Luke 1:41-45). Later, an angel of the Lord appeared to Joseph in a dream to inform him that the baby who was in Mary's womb had been supernaturally conceived *by* "the Holy Spirit" (Matthew 1:20; see also verse 18).

After Jesus was born, "the Holy Spirit" came upon "a just and devout man" in Jerusalem named Simeon, leading him to take Jesus in his arms and bless God because of the salvation that was to eventually come through the

Christ child (Luke 2:25-35). In the following years, Jesus the child grew and became "strong in spirit," filled with wisdom, and the grace of God was upon Him (Luke 2:40). When John baptized the Nazarene, the Spirit of God again bore witness of Jesus as the Son of God, descending as a dove and remaining on Christ. After that happened, John the Baptist then declared that Jesus Christ was the One who would baptize *with* "the Holy Spirit" (John 1:31-34).

After Jesus ascended to heaven, following His crucifixion and resurrection, the Holy Spirit of God again testified about the Son of God in a powerful way by miraculously ushering in the church age on the Day of Pentecost. As Jesus had prophesied, the disciples were all filled with the Holy Spirit on that day (Acts 1:8; 2:1-21).

The New Testament teaches that the Holy Spirit not only testifies through the Word of God but also through each and every Christian's life that Jesus, the Son of God, is Redeemer, Savior, and Lord (Romans 8:1-17; II Corinthians 3:1-18; Galatians 5:22-25).

In the first century, apostles like Peter knew that "the gospel" of Christ was preached "by the Holy Spirit sent from heaven" (I Peter 1:12). And today the Spirit still testifies that Jesus of Nazareth is the Son of God: "The Spirit [Jesus] and the bride [the church] say, 'Come!' And let him who hears say, 'Come!' And let him who thirsts come. And whoever desires, let him take the water of life freely" (Revelation 22:17, NKJV).

When Jesus died on the cross for our sins, a soldier pierced His side with a spear, and immediately "*blood and water*" came out as a witness for His death. The writer of these words, the same John who wrote I John 5:5-9, stated that he who saw these things has testified so that we may *believe* (John 19:31-37).

The three witnesses of the Spirit, the water, and the blood have a profound relationship with one another in many passages of Scripture. Paul explained in Romans that when we receive *water* baptism because of our faith in Jesus, we are baptized into His *death* (Romans 6:3-4). It is because of Jesus' atoning death and the shedding of His *blood* that our sins are forgiven (Hebrews 9:11-15). It was by "the *blood* of Christ" that He became a perfect sacrifice offered to a holy God through "the eternal Spirit" (Hebrews 9:14).

As we noted earlier, John the Baptist testified that Jesus would baptize His disciples *with* the Holy Spirit. Christians are all baptized "by one Spirit" into one body (I Corinthians 12:13). The apostle Peter promised in the first gospel sermon that when we repent and are *baptized* in the name of Jesus Christ for the forgiveness of sins, we will receive the *gift* of the Holy Spirit (Acts 2:38). Earlier, Jesus had promised that the Holy Spirit would come after His physical departure, and this Spirit is the Spirit of truth that would "testify" of Jesus Christ (John 15:26). This Spirit of truth would guide Jesus' disciples into all truth and would also "glorify" Jesus (John 16:13-14).

In summary, the three witnesses of I John 5—the Spirit, the water, and the blood—are a strong, interrelated, unified testimony of Jesus Christ as the Son of God. They have given testimony before, during, and after Jesus' ministry, death, resurrection, and ascension to heaven.

On the other hand, the three witnesses in the latter part of I John 5:7 do not correspond to the discussion of the three witnesses of the Spirit, the water, and the blood in verses 6 and 8. In addition, the words "the Father, the

Word, and the Holy Spirit" in verse 7 do not even have the title "the Son," which appears later in the trinitarian creeds of church history. Concerning this, in his book, *The Oneness of God*, David K. Bernard commented appropriately:

> It is also interesting to note that this verse [verse 7] does not use the word *Son*, but *Word*. If *Son* were the special name of a special person in the Godhead, and if this verse were trying to teach separate persons, why did it use *Word* instead of *Son*? *Son* does not refer primarily to deity, but *Word* does. The Word is not a separate person from the Father any more than a man and his word are separate persons. Rather, the Word is the thought, plan, or mind of God and also the expression of God.[3]

To summarize our discussion of I John 5:5-9 in general and verses 7 and 8 in particular, we cite these important points: (1) Many other passages in the New Testament substantiate the threefold testimony of "the Spirit, the water, and the blood" of verse 6. (2) If one accepts the additional words of verses 7 and 8, then the Spirit becomes a superfluous witness since the Spirit is one of the three witnesses of "the Spirit, the water, and the blood" (verses 6 and 8) and then one of the three witnesses of "the Father, the Word, and the Holy Spirit" (verse 7). (3) The doubtful words of verses 7 and 8 do not appear in *any* of the thousands of ancient Greek manuscripts that have been preserved. (4) It is well documented in church history how the questionable words found their way into Erasmus's Greek text in the sixteenth century and from there into the KJV and the NKJV. (5) The controversial passage does not fit the context of I John 5 and is an obvious interpolation. (6) The title "the Son" is not even in the passage. (7) An attempt to interpret the doubtful words to mean that there are three distinct *persons* in the Godhead who bear witness would require a tritheistic and polytheistic view of God. (8) Whatever the post-biblical scribe's reasons for adding the words, the passage itself does state that these three are "one," not "three."

One Spirit

A Christian writer has suggested that "God, Jehovah, is a Holy Spirit, but not the same spirit . . . as God, the Holy Spirit."[4]

Evidently, the author of this quote believes in and worships more than one Spirit-Being known as God. But nowhere does the Bible give any indication that Yahweh God is a "different" Holy Spirit from "God, the Holy Spirit." On the contrary, the Scriptures are consistent in teaching that the God of the Bible is one Spirit, not two or three. The apostle Paul stated plainly that there is "one Spirit" (Ephesians 4:4). The writer of Hebrews called this one Spirit "the eternal Spirit" (Hebrews 9:14). Jesus Himself declared:

"God is a Spirit [not "Spirits"]: and they that worship him [not "them"] must worship him in spirit and in truth" (John 4:24, KJV).

As early as Genesis, Yahweh referred to this Spirit as "My Spirit" (Genesis 6:3). But even though the Bible portrays God as one eternal Spirit, we must not attempt to place limits on *this* Spirit. The psalmist cried out to Yahweh: "To where shall I go from Your Spirit? Or to where shall I flee from Your presence? If I ascend to heaven, You are there! If I make my bed in Sheol, You are there!" (Psalm 139:7-8). The humbled Job acknowledged the *power* of that Spirit when he proclaimed: "The Spirit of God has made me, and the breath of the Almighty gives me life" (Job 33:4). Thus in Job's language the *Spirit* of God is from the "Almighty" Himself.

Some apparently believe that the expression "the Holy Spirit" is a *name* for God, and perhaps they have this concept because both "Holy" and "Spirit" usually begin with capital letters in our English translations. But if this is really a name for God, it is strange that the Bible never reveals that it is a name. Furthermore, it is interesting that the Bible also refers to the Holy Spirit as "the Spirit of God," "the Spirit," and "the Spirit of Christ."

Is the "Holy Spirit" actually a name, or is it in reality a title—a title of distinction that describes our God for what He is? In at least *some* passages the English versions evidently recognize that the phrase must be a title, and not a name, for in such cases these translations do *not* capitalize the phrase. For example, the King James Version translates a prayer of David as follows: "Take not thy holy spirit from me" (Psalm 51:11).[5] It is rather obvious that in David's cry to Yahweh, he used a title of description, not God's name.

The God whom King David worshiped *is* holy. Through His prophets, God reminded the people of Israel time and again: "I am Yahweh your Holy One, the Creator of Israel, your King" (Isaiah 43:15). "To whom then will you compare Me, that I should be like him? says the Holy One" (Isaiah 40:25). "For I am Yahweh your God, the Holy One of Israel, your Savior" (Isaiah 43:3).

The God of Israel is *the* Holy One. It is always "He." It is never "they." It is always the "Holy One"; it is never the "Holy Ones." If God is the Holy One, and if He is, in reality, a Spirit (and not flesh), then He *should* be called the Holy Spirit; and so He is—according to the testimony of the Scriptures.

Before his martyrdom, Stephen accused the Jews of rejecting this Holy Spirit, even as their fathers had.[6] Their fathers had, indeed, rejected Yahweh—God Almighty.

In Isaiah 6, that prophet described his personal encounter with God, and Yahweh gave him a message to deliver to his people.[7] Seven hundred years later in Rome the apostle Paul quoted a major portion of that message.[8] In Isaiah, the One who was responsible for the message was the LORD—Yahweh.[9] But according to Paul, He is the "Holy Spirit."[10]

The Old Testament states that the ancient Israelites tested *Yahweh* following their exodus from Egypt.[11] By inspiration, the writer of Hebrews recorded that the Israelites had, in fact, tested the "Holy Spirit."[12]

The New Testament writers knew of only *one* Spirit that could impart spiritual gifts and spiritual guidance: "To one is given through the Spirit the utterance of wisdom, and to another the utterance of knowledge according to the same Spirit, to another, faith by the same Spirit; to another, gifts of healing by the one Spirit. . . . But one and the same Spirit works all these things, distributing to each one individually as *He* wills" (I Corinthians 12:8-9, 11, NKJV). "For in *One* Spirit we were all baptized into one body . . . and all were made to drink of one Spirit" (I Corinthians 12:13).

Several hundred years previously Yahweh had promised through His prophet Joel: "I am Yahweh your God and there is no other. . . . And it shall come to pass afterward that I will pour out My Spirit in those days" (Joel 2:27-28, NKJV). "My Spirit," predicted Yahweh. The one and only Holy Spirit of which we can partake is none other than the Spirit of Yahweh!

The Lord Is That Spirit

Although Jesus of Nazareth did have a human mother, His physical birth had its very source in the Holy Spirit of God. As the angel promised Mary: "The Holy Spirit will come upon you, and the power of the Most High will over-shadow you. Therefore, the child to be born will be called the Son of God" (Luke 1:35).

The Christ child did not need a human father since the *spiritual* presence of God Himself supernaturally over-shadowed Mary. And it is interesting that the foregoing passage designates the Holy Spirit as the "Most High."

Since Mary was "found with child from the Holy Spirit,"[13] this One to be born of her was to be *"full* of the Holy Spirit" (Luke 4:1). And if Jesus was full of the Spirit, is it really possible for us to limit the measurement of the Spirit that *He* possessed? As John exclaimed: "For the One whom God sent speaks the authentic words of God—and there can be no measuring of the Spirit given to *him!*" (John 3:34, Phillips).

Try as we may, can we truly comprehend the unlimit-ed presence of God's Spirit? Yahweh challenged through His prophet: "'Can anyone hide himself in secret places, so I shall not see him?' says the LORD; 'Do I not fill heaven and earth?' says the LORD" (Jeremiah 23:24, NKJV).

In a unique way the Almighty Spirit came to reside in the person of Jesus of Nazareth: "For in *Him* all the fullness of God was pleased to dwell" (Colossians 1:19). And that Almighty Spirit *continues* to reside in the immortal being of Jesus: "For in Him the whole fullness of deity [the Godhead], continues to dwell in bodily form—giving expression of the divine nature" (Colossians 2:9, Amplified).

Some have wondered what the blasphemy against the Holy Spirit is. Christ commented on this very thing, and He did so because certain ones "said that He had an *unclean* spirit" or evil spirit—when in fact He possessed the Holy Spirit of God Himself.[14] May we never be guilty of blasphemy against the Holy Spirit. May we never be guilty of accusing Jesus with possessing anything other than the very Spirit of God.

We cannot, in any sense of the term, "separate" God into two or three spirits. He is One, and there is no other (Deuteronomy 6:4; Isaiah 46:9). Let us compare Matthew 10:20 with Mark 13:11. These are definitely parallel passages. Matthew calls the Spirit "the Spirit of your *Father*," while Mark designates Him as "the *Holy* Spirit." If no other verses of Scripture were available to us, these two alone would establish that our heavenly Father is none other than the Holy Spirit—as God!

But other passages of Scripture *are* available, and they make the same point. In Acts 5, Ananias and Sapphira tried the unfortunate experiment of lying to the apostles. As a result, they were struck dead; but before that happened, Peter declared to them that they had actually lied to God, not simply to humans. And may we notice especially the terminology in this context. In Acts 5:3 we learn that they lied to "the Holy Spirit." Then, in verse 4 we find that they lied to "God" Himself. Finally, in verse 9 we read that they tested "the Spirit of the *Lord*." Whether He is called "the Holy Spirit," "God," or "the Spirit of the Lord," He is the one divine Spirit against whom Ananias and his wife committed their sin.

Although Jesus was put to death as a man, He was not *only* a man. Some have called Him the "God-Man," an appropriate designation. Because the Christ possessed the very Spirit of God in its fullness, He—as God—raised Himself from the grave by the power of His eternal Spirit: "For Christ also suffered once for sins, the just for the unjust, that He might bring us to God, being put to death in the flesh but made alive by the Spirit" (I Peter 3:18, NKJV). (See also John 2:19-22.)

During His public ministry, Jesus had already stated: "It is the *Spirit* that gives life; the flesh is of no avail" (John 6:63). If only we human beings would recognize the truth in this statement, then we would stop trying to "play God" with others and with ourselves. Then, we would quit trying to deceive others and ourselves with the unspoken lie that we will somehow live forever in our present situations. People are dying all around us. World leaders are here today and gone tomorrow. We attend the funerals of our friends, our parents, our brothers and sisters, and sometimes even our own children! Why cannot we humans believe Jesus? It is so obvious that it is the "Spirit" who gives life; the flesh is of no avail!

A New Testament writer stated categorically that this Spirit *is* the Spirit of Christ—Christ Himself: "But you are not in the flesh; you are in the Spirit, if the Spirit of *God* really dwells in you. Anyone who does not have the Spirit of *Christ* does not belong to Him. But if Christ is in you . . . " (Romans 8:9-10).

Similarly, Ephesians 3 refers to God and His Spirit. Verse 14 calls Him "the Father." Verse 16 refers to the Holy Spirit as "His Spirit." Finally, verse 17 specifically identifies this One as "*Christ*."

Thus both Romans 8:9-10 and Ephesians 3:16-17 state that Jesus Christ Himself resides in the believer—through *His* Spirit! In this very regard, Jesus had declared to His disciples that they would eventually receive "the Spirit of truth." And in His declaration He identified this Spirit of truth to be *Himself*:

> "*Even the Spirit of truth, whom the world cannot receive, because it neither sees Him nor knows Him. You know Him, for He abides with you and will be in you. I will not leave you as orphans; I will come to you*" (John 14:17-18).

Jesus also referred to the Holy Spirit as "the Comforter," the *Parakletos* (Greek), that would be sent *in His name*.[15] And even as the Spirit is the Comforter, we learn from another passage of Scripture that *Jesus* is the One who is this Comforter, this *Parakletos*,[16] for the same Greek term for "Comforter" occurs in both references.

In addition, "comfort" is used two times, as a noun (*paraklesis*) and as a verb (*parakaleo*), in II Thessalonians 2:16-17. This is the passage that we showed earlier to have four singular verbals (including "comfort") that are associated with "our Lord Jesus Christ, even God our

Father." Therefore, this passage confirms that our Lord Jesus Christ *as* God our Father is the One who "comforts" us and is "the One who gave" us this "eternal comfort." Of course, Jesus can do this because He Himself is "the Comforter"—the Holy Spirit (John 14:26; I John 2:1).

The apostle Peter, by inspiration, accused the Jewish people of that generation of rejecting their own Messiah, the "Holy One," when they crucified Jesus: "But you denied the Holy One—the Righteous One!" (Acts 3:14). Christians were later reminded: "But you have an *anointing* from the Holy One, and you know all things" (I John 2:20, NKJV). (Compare with I John 2:27, John 14:26; Acts 10:38.)

So we see that—as far as the New Testament is concerned—the "Holy One" who was rejected and crucified by humans rose from the grave to *anoint* humans with His Spirit. In describing His resurrection, the apostle to the Gentiles recorded: "The first man, Adam, was made a living soul. The last Adam [Christ] was made a life-giving Spirit" (I Corinthians 15:45).

Jesus no longer possesses the Spirit of God in a tabernacle of mortal flesh as He did in His earthly sojourn. In the terminology of Paul, He is presently a life-giving Spirit! And as the Holy One who anoints His people *with* His Spirit, Jesus can rightly be called *the* Holy Spirit.

Two passages from the letters of Peter substantiate that the Holy Spirit which moved God's prophets was the Spirit of Jesus Christ:

"For prophecy never came by the will of man, but holy men of God spoke as they were moved by the Holy Spirit" (II Peter 1:21, NKJV).

185

"Of this salvation the prophets have inquired and searched diligently, who prophesied of the grace that would come to you, searching what, or what manner of time, the Spirit of Christ *who was in them was indicating when He testified beforehand the sufferings of Christ and the glories that would follow" (I Peter 1:10-11, NKJV; see also verse 12).*

From the Book of Acts, we read that the Lord, as "the Spirit," continuously guided the believers. In Acts 8:29 "the Spirit" spoke to Philip. Ten verses later He is called "the Spirit of the Lord" (verse 39).

In Acts 16 He who guided Jesus' disciples is "the Holy Spirit" (verse 6). In the next verse He is simply "the Spirit" (verse 7), according to the KJV and NKJV (from the Greek Byzantine manuscripts). Several English versions have "the Spirit of Jesus" in Acts 16:7 because of the textual evidence of other ancient Greek manuscripts.

Whether one accepts the correct reading in Acts 16:7 to be "the Spirit" or "the Spirit of Jesus," a comparison of Acts 16:6-8 and II Corinthians 2:12 shows that "the Spirit" who guided Paul and his companions *was* "the Lord" Himself. And Acts 16:10 says the same thing. Later, the same chapter specifically identifies this Spirit, who is "the Lord," as "the Lord Jesus Christ" (Acts 16:14, 31-32), just as Jesus is the Lord who guided His disciples *throughout* the Book of Acts (e.g., Acts 9:5, 10-17, 20:29).

The Book of Revelation also reveals "the Spirit" to be our Lord Jesus Christ. From the last book of the New Testament, "the Spirit" is the One who repeatedly speaks. He admonished: "He who has an ear, let him hear what *the Spirit* says to the churches" (Revelation 2:7). The next verse identifies the Spirit as Jesus Christ: "The words of the First and the Last, He who died and came to life" (Revelation 2:8).

And so it is with several passages from Revelation. "The Spirit" is the One who offers "the crown of life" to those who are "faithful unto death" (Revelation 2:10-11). "The Spirit" is the One who exhorts us to "hold fast" until He comes (Revelation 2:25, 29). "The Spirit" says:

"He who has an ear, let him hear what the Spirit *says. . . . To the angel of the church in Philadelphia write . . . I know your works. . . . You . . . have kept My word, and have not denied My name. . . .* Behold, I come quickly. *Hold fast what you have, that no one may take your crown" (Revelation 3:6-8, 11, NKJV).*

"He who has an ear, let him hear what the Spirit *says to the churches. And to the angel of the church of the Laodiceans write . . . I know your works, that you are neither cold nor hot. . . . I will spew you out of My mouth. . . . As many as I love, I rebuke and chasten. Therefore, be zealous and repent.* Behold, I stand at the door and knock. *If anyone hears my voice and opens the door, I will come in to him and dine with him and he with Me. . . . He who has an ear, let him hear what* the Spirit *says to the churches" (Revelation 3:13-16, 19-20, 22, NKJV).*

A comparison of Revelation 3:20 with Luke 12:36-37, 40 shows that "the Son of Man," Jesus, is "the Spirit" in Revelation who is standing at the door and knocking. Also, the context in Revelation itself establishes that Jesus is the Spirit who is speaking in Revelation 1:17-3:22. Red-letter editions of the New Testament have this entire section in red because they recognize that it is from Jesus. Therefore, the epistles from "the Spirit" to the churches are definitely messages from Jesus Christ.

In Revelation 2, "the Spirit" identifies Himself to be "the Son of God, who has eyes like a flame of fire, and His feet like fine brass" (Revelation 2:17-18, NKJV).

The Book of Hebrews gives our Lord the lofty title of "*Father of Spirits*" (Hebrews 12:9).[17] It was logical, then, for the dying Stephen, looking up into the heavens and seeing the Lord of glory, to cry out to Him: "Lord Jesus, receive *my* spirit" (Acts 7:59).

At times, the Bible refers to the *presence* of God when speaking of His Spirit: "To where shall I go from your Spirit? Or to where shall I flee from your presence? If I ascend to heaven, You are there! If I make my bed in Sheol, You are there!" (Psalm 139:7-8).

Other passages of Scripture emphasize God's very nature or *essence*: "God is a Spirit" (John 4:24, KJV).

Still other references consider the *mind* of God: "Who has directed the Spirit of Yahweh, or as His counselor has instructed Him?" (Isaiah 40:13).

It is significant that an inspired author of the New Testament took the above reference from Isaiah and applied it to Jesus Christ: "For 'Who has known the mind of the LORD that he may instruct Him?' But we have the mind of *Christ*" (I Corinthians 2:16, NKJV.)

The commentators recognize that Paul quoted the Isaiah passage. In the words of one scholar: "The Lord (Isaiah 40:13, referring to God) is here applied to Christ."[18] Thus, to the apostle, the Spirit of Yahweh is actually "the mind of Christ."

Another illuminating text is II Corinthians 3. Because the Lord Jesus Christ is the theme of this entire chapter, we cannot misunderstand Paul when he wrote about Jewish people who reject their own Messiah:

"But their minds were hardened. For until this day the same veil remains unlifted in the reading of the Old Testament, because the veil is taken away in Christ. But even to this day, when Moses is read, a veil lies on their heart. Nevertheless when one turns to the Lord, the veil is taken away. Now the Lord is the Spirit; and where the Spirit of the Lord is, there is liberty" (II Corinthians 3:14-17, NKJV; see also verse 18).

In view of this inspired declaration by an apostle of God that "the Lord is the Spirit" (verse 17), a Baptist publication has properly acknowledged this great truth: "The Holy Spirit *is* Jesus, present here and now, knowable, communicable, effective friend and Lord."[19]

And John Stott well advised us when he wrote: "The Holy Spirit is God the Lord. He is the divine Spirit, the mighty Spirit; we should not attempt to limit his sovereignty."[20]

To conclude this section, we have these words by the apostle Paul:

Now there are diversities of gifts, but the same *Spirit . . . the* same *Lord . . . the* same *God who works all in all. But one and the* same *Spirit works* all *these things, distributing to each one individually as He wills (I Corinthians 12:4-6, 11, NKJV). (Note also the emphasis on "the same Spirit" in verses 8 and 9.)*

Born of the Spirit

When Nicodemus came to Jesus, the Nazarene informed this Jewish leader:

"Truly, Truly, I say to you, Unless one is born from above, he cannot see the kingdom of God" (John 3:3).

Although some versions render the phrase as "born again," the more literal rendering is "born from above." (If one is "born from above," he, of course, would be born *again*.) And we can be born from above by being born of the very Spirit of God:

"Jesus answered, 'Truly, truly, I say to you, unless one is born *of water and the Spirit, he cannot enter the kingdom of God'" (John 3:5).*

What does "born of water" mean here? Some have suggested that it refers to physical birth. While this might be a possibility, it is not a logical explanation. Jesus was speaking of water baptism, as confirmed by the reality of baptism in the four Gospels as well as the important role that it came to play in the apostolic church as recorded in the Book of Acts. The converts in the first century were commanded to "repent and be baptized" in water if they were to have their sins forgiven and receive God's Spirit. Peter proclaimed:

"Repent and be baptized every one of you in the name of Jesus Christ for the forgiveness of your sins. And you shall receive the gift of the Holy Spirit" (Acts 2:38).

Those who accepted Peter's inspired instructions on the Day of Pentecost "were baptized, and there were added that day about three thousand souls" (Acts 2:41).

In like manner, chapters 8, 9, 10, 16, and 19 of the Book of Acts demonstrate conclusively that water baptism played a prominent part in the new birth of the believers. An unusual case in which the converts received the Holy Spirit *before* water baptism is in Acts 10; and this occurred to show the apostle Peter and the other Jews present that the Spirit was to be poured out on Gentiles as well as on Jews.[21] Yet even here, when Peter realized that these Gentiles had received the Spirit, *immediately* "he commanded them to be baptized in the name of Jesus Christ" (Acts 10:48).

Saul of Tarsus had apparently already repented of his sins when Ananias came to him, for he had been fasting for three days. Therefore, Ananias exhorted him: "And now why do you wait? Rise and be baptized, washing away your sins, calling on the name of the Lord" (Acts 22:16). In his instructions Ananias merely followed the apostolic authority of Peter who had told the multitude: "Repent *and* be baptized" (Acts 2:38).

Water baptism is not "salvation by works." It *is* an act of obedience to the Word of God. And if we expect to receive the Spirit of God, we must be willing to obey God.

The apostles testified in this regard: "We are witnesses to these things; and so is the Holy Spirit whom God has given to those who *obey* Him" (Acts 5:32).

Why was water baptism a Biblical preparation for receiving God's Spirit? To be baptized in water is to display an act of faith. It shows that we *believe* in the power of the death, burial, and resurrection of Jesus. It shows that we believe that God can enter into our very beings and make a "new creation" in us—even in this life. It shows that we believe that as Jesus rose from the grave we likewise shall rise from the dead at the last day to inherit eternal life—if we are faithful until death (Revelation 2:10). Water baptism is a beautiful, symbolic picture of these things—death, burial, and resurrection.

This is why it is *immersion* in water. The watery grave pictures death—and a glorious resurrection from that death. In Paul's language: "Do you not know that all of us who have been baptized into Christ Jesus were baptized into His death? We were buried therefore with Him by *baptism* into death, so that as Christ was raised from the dead by the glory of the Father, we too might walk in newness of life. For if we have been united with Him in a death like His, we shall certainly be united with Him in a resurrection like His" (Romans 6:3-5).

Even though most of the English translations have failed to translate the word "baptism," the detailed Biblical record still makes it plain in all the English versions that baptism is, in fact, immersion. Actually, the word "baptism" itself is a *Greek* term and not really an English rendering. And scholars have no doubt of its meaning. The *New Catholic Encyclopedia* truthfully states: "The word 'baptism' is derived from the Greek . . . meaning 'plunge' or 'dip' (as in John 13:26)."[22] The same source also says: "That baptism took place by immersion is evidenced by Paul's presenting it as being buried with Christ" (Romans 6:3-4; Colossians 2:12).[23]

Romans 6 clearly illustrates that water baptism is a kind of new birth out of water; but if we are to be "born of water," we should have as our ultimate goal to be "born of the Spirit."

Some New Testament references indicate that when the believer rises from the dead to inherit an immortal body, *that* will be a new birth. For the risen Christ Himself was the "firstborn from the dead."[24]

However, many passages of Scriptures show that we can be "born of the Spirit" in *this* life. As a matter of fact, to be a Christian in the Biblical sense, according to Romans 8 we must have "the Spirit of Christ" *in* our lives; otherwise, we are "not of Him" (literal Greek).[25]

As we saw earlier, we can even receive "the mind of Christ" when we receive that Spirit.[26] But it is not sufficient for us to accept water baptism merely to get wet. In order for our sins to be forgiven and for the Spirit to come into our lives, our baptism in water must coincide with real faith and genuine repentance: "He who *believes* and is baptized shall be saved" (Mark 16:16). "*Repent* and be baptized . . . and you shall receive the gift of the Holy Spirit" (Acts 2:38).

The Word of God explains the importance of having the Spirit of Christ in our lives: "You, however, are controlled not by the sinful nature but by the Spirit, if the Spirit of God lives in you. And if anyone does not have the Spirit of Christ, he does not belong to Christ" (Romans 8:9, NIV). (See also verses 10-17.)

Peter reminded first-century disciples that their new birth was the result of the Word of God: "having been born again, not of corruptible seed but incorruptible, *through* the word of God which lives and abides forever" (I Peter 1:23, NKJV; see also the NIV and RSV). The literal Greek is not "by," as some versions have; but "through" the Word of God. Just as water flows through a riverbed, so the living waters of the Holy Spirit flow through the riverbed of God's Word—into our very lives.

Our heavenly Father is willing to give us His Spirit if we are willing to "ask," "knock," and "seek" for it on His terms.[27] The first word of John the Baptizer was "Repent."[28] The first word of Jesus was "Repent."[29] The first word of Peter and the apostles was "Repent" (Acts 2:38; 3:19).

When John appeared in the wilderness, he began to preach a "baptism of repentance." But John's baptism was a baptism in water only. We have already seen that Christian baptism was different; it consists of two elements. John 3:5 speaks of being born (1) of water and (2) of the Spirit. When the converts in Acts received Jesus' baptism, they received water baptism in the name of Jesus—in *His* authority—and they received a baptism of *His* Spirit (Acts 2:38; Romans 8:9). Thus Jesus' baptism is different from John's. And the latter presented a striking contrast between his baptism and the baptism that Jesus was to introduce. John freely acknowledged: "There comes One after me who is mightier than I, whose sandal strap I am not worthy to stoop down and loose. I indeed baptized you with water, but He ["Himself," literal Greek] will baptize you *with* ["with" or "in," literal Greek] the Holy Spirit" (Mark 1:7-8, NKJV). The preposition "in" is probably a more accurate translation than "with." (See Alfred Marshall's *Interlinear Greek–English New Testament*.)

According to John, the One coming after him would Himself baptize with His own Spirit. To whom was John addressing his remarks? The twelve apostles? Was the baptism in the Holy Spirit only meant for the apostles? No, John could not have limited his remarks to the apostles, for he spoke before Jesus chose the apostles—even before Jesus began His ministry. When John stated that Jesus Christ "will baptize you in the Holy Spirit," he spoke to the multitudes of Judea. He promised the baptism in the Holy Spirit to the masses of the people, for Mark informed us that John preached to "all the land of Judea, and those from Jerusalem" (Mark 1:4-8, NKJV).

When was this Holy Spirit given? Some might think that it was given immediately following the resurrection of Christ. John recorded that Jesus "breathed on them, and said to them, Receive the Holy Spirit" (John 20:22, RSV).

This verse, as translated, could lead us to believe that the apostles may have received the Spirit when Christ "breathed on them." However, we should observe that the word for "them" is not in the Greek text. Also, the Greek lexicons state that the Greek verb can mean either "breathed on" or "breathed in." (Marshall's *Interlinear* has the latter.)

Whether "breathing in" or "breathing on," the risen Christ showed His disciples that even as *He* was filled with the Spirit, they too could eventually partake of that selfsame Spirit. We know that the Holy Spirit did not come over them at that time, for it was later when Jesus told His followers: "John baptized with water; but before many days you *shall* be baptized in the Holy Spirit. . . . You *shall* receive power when the Holy Spirit has come upon you" (Acts 1:5, 8).

As we read the dramatic second chapter of Acts, we see that those disciples did receive power—when God's Spirit came over them. They were all "filled" with that Spirit, and this experience transformed their lives.[30]

God promised to pour out His Spirit not only upon a select few but upon all who would come to Him. Yahweh had promised through His prophet Joel: "I will pour out My Spirit upon all flesh" (Joel 2:28).

On the day the church was born, Peter proclaimed to the inhabitants of Jerusalem that this prophecy of Joel was at that very time beginning to be fulfilled.[31] But the promise is for "all" flesh—both Jew and Gentile. The Spirit is not only for the Gentile, not only for the Jew, and not only for that generation. The apostle continued: "Repent, and let every one of you be baptized in the name of Jesus Christ for the remission of sins; and you shall receive the gift of the Holy Spirit. For the promise is to you and your children, and to all who are afar off, as many as the Lord our God will call" (Acts 2:38-39, NKJV).

In the Book of Acts the Holy Spirit "fell" on the disciples.[32] The Spirit was "poured out"[33] upon the believers—in fulfillment of Joel 2:28. And not only in Jerusalem or Judea was the Spirit available; according to the Biblical account, people of Samaria, Ephesus, Philippi, Corinth, Rome, and even Ethiopia and beyond began to feel the spreading influence of that Spirit. As a result, the disciples were accused of "turning the world upside down." (See Acts 17:6.)

Of course, in reality, the world was being turned right side up (it was already "upside down," floundering in the confusion of pagan religions). The truth and guidance of God's Spirit and the powerful message of the good news of Jesus Christ spread throughout the Roman Empire; and it had its effect: "The disciples were *filled* with joy and the Holy Spirit" (Acts 13:52).

The apostle Paul prayed to God that the believers would "be strengthened with might through His Spirit in the inner man" (Ephesians 3:16). Moreover, it was Paul's hope that "Christ" would dwell in their hearts (Ephesians 3:17).

With Christ "in" our lives, we can partake of the *love* of God through His Spirit: "the love of God has been poured out into our hearts *through* [literal Greek] the Holy Spirit that was given to us" (Romans 5:5). We can receive the *love* of God through the reception of His Spirit simply because "God is love" (I John 4:8).

If we possess His Spirit, we can possess His spiritual characteristics—to a lesser or a greater degree, according to our faith. And we are warned in this regard: "Do not quench the Spirit" (I Thessalonians 5:19).

Genuinely Spirit-filled believers will naturally possess the *fruit* of the Spirit: "the fruit of the Spirit is love, joy, peace, longsuffering, kindness, goodness, faithfulness, gentleness, self-control" (Galatians 5:22-23, NKJV).

The *world* cannot give these attributes to us—not in depth. Yes, the world offers to us substitutes—sex . . . *without* love, excitement . . . *without* joy, leisure . . . *without* peace. But God's Spirit offers to us "the real thing." To the extent that we yield our wills to His will—our spirits to His Spirit—to that extent we can possess and cultivate real love, real joy, real peace, real goodness *in* our lives. The New Testament calls this new birth within us a "new creation." And whereas God's first creation was physical, this creation is spiritual.

Paul reminded the disciples in Corinth: "For *in* [literal Greek] one Spirit we were all baptized *into* one body— whether Jews or Greeks, whether slaves or free—and have all been made to drink *into* one Spirit" (I Corinthians 12:13). We are baptized "in" one Spirit (not merely "by" one Spirit, as some popular English versions have). And to be baptized—immersed—in the Spirit is to be completely filled with that Spirit. Furthermore, it was Paul's hope that the Christians would stay filled with that Spirit, for he encouraged Spirit-filled believers in Ephesus: "Be filled with the Spirit" (Ephesians 5:18).

If we are all baptized "in one Spirit" and filled with that Spirit, we could ask, "Whose Spirit is it?" And again, the Bible's response is clear: "I am Yahweh your God; and there is none else. . . . I will pour out *My* Spirit upon all flesh" (Joel 2:27-28).

We saw in the previous section of this chapter that the Spirit of Yahweh is the Spirit of the Lord—the Spirit of Jesus. In this regard, Jesus Christ said: "'If anyone thirsts, let him come to *Me* and drink. He who believes in Me, as the Scripture has said, out of his heart will flow rivers of living water.' But this He spoke concerning the Spirit, whom those believing in *Him* would receive; for the Holy Spirit was not yet given, because Jesus was not yet glorified" (John 7:37-39, NKJV).

Jesus spoke of His Spirit as being living waters; and He made the correlation at a most opportune time, for He spoke in Jerusalem during the Feast of Tabernacles. What happened during the Feast of Tabernacles in Jerusalem? Among other things: "For seven days water was carried in an olden pitcher from the pool of Siloam to the temple as a reminder of the water from the rock in the desert (Numbers 20:2-13), and as a symbol of hope for the coming Messianic deliverance."[34]

At this exact time Christ proclaimed to the people

that He possessed living waters! Jesus had already made this same parallel when He spoke to a woman of Samaria about the Holy Spirit: "Whoever drinks of the water that *I Myself* [literal Greek] shall give him will never thirst. But the water that I shall give him will become in him a fountain of water springing up into everlasting life" (John 4:14). Still earlier, John had testified concerning the Messiah: "He Himself [literal Greek] will baptize you in the Holy Spirit" (Mark 1:8).

Since Jesus Himself baptizes the believer in His Spirit, Paul described Him as "the One who is *supplying* to you the Spirit [literal Greek]" (Galatians 3:5). There is One who supplies to us His Spirit, and the apostle identified Him as Jesus when he wrote of "the *supply* of the Spirit of Jesus Christ" (Philippians 1:19). The same root word in the Greek for "supply" appears in both of these references. Thus, we can be sure that Jesus is the One who "supplies" to us the Holy Spirit, His Spirit—even as He promised He would do.

It is appropriate to conclude the present chapter by reiterating statements from two apostles. The first comes from Paul, the second from John:

- *"The first man, Adam, was made a living soul. The last Adam was made a life-giving Spirit"* (I Corinthians 15:45).
- *"And now little children, abide in Him, so that when He appears we may have confidence and not shrink from Him in shame at His coming. If you know that He is righteous, you may be sure that everyone who does right is born of Him"* (I John 2:28-29).

It is *because* Jesus is a life-giving Spirit that we can be "born of Him" (I John 2:29)—"born of the Spirit" (John 3:5).

Chapter 6

Lord of All

One Lord

We have already presented much important information concerning the Lordship of Jesus in previous chapters. Therefore, it would be worthwhile to review those chapters before continuing.

In the first part of Chapter 3, we discussed in detail a thought-provoking question from the Gospel of Matthew that Jesus presented to the inhabitants of Jerusalem regarding His Sonship. Because Jesus' intriguing question is also central to His Lordship, we return to His comments, this time according to the Gospel of Mark:

"And as Jesus taught in the Temple, He said, 'How can the scribes say that the Christ [Messiah] is the son

of David? David himself, inspired by the Holy Spirit, declared, "The LORD said to my Lord, 'Sit at My right hand, till I put your enemies under your feet.'" David himself calls Him Lord; so how is He his son?" (Mark 12:35-37).

Matthew added, "No one was able to answer Him a word, nor did anyone dare to ask Him any more questions" (Matthew 22:46). Even the Jewish experts of the law could not understand how the Lord could possibly be a son—and a son of David, at that. And perhaps they could not comprehend what David might have meant when he also wrote: "The LORD said to my Lord." However, the problem is resolved if we take David's proclamation in a figurative sense. We learned in chapter 3 that Yahweh's dialogue with Adonai is metaphorical because David himself and other Old Testament writers revealed Yahweh to *be* Adonai (as well as Adon or Adoni).

Psalm 2:6-7 refers to David *himself* as the "Son" who is begotten on a certain day. However, when Hebrews 1:5-6 quotes Psalm 2:6-7, it shows that the prophecy has a *dual* sense (a Biblical pattern), with (1) King David as the type (shadow) and (2) Jesus, his royal descendant through Mary, as the antitype (reality). For Psalm 2:6-7 pointed ultimately to the coming of a divine Messiah who was to be both an Israelite and a descendant of the house of David.

It is interesting that only a few verses before Christ asked His unusual questions—as recorded by Mark—Jesus Himself had just emphasized that the Lord God is "one Lord" (Mark 12:29). From Genesis to Revelation, the Scriptures are persistent in their declaration that the

God of the Bible is "one Lord."

This study has established that the Lordship of God—according to the Biblical record—was extended to the Messiah approximately two thousand years ago. In the inspired language of the apostle Peter, Jesus of Nazareth was "*made . . . both Lord and Christ*" (Acts 2:36, NKJV; see also KJV, RSV, and NIV).

From what we have seen thus far, we know that the Bible does not depict Jesus of Nazareth as "another" Lord or "another" God. According to Paul, the true "God was in Christ, reconciling the world to Himself" (II Corinthians 5:19). If we are going to believe Jesus, we must take Him at His word that the Father was in Him (and not merely "with" Him). Christ still asks: "Do you not *believe* that I am in the Father and the Father in Me?" (John 14:10).

We should ponder Jesus' reply to a scribe's question—a reply that sums up the Biblical teaching of the oneness of our God:

"Then one of the scribes . . . asked Him, 'Which is the first commandment of all?' Jesus answered him, 'The first of all the commandments is: "Hear, O Israel, the Lord our God, the Lord is one. And you shall love the Lord your God with all your heart, with all your soul, with all your mind, and with all your strength." This is the first commandment'" (Mark 12:28-30, NKJV). (See Deuteronomy 6:4-5.)

The Jewish scribe was pleased with Jesus' answer, for he told Christ: "Well said, Teacher, You have spoken the truth, for there is one God, and there is no other but He" (Mark 12:32, NKJV). In like manner, Jesus was pleased with the *scribe's* response, for Mark continued: "When Jesus saw that he answered wisely, He said to him, 'You are not far from the kingdom of God'" (Mark 12:34).

In Mark's inspired words Jesus "saw" that the scribe had answered wisely. And what had the scribe said? That the Lord God is "one"—that "there is no other but He."

The Bible declares—indeed Jesus Christ Himself declares—that our Lord God is one Lord. So it is not a light claim that Jesus made when He consistently (1) permitted *others* to call Him Lord and (2) referred to *Himself* as "the Lord." (See also Luke 6:5, 46-49.)

Jesus once told His followers: "You call Me Teacher and Lord. And you say well; for so I am" (John 13:13). The Greek in John 13:13 says it even more vividly, for it literally reads: "You yourselves call Me *the* Teacher and *the* Lord. And you say well, for I am" (John 13:13, literal Greek).

Christ did not consider Himself simply as "a" Lord or "another" Lord. He called Himself "*the* Lord." And He commended His disciples for recognizing who He was.

The inspired authors of the New Testament spoke with one voice that they worshiped and served one Lord. And their voice testified that this Lord is none other than the "Lord Jesus Christ." The apostle Paul said that there is "one Lord" (Ephesians 4:5). And the only Lord that Paul recognized was Jesus: "Yet for us . . . there is but one Lord, Jesus Christ, through whom all things came and through whom we live" (I Corinthians 8:6, NIV). The context of this verse identifies the Lord Jesus with God Himself. Here is Paul's complete statement:

"'There is no God but one.' For although there may

be so-called gods in heaven or on earth—as indeed there are many "gods" and many "lords"—yet for us there is one God, the Father, from whom are all things and for whom we exist, and one Lord, Jesus Christ, through whom are all things and through whom we exist" (I Corinthians 8:4-6, RSV).

In I Corinthians 8 itself, we should note that the apostle Paul equated the "so-called gods" with the "many 'gods' and many 'lords'" in verse 5. For Paul, "gods" meant "lords" in verse 5, just as "God" meant "Lord" for him in verse 6. May we also notice that the passage begins with the statement that "there is no God but one." This is another confirmation that the "one God, the Father" and the "one Lord, Jesus Christ" are two manifestations or roles of one Lord God!

While the foregoing passage states that "from" God the Father come all things, and "through" the Lord Jesus come all things, *another* passage by the same writer, Paul, states that "all things" come to us both "from" and "through" the *Lord*:

"For who has known the mind of the Lord? . . . For from Him and through Him and to Him are all things" (Romans 11:34, 36).

When we compare these two passages from Romans and I Corinthians, we see that, for Paul, there was no real distinction between "God the Father" and "the Lord." In Romans 11, the NIV has no justification for having "God" in verse 35. Only pronouns appear in the Greek in verse 35, and they refer back to "the Lord" of verse 34. Thus

Paul stated that it is "from" [*ex*, "out of"] *the Lord* that all things come, and the same writer stated in I Corinthians 8:6 that all things come "from" ["out of"] *God the Father.* So as far as the apostle Paul is concerned, according to Romans 11:34-36 and I Corinthians 8:6 all things "come out of" the Lord, who is God the Father.

Furthermore, a comparison of Romans 11:34, I Corinthians 2:16, and Isaiah 40:13 establishes that "the mind of the Lord" in the two New Testament passages is, in fact, (1) "the mind of Christ" (I Corinthians 2:16), (2) "the mind of the LORD" (Yahweh), *and* (3) "the Spirit of Yahweh"! For Paul was definitely quoting Isaiah 40:13 in both Romans 11:34 and I Corinthians 2:16. Consequently, according to this apostle, there is no difference between Yahweh (the Lord of the Old Testament) and Christ (the Lord of the New Testament)! This is why the apostle Paul made no distinction in person between the Lord and God the Father in Romans 11:34-36 and I Corinthians 8:6.

As a matter of fact, it is important to remember that the New Testament writers *often* applied Yahweh passages in the Old Testament to our Lord Jesus Christ in the New Testament.

Returning to I Corinthians 8:6, Bible scholars realize that the divine title "Lord" in the New Testament means the same thing as "God." In commenting on I Corinthians 8:6, a respected source has stated that *Kurios*, "Lord," is "a title used to indicate deity of Jesus Christ." The same source also refers to "a collection of the evidence proving that the Jews at the time of Christ used the term for God."[1]

For the Jew, God was the Lord, and the Lord was God.

For the Gentile also, these two divine titles were equivalent. And both Jews and Gentiles in the first century read I Corinthians 8:5-6 in this light. Modern scholarship has given us two relevant statements in this regard: (1) Among the Gentile nations the title "Lord" was "regularly employed for the divine heads of the different Graeco-Oriental salvation cults." (2) Therefore, when the Gentiles heard Paul and other Christians say that "Jesus is Lord," it signified to them that "Jesus was a divine redeemer-god."[2] In fact, the Christians in the first century made it very clear that they considered Jesus to be the *only* Redeemer-God with whom we have to do.

Several years ago, I had a professor who once correctly wrote in a scholarly, historical work about Christian origins that in the first century "every Jew must have known that in Hebrew God is called 'the Lord.'"[3] Because of this, as a Hebrew Christian the apostle Paul made no distinction in person between God the Father and the Lord Jesus Christ in Romans 11:34-36 and I Corinthians 8:4-6.

With this information before us, let us once again look at Paul's passage in I Corinthians, this time according to the original, inspired language:

"There is no God but one. For although there are so-called gods, whether in heaven or on earth—as indeed there are many 'gods' and many 'lords'—yet for us there is one God, the Father, out of [ex] whom are all things and we ourselves into [eis] Him—even [kai] one Lord, Jesus Christ, through [dia] whom are all things and we ourselves through [dia] Him" (I Corinthians 8:4-6, literal Greek).

This is yet another important passage of Scripture that does not mention the Holy Spirit at all, because Paul was discussing two roles of one Lord God, not three divine persons of a trinity. And it is interesting how the apostle *emphasized* these two roles by the use of the prepositions. All things originally came "out of" God as Father and Creator, and we ourselves "into" Him—even one Lord, Jesus Christ, "through" whom are all things and we ourselves "through" Him. Of course, the use of the preposition "through" stresses the role of Jesus as *Mediator*. (See I Timothy 2:5.)

As this apostle recorded elsewhere, there are varieties of service "but the same Lord"; there are varieties of working "but the same God" (I Corinthians 12:5-6).

He also told believers in the first century: "Masters, treat your servants justly and fairly, knowing that you also have a Master in heaven" (Colossians 4:1). The Greek term for "Master" here is *Kurios*—"Lord." Who is this *Kurios* in heaven? Paul told us just two verses earlier: "You are serving the Lord Christ" (Colossians 3:24).

If we deny the Lord Jesus, we deny the only Lord and Master who exists. Jude warned: "For certain men have crept in unnoticed, who long ago were marked out for this condemnation, ungodly men, who turn the grace of our God into licentiousness and deny the only Lord God and our Lord Jesus Christ" (Jude 4, NKJV).

The Byzantine family and other ancient sources have "God" in the phrase "the only Lord God," and the KJV and NKJV are correct in following the Byzantine family text. Even the context clearly establishes that "God" is discussed, since this divine title appears earlier in the same sentence. Also, "the only Lord" is, of course, God Himself.

In short, "God" belongs in the verse, and the context of the verse itself simply confirms the reliable Byzantine textual evidence. In view of this context, the word "and" between the divine titles, which is *kai* in the Greek, is better translated as "even": "the *only* Lord God, even *our* Lord Jesus Christ."

Jude 4 alone proves that Jesus Christ is the only Lord and the only God that the first-century Christians worshiped and served. The verse is so clear that even when *kai* is translated as "and" instead of "even," everyone still understands that our Lord Jesus Christ is the only One whom the text is talking about.

The verse has other points that glorify Jesus. In the Greek, Jude used two different exalted titles for "Lord": *Kurios* and *Despotes*. In earlier chapters, we have shown that *Kurios* is a majestic title for God in the Bible. In the Septuagint, the ancient Greek translation of the Hebrew Old Testament (which New Testament writers often quoted, instead of translating the Hebrew directly), it means "Lord" or "Master." In the New Testament itself, *Kurios* is the Greek title for the English word "Lord," referring to the true God. In addition, *throughout* the New Testament the inspired authors demonstrated the deity of Jesus by calling Him *Lord*—"Lord Jesus Christ"—as Jude did.

Besides "*Kurios*," Jude 4 also refers to Jesus as "the only *Despotes*." This is another majestic title, and it means "Master," "Lord," or "Owner." (We will discuss *Despotes* in greater detail later in this chapter when we examine Acts 4:24, a verse that has this exalted, divine title in a prayer to God.) In light of the context of Jude 4, it is not surprising that the Greek lexicons state that *Despotes* applies to Jesus Christ here, for Jesus is the only One who is praised. This declaration specifically reveals Him to be "the only *Despotes*"—the only Lord, Master, and Owner whom we are to serve. And we are warned in this verse and, indeed, in the context of the entire chapter *not* to deny Him.

It is significant that the very next verse refers to "the Lord" as the Lord of the Old Testament, who delivered those who believed in Him and who brought under judgment those who rejected Him and His ways. (See verses 3-11.) Verses 4 and 5 alone show that our Lord Jesus Christ *is* the Lord of the Old Testament.

Earlier, we noted Isaiah's Yahweh passage that Paul utilized when he wrote: "At the name of Jesus every knee shall bow . . . every tongue confess that *Jesus* is Lord" (Philippians 2:10-11). By applying Isaiah's reference of Yahweh to Jesus, Paul simply acknowledged that he considered Christ to be his Lord—his only Lord.

Similarly, when the apostle Thomas worshiped Jesus, he cried out to the Messiah: "My Lord and my God!" (John 20:28). It is not a small matter for us to call Jesus "Lord." If He is Lord, He is our Lord God. And if He is our Lord God, He is our only Lord—the only Master of our lives. In the words of a contemporary Christian author:

> The earliest Christian confession was the phrase "Jesus is Lord" (see Romans 10:9; Philippians 2:11; I Corinthians 12:3). The first Christians were Jews, believers in the one God of Jewish monotheism. But they dared give Jesus the title of "Lord" (which the Old Testament applies to God) because they had experienced salvation and new life in him. He had done for them what only God could do.[4]

Lord of All

If there is one Lord, He is Lord of all. The very word "lord" signifies "master" or "owner." When the New Testament recorded Jesus' warning that no one can serve "two masters,"[5] it uses the regular Greek term for "lord"—*kurios*. "No one," said Jesus, "can serve *two* lords." In the immediate context of His statement, Christ reminded us that we cannot serve both our Lord God and "mammon" (wealth) as "lords" over our lives; a person can serve one *or* the other but not both at the same time.

In addition to the particular focus on mammon, Jesus said unconditionally that "no one can serve two lords," whoever or whatever they may be. If we are to worship and serve the God of two Testaments, we must realize that He is one Lord—indeed the only one who has the authority to demand our total allegiance and commitment. For the Bible depicts God as "Lord of all."

The One who created this universe is the "Lord of heaven and earth" (Acts 17:24). How can we limit the sovereignty of the Lord? What mere mortal can we compare to the Lord? For the Lord is the Creator and owns it all: "The earth is the Lord's and everything in it" (I Corinthians 10:26; see Psalm 24:1).

We are asked: "Have you not known? Have you not heard? The Lord is the eternal God, the Creator of the ends of the earth. He does not faint or grow weary; His understanding is unsearchable" (Isaiah 40:28).

Although the Lord's understanding is "unsearchable" by humans with their limited mentality, the Lord Himself can search the human heart: "I the Lord search the heart" (Jeremiah 17:10). It was precisely because Jesus was the Lord that in His earthly sojourn "He Himself knew what was in man" (John 2:25). The apostle Peter acknowledged to the risen Christ that He is Lord of all when the fisherman confessed to Him: "Lord, You know all things" (John 21:17).

At times, humanity bestows undue honor and glory upon the wealthy, the powerful, the renowned of this world. But God alone should be honored and glorified as God, for He alone is the Lord of glory.

The fourth book of the New Testament informs us that the prophet Isaiah saw the *glory* of Jesus and spoke of Him.[6] And that Hebrew prophet *had* seen the glory of Christ—the glory of Yahweh—in a spectacular vision, which Isaiah 6 describes. (Compare John 12:39-41 with Isaiah 6:1-10.) Here is a portion of that vision:

> *"And above the firmament . . . was the likeness of a throne, in appearance like a sapphire stone; on the likeness of the throne was a likeness with the appearance of a man high above it. Also from the appearance of His waist and upward I saw, as it were, the color of amber with the appearance of fire all around within it; and from the appearance of His waist and downward I saw, as it were, the appearance of fire with brightness all around. Like the appearance of a rainbow in a cloud on a rainy day, so was the appearance of the brightness all around it. This was the appearance of the likeness of the glory of the LORD. So when I saw it, I fell on my face, and I heard a voice of One speaking" (Ezekiel 1:26-28, NKJV).*

David praised his Lord God as the King of glory:

> *"Lift up your heads, O you gates! And lift them up,*

you everlasting doors! And the King of glory shall come in. Who is this King of glory? The LORD of hosts, He is the King of glory" *(Psalm 24:9-10, NKJV).*

Very possibly, the apostle Paul was thinking of David's exaltation when he later gave *Jesus* the majestic title "the Lord of glory" (I Corinthians 2:8). And very likely, James also was considering David's praise when *he* referred to Jesus as "our Lord Jesus Christ, the One of glory" (James 2:1, literal Greek). Because Jesus is the Lord of glory, He deserves to be honored and glorified as Lord—by all.

The author of Hebrews glorified Jesus Christ as the Lord of history: "Your throne, O God, is forever and ever. . . . You, LORD, in the beginning laid the foundation of the earth, and the heavens are the work of Your hands; they will perish, but You remain; and they will all grow old like a garment; like a cloak You will fold them up, and they will be changed. But You are the same, and Your years will not fail" (Hebrews 1:8, 10-12, NKJV). (See Psalm 102:25-27.)

Yahweh proclaimed through His prophet: "I am the LORD; I do not change" (Malachi 3:6, NKJV). And this is the very claim that the New Testament makes for Jesus: "Jesus Christ is the same yesterday and today and forever" (Hebrews 13:8).

The Lord of the Bible is the God who is there, and He has always been there. Thus in the true sense of the word, the Lord Jesus Christ *is* the Lord of history—all of history—"yesterday and today and forever." And we can rightly call Him "*Lord* of history," not only because He has always "been there" but because the God of two Testaments controls and guides history. What about

Alexander the Great? Genghis Khan? Napoleon Bonaparte? Joseph Stalin? Adolf Hitler? Mao Tse-tung? True they were powerful men and powerful lords—as far as humans are concerned. However, humans are here today and gone tomorrow (including Saddam Hussein). Jesus Christ is here today and *here* tomorrow.

As the divine Lord of the universe, Jesus is "Lord of lords and King of kings" (Revelation 17:14). Since He is Lord of lords and King of kings, He is the only *real* "Sovereign"—as the following passage shows:

> *"I urge you in the sight of God who gives life to all things . . . that you keep this commandment without spot, blameless until our Lord Jesus Christ's appearing, which He will manifest in His own time, He who is the blessed and only Potentate, the King of kings and Lord of lords, who alone has immortality, dwelling in unapproachable light, whom no man has seen or can see, to whom be honor and everlasting power. Amen" (I Timothy 6:13-16, NKJV).*

In this majestic passage of Scripture Jesus, as the Lord of lords, is the "only" Sovereign—the only Potentate, and the only One who possesses immortality.

On more than one occasion, Jesus referred to Himself as "the Master of the house" (Matthew 10:25). In the Gospel of Luke Jesus encouraged: "Strive to enter through the narrow gate, for many, I say to you, will seek to enter and will not be able. When once the Master of the house has risen up and shut the door, and you begin to stand outside and knock at the door, saying, 'Lord, Lord, open for us,' and He will answer and say to you, 'I do not know you, where you are from. . . . Depart from Me, all you workers of iniquity'" (Luke 13:24-25, 27, NKJV).

On that day—the day of judgment—"the day of the Lord"—many will *call* Jesus Christ "Lord" as they always did. But Christ warned: "Not everyone who says to Me, 'Lord, Lord,' shall enter the kingdom of heaven, but he who does the will of My Father in heaven. Many will say to Me in that day, 'Lord, Lord, have we not prophesied in Your name, cast out demons in Your name, and done many wonders in Your name?' And then I will declare to them, 'I never knew you; depart from Me, you who practice lawlessness!'" (Matthew 7:21-23, NKJV).

We may talk about "knowing the Lord." However, Jesus Christ has already asked: "Why do you call Me, Lord, Lord, and not do what I tell you?" (Luke 6:46).

But the time will eventually come when all will comprehend that Jesus is Lord—Lord of all (Romans 14:10-11).

Revelation 19 designates Jesus, "the Lamb," as "the Lord God Almighty" (Revelation 19:6-7). He is the Almighty—as Lord of all. And Jesus has given to us His own testimony concerning Himself: "He who comes from above is *above* all; he who comes from the earth belongs to the earth, and of the earth he speaks. He who comes from heaven is above all" (John 3:31). (See Psalm 97:9.)

Paul told us: "For none of us lives to himself, and no one dies to himself. For if we live, we live to the Lord; and if we die, we die to the Lord. Therefore, whether we live or die, we are the Lord's. For to this end Christ died and rose and lived again, that He might be Lord of both the dead and the living" (Romans 14:7-9, NKJV).

Wherever we turn, the Biblical testimony is the same:

Jesus Christ is Lord. Consequently, these words of an apostle are still relevant for us today:

"The same Lord is Lord of all and bestows His riches upon all who call upon Him" (Romans 10:12).

And the words of another apostle shout to us even today:

"Jesus Christ: He *is Lord of all" (Acts 10:36).*

"If the Lord Wills"

Some speak of serving "the Lord Jesus," and others sometimes refer to "the baby Lord Jesus." If we are to actually serve the Lord Jesus Christ, we cannot think of Him merely as a babe in a manger. If we are to serve Jesus as Lord, we should serve Him as the New Testament Christians served Him—as Master and God.

The Lord was the One who added to His church daily those who were being saved.[7] When the disciples in Acts came together to pray, they came together to pray to the Lord as their God: "Lord, You are God, who has made heaven and earth, and the sea, and all that is in them" (Acts 4:24).

It was God who struck the persecutor Saul with blindness on the road to Damascus, and He identified Himself to Saul as "the *Lord Jesus"* (Acts 9:5, 17). Because of the shock of that experience, the persecutor Saul eventually became the apostle Paul, and he worshiped Jesus Christ as Lord and God.

Later, the Lord spoke to Paul in a vision: "Do not be afraid, but speak, and do not keep silent; for I ["I Myself," literal Greek] am with you, and no one will attack you to hurt you; for I have many people in this city" (Acts 18:9-10, NKJV). Subsequently, this apostle wrote concerning His Lord: "The Lord stood by me and gave me strength to proclaim the Word fully. The Lord will rescue me from every evil and save me for His heavenly kingdom" (II Timothy 4:17-18).

As disciples of Jesus, the Christians of the first century considered Him Lord of their lives. Thus no matter what situation they found themselves in, their prayer was: "If the Lord wills . . . if the Lord permits," as we see in the following statements by Paul and James:

- *"I hope to spend some time with you, if the Lord permits" (I Corinthians 16:7).*
- *"You ought to say, 'If the Lord wills, we shall do this or that'" (James 4:15).*

The disciples in the New Testament knew by whom they stood, for they worshiped their Lord as God; and in worshiping and serving the Lord Jesus, they gave Him their all. They did this because they understood that their lives were in His hands. Jesus Himself had declared: "You shall worship the Lord your God; and Him only shall you serve" (Matthew 4:10).

"Come, Lord Jesus!"

On a beautiful April day in 1970 I was leaving a restaurant in Los Angeles when my eyes fell upon the headlines of a national newspaper. I was surprised at what I saw, because a headline read in large, bold type: "NATION PRAYS." Undoubtedly many Americans *were* praying—

perhaps some for the first time. But it was a surprise to see it acknowledged on the front page of a sophisticated newspaper in Los Angeles, California.

The nation was praying because at that very time three American astronauts were limping home in a crippled spacecraft, still thousands of miles away from earth. Tragedy had struck the moon mission, and many were beginning to wonder if any of the three men would return to this planet alive. But millions prayed. And the astronauts were spared.

Prayer comes easily in a crisis—a real crisis. Even the agnostic and the "atheist" quickly learn how to pray to God in a crisis. But how many people pray to the Lord God on a daily basis? How many people thank their Creator for giving them every breath of air that they breathe? How many people pray to their Lord in gratitude for life itself, which He has given them? How many people truly pray to the Lord God, addressing Him as "Lord Jesus," as the Spirit-filled Stephen did? (Acts 7:59-60).

The Christians in the New Testament did this, and they were blessed for doing so. The apostle Peter wrote: "For the eyes of the Lord are upon the righteous; and His ears are open to their prayer" (I Peter 3:12). (I Peter 3:10-13 is a quotation of a Yahweh passage in Psalm 34:12-16.) In Peter's inspired language "the eyes of the Lord are upon the righteous . . . His ears are open." In other words, the Lord can see; the Lord can hear.

A few years earlier Jesus Himself had instructed Peter and the other apostles: "Pray to the Lord of the harvest" (Matthew 9:38). Who is this Lord of the harvest? The New Testament elsewhere indicates that the Lord of the harvest is the Lord of the second coming—the Lord of judgment—the Lord Jesus Christ.[8] In Luke's account, Jesus identified *Himself* as the Lord of harvest who sends out laborers into His harvest: "The harvest truly is great, but the laborers are few; therefore pray [to] the Lord of the harvest to send out laborers into His harvest. Go your way; behold I ["I Myself," the literal Greek of the Byzantine manuscripts] send you out as lambs among wolves" (Luke 10:2-3, NKJV).

In His explanation of the parable of the tares in Matthew 13:36-43, Jesus indicated that He is the Lord of harvest, the Son of Man who is coming again as Judge. In addition, Jesus Christ revealed here that He was actually the Father when He referred to "the Son of Man" and "*His* kingdom" in verse 41 and then referred to the kingdom of the "*Father*" only two verses later. At that time He immediately said, "He who has ears to hear, let him hear" (Matthew 13:43). Jesus specifically revealed that *He* is the Father, and He admonished us to listen to His revelation, because He gave it in reference to Himself as both Lord and Judge at His second coming!

At least three times the apostle from Tarsus prayed to the Lord Jesus about an affliction with which he was suffering. Paul wrote later: "Three times I besought the Lord about this, that it might leave me" (II Corinthians 12:8).

Who is "the Lord" in this context? In the very next verse (verse 9) Paul first quoted the Lord who had spoken of His "power." (See NIV and RSV; both the KJV and NKJV have "strength.") Then he designated it as "the power of *Christ*." (*Dunamis*, the Greek word for "power," appears both times in verse 9). This proves conclusively that the Lord to whom the apostle prayed was none other than the Lord Jesus Christ!

On another occasion, the apostle to the Gentiles wrote of "thanking" Jesus Christ for blessing him: "I thank Christ Jesus our Lord, the One who *empowered* me [literal Greek] because He considered me faithful, putting me into the ministry" (I Timothy 1:12). The Lord Jesus Christ was the One who empowered Paul, whether in dealing with a specific affliction (II Corinthians 12:8-9) or helping the apostle fulfill His ministry in general (I Timothy 1:12). And according to these two passages of Scripture, it was the *Lord Jesus* to whom Paul was in the habit of praying, both for petitions and in giving thanks!

Similarly, the dying Stephen prayed to Jesus Christ after he had just seen a vision of the Lord Jesus standing in the heavens:

"'Lord Jesus, receive my spirit.'" Then he knelt down and cried out with a loud voice, "'Lord, do not charge them with this sin.' And when he had said this, he fell asleep" (Acts 7:59-60, NKJV).

After Peter warned a recent convert to pray to "the Lord" for forgiveness (Acts 8:22), the man immediately begged the apostle to pray to "the Lord" on His behalf (verse 24). The context identifies the Lord only a few verses earlier as "the Lord Jesus" (verse 16)!

According to an esteemed scholar, "Personal prayer to Christ developed from the church's invocation of the Lord in public. We encounter such personal prayer in the writings of Paul, who prayed directly to the Lord Christ at decisive times (II Corinthians 12:8; I Thessalonians 3:12; II Thessalonians 3:2ff.)."[9]

In other words, according to this reference, personal prayer to Jesus developed from praying to Him in the *public* worship services. But one might ask, "How do we know that personal prayer to Jesus did not come before or at least contemporaneous *with* the public prayers?" Whatever the answer, we can be certain that the early disciples prayed directly to Jesus Christ in both public and private worship. Here is an example of prayer to the Lord in a public service:

"They raised their voice to God with one accord and said: 'Lord [Despotes], You are God, who made heaven and earth and the sea, and all that is in them'" (Acts 4:24, NKJV).

The disciples prayed to God, the Lord, whom they praised as the Creator (i.e., the *Father*) of all things. This Lord God, the Creator, is the same Lord Jesus who is magnified as the Creator in Hebrews 1:10-12. This is the same Lord Jesus who is both the Word and the Creator in John 1:1-3, 14-18. This is the same Lord who, as "the only Lord," is specifically the Lord Jesus Christ in Jude 4. And it is significant that the Greek word for "Lord" in Jude 4, *Despotes* ("Lord, Master, Owner"), is the same exalted word for "Lord" in Acts 4:24. Thus, we cannot distinguish the Lord to whom the disciples prayed in Acts 4 from the Lord Jesus of Jude 4.

Furthermore, the apostle Peter called Jesus our *Despotes* when he wrote that some would deny "the Lord" who *bought* them (II Peter 2:1). And when the disciples in Acts 4 referred to their *Despotes* also as "Lord" (*Kurios*) in verse 29 and as "God" in verse 24, they were praying to the same Lord God who *purchased* the church "with His own blood" (Acts 20:28).

The disciples' prayer of Acts 4 begins in verse 24 and ends in verse 30, and the prayer emphasizes the role of the Lord as a Son by referring to Jesus in the third person. In this prayer these Christians quoted David's Messianic prophecy of Psalm 2, where King David anticipated God's two roles in the Messianic age in his phrase "the LORD [*Yahweh*] and His Christ [*Anointed One*]" (verse 2). In that psalm, David foretold the physical incarnation of God in the coming Messiah. After quoting David's words in their prayer, the disciples then *emphasized* the marvelous Sonship of God in Jesus.

Like Psalm 2:2, the prayer in Acts 4 focuses on the wonderful, saving, redemptive Sonship of God when the disciples referred to Jesus of Nazareth as "Your holy Servant Jesus, whom You anointed" (verse 27) and "the name of Your holy Servant Jesus" (verse 30). The title "holy Servant" both times brings to mind the suffering *Servant* of Isaiah 53 and the coming into the world of the perfect sacrifice, the Lamb of God.

It is interesting that the disciples' prayer does not have any of the usual New Testament Greek words for "servant" (e.g., *doulos*). Instead, the Greek word for "servant" here is *pais*, which means both "servant" and "son." In fact, the Greek lexicons give Acts 4:27, 30 as verses in which *either* "son" *or* "servant" can be the meaning of the Greek term. In regard to this, we suggest that *both* concepts were probably intended in the prayer because of (1) the apparent meaning of *pais* as "servant" in verse 25 in reference to King David, (2) the two inherent meanings of "son" and "servant" in the Greek word itself, and (3) the

Biblical doctrine of the Sonship and the Servanthood of the Messiah, which are interrelated (Isaiah 9:7, 53:11).

"Child" or "son" is a basic meaning of the Greek term, which is why the King James Version uses the word "child" in Acts 4:27, 30. We see this meaning in other Greek words that are directly related to *pais*: *paidarion*, "boy"; *paidiothen*, "from childhood"; and *paidion*, "child, infant." Indeed, *paidion* is the very word for the "child" Jesus in Matthew 2:13-14, 20-21. On the other hand, we see the concept of "servant" in other related words: *paidagogos*, "attendant (slave)"; *paideia*, "training, discipline"; *paideuo*, "instruct, train, discipline, whip, scourge"; *paidiske*, "maid, servant-girl"; *paio*, "strike, hit, wound." In fact, the last word, *paio*, appears in Matthew 26:68 and Luke 22:64 when Jesus was "struck" and "wounded" shortly before His crucifixion.

We clearly see the suffering servanthood of Jesus in the word *pais* and its related terms. Therefore, it is evident that in Acts 4:27, 30 and *other* New Testament passages, *pais* applies to Jesus in a profound way the dual concept of "Servant" and "Son."

In short, the believers referred to the Nazarene in the third person in this prayer because they were praising the role of the *Sonship* of God as a human Servant. They knew that the Spirit of the Lord God, to whom they were praying, had been *in* Jesus, the Son. They did not worship two Lords anymore than King David did. However, they did worship and pray to one Lord God who had manifested or revealed Himself in His "holy Son and Servant, Jesus" (verses 27, 30).

The early saints continually "called upon" the one Lord in their prayers. Paul exhorted Timothy:

"Shun youthful passions and aim at righteousness, faith, love, and peace, along with those who call upon the Lord from a pure heart" (II Timothy 2:22).

In the context of this verse, Paul not only spoke of the one time when new converts called upon the Lord to save them from their sins when they were born again. In this passage the apostle referred to saints who *continually* "call upon" the Lord from a pure heart. And Paul associated the evangelist Timothy with these ones who "call upon" the Lord. The present-tense participle in the original language indicates repeated action and shows that the believers were continually calling on the Lord in their prayers.

In fact, the New Testament reveals that *all* the Christians in the New Testament era regularly called on the Lord Jesus Christ in their prayers. With regard to the believers of that age, Paul testified: "To the church of God which is at Corinth, to those who are sanctified in Christ Jesus, called to be saints, with *all* who *in every place* call on the name of Jesus Christ our Lord, both theirs and ours" (I Corinthians 1:2, NKJV).

Greek scholars are aware that the present-tense verb, "call on," in this verse "emphasizes the habitual act which characterizes their life."[10] By "calling on" the Lord Jesus in prayer, the early Christians naturally realized that they were "calling on" God the Father. Indeed, when the apostle Peter said, "If you call upon the Father . . ." (I Peter 1:17), he used the same Greek verb for "call on" that Paul used in I Corinthians 1:2!

The expression "call upon" or "call on" definitely has the connotation of praying and can be properly rendered as "invoke." In I Peter 1:17, the Revised Standard Version is correct in translating the verb as "invoke." Consequently, when the Christians in the first century were "calling upon" the Lord Jesus (I Corinthians 1:2), they were also calling upon, or "invoking," the Father (I Peter 1:17).

It is right and proper for us to address God as "Father" when we go to Him in prayer (Matthew 6:9). And the New Testament Christians did this, as we observe in I Peter 1:17. However, they also consistently identified the God of two Testaments as Lord, "the" Lord. And the apostles and other Christians throughout the Book of Acts (as well as the entire New Testament) constantly addressed their prayers to "the Lord" (Acts 1:24; 4:24; 7:59; 10:4, 14).

What is significant about the early Christians addressing their prayers to the Lord? It is significant simply because of the well-documented fact that the only Lord whom those disciples worshiped was the Lord Jesus Christ! "For us there is but . . . one Lord, Jesus Christ" (I Corinthians 8:6). "No one can say, 'Jesus is Lord,' except by the Holy Spirit" (I Corinthians 12:3). "Jesus Christ: He is Lord of all" (Acts 10:36).

When the Christians of the first century called upon or invoked the Lord, were they *really* invoking the Lord Jesus Christ? This question is paramount; we cannot ignore it. And instead of ignoring the question, God's Word—the Bible—answers the question with a resounding affirmative.

In addition to the above passages of Scriptures confirming the truth that those Christians prayed to Jesus as Lord, another Biblical passage is available that establishes the same thing. An honest look at Acts 9 shows us once and for all that the Lord with whom the early disciples communed was Jesus Himself.

In the first portion of Acts 9 we learn how Saul was temporarily struck blind by the Lord on a road outside the city of Damascus (verses 1-9). This same Lord proceeded to identify Himself to Saul as Jesus Christ (verse 5). And this Jesus, as Lord and God, summarily instructed the terror-stricken Saul to go on into Damascus, for there he would be told what to do (verse 6). The blinded Saul was then led into the city by his companions (verse 8). At this point we shall pick up the account as the inspired writer of Acts related it. We do so because every thoughtful Christian should carefully examine the following verses. Here is Luke's account in Acts 9:10-19:

"Now there was a certain disciple at Damascus, named Ananias; and the Lord said to him in a vision, 'Ananias.' And he said, 'Behold, here am I, Lord.' And the Lord said to him, 'Arise and go to the street called Straight, and inquire at the house of Judas for a man from Tarsus named Saul, for behold he is praying, and he has seen in a vision a man named Ananias come in and lay his hands on him, so that he might regain his sight.' But Ananias answered, 'Lord, I have heard from many about this man how much harm he did to Your saints in Jerusalem; and here he has authority from the chief priests to bind all who call upon Your name.' But the Lord said to him, 'Go, for he is a chosen instrument of Mine, to bear My name before the Gentiles and kings and the sons of Israel: for I will show him how much he must suffer for My name's sake.' And Ananias departed and entered the

house, and after laying his hands on him said, 'Brother Saul, the Lord Jesus, who appeared to you on the road by which you were coming, has sent me so that you may regain your sight, and be filled with the Holy Spirit.' And immediately there fell from his eyes something like scales, and he regained his sight, and he arose and was baptized; and he took food and was strengthened."

In examining this passage we quickly see several outstanding facts: (1) The One who suddenly appeared in a vision to Ananias is "the Lord" (verse 11). (2) "The Lord" is none other than "*the Lord Jesus*" (verse 17). (3) Thus it was the Lord Jesus who called Saul "a chosen instrument of Mine" (verse 15). (4) Thus it was the Lord Jesus who informed Ananias that Saul would "bear My name before the Gentiles and kings and the sons of Israel" (verse 15). (5) Thus it was the Lord Jesus who told Ananias that Saul "must suffer for My name's sake" (verse 16). (6) Thus it was the *Lord Jesus* to whom Ananias was speaking when he referred to Christians "who call upon [invoke] Your name" (verse 14).

Thus, according to Acts 9:17, Ananias communed with the Lord Jesus during the course of this remarkable vision! And thus, according to Acts 9:14, Christians were continually calling upon or "invoking" the Lord Jesus as their Lord and God!

We see a classic case of a short but urgent prayer to our Lord at the close of I Corinthians:

"If any one has no love for the Lord, let him be accursed. . . . Our Lord, come!" (I Corinthians 16:22).

This petition—"Our Lord, come!"—is actually from the Aramaic language: *Maranatha* (which the King James Version has left untranslated). A responsible source has pointed out: "*Our Lord, come*! is the preferable rendering of the word *Maranatha* (transliterated from two Aramaic words); another legitimate rendering, but less probable in this context, is 'Our Lord has come.'"[11]

The modern English versions have normally translated *Maranatha* as a petition and prayer to the Lord Jesus, and Biblical scholarship is in general agreement. Very possibly, this is because it occurs *as* a petition in another passage. In the last chapter of the Bible, immediately after Jesus Himself spoke of His second coming, John uttered this petition:

"Come, Lord Jesus!" (Revelation 22:20).

Unlike the previous example from Paul, this time we find the petition in the precise Greek language, not the Aramaic. To be more specific, here we find an "imperative of entreaty" in the Greek. This means that we *must* take it as a prayer from John to Jesus!

Even as the people of the United States prayed that three American astronauts might return safely to this planet, so also we—like the apostle John—should be eager to pray to the Lord Jesus Christ that He will soon come again: "Come, Lord Jesus!"

Chapter 7

The True God

Why Jesus Was Worshiped

Throughout His earthly ministry, Jesus Christ was constantly being worshiped. A leper who wanted to be healed worshiped the Christ.[1] A certain ruler, desiring Jesus to come and raise his daughter from the *dead*, worshiped the Nazarene.[2] After the Lord's disciples saw Him walking on the sea in the midst of a storm, in amazement they worshiped Him.[3] Even a Canaanite woman came to Jesus and worshiped Him.[4] Let us consider Simon Peter's encounter with Christ:

"Now so it was, as the multitude pressed about Him to hear the word of God, that He stood by the Lake of Gennesaret, and saw two boats standing by the

lake; but the fishermen had gone from them and were washing their nets. Then He got into one of the boats, which was Simon's, and asked him to put out a little from the land. And He sat down and taught the multitudes from the boat. Now when He stopped speaking, He said to Simon, 'Launch out into the deep and let down your nets for a catch.' But Simon answered and said to Him, 'Master, we have toiled all night and caught nothing; nevertheless at Your word I will let down the net.' And when they had done this, they caught a great number of fish, and their net was breaking. So they signaled to their partners in the other boat to come and help them. And they came and filled both the boats, so that they began to sink. When Simon Peter saw it, he fell down at Jesus' knees, saying, 'Depart from me, for I am a sinful man, O Lord!' For he and all who were with him were astonished" (Luke 5:1-9, NKJV).

Simon Peter had seen the sign of the great catch. He had looked at Jesus. And then he looked at *himself*. Peter's response? "Depart from me, for I am a sinful man, O Lord!" But was not the fisherman's reaction similar to Isaiah's? For when that prophet saw the holiness of Yahweh, *he* cried out:

"Woe am I, for I am lost! For I am a man of unclean lips, and I dwell in the midst of a people of unclean lips. For my eyes have seen the King, Yahweh of hosts!" (Isaiah 6:5).

Like Isaiah of old, Simon Peter simply recognized that

"before the holy God, sinful man cannot stand."[5]

The people of Palestine who worshiped Jesus did so under various circumstances. Some desired to be healed of horrible afflictions. Others wanted Jesus to heal their loved ones. Still others, like Peter, responded after recognizing that they were sinners standing in the presence of something holy and good. Those people observed the Nazarene—His miraculous signs and healings, His teaching and good works, His power and serenity.

After a leper was healed, he was truly grateful; and his worship was an expression of that gratitude: "When he saw that he was healed, he turned back, praising God with a loud voice. And he fell on his face at *Jesus'* feet, giving *Him* thanks" (Luke 17:11-16). It did not matter to that former leper that he himself was a Samaritan and Jesus a Jew. It did not matter to him that Samaritans were supposed to "hate" Jews. For he knew that this Jew had healed him from "the living death" (as the disease was called). And he *knew* that this Jew was no ordinary man. So he worshiped Him—bursting with gratitude.

After a blind man was healed by Jesus, he was capable of seeing not only physical things, but he could visualize spiritual things as well. Otherwise, he would not have said to Christ: "'Lord, I believe!' And he worshiped Him" (John 9:38, NKJV).

Later, when the followers of the crucified Jesus saw that He had *indeed* risen from the grave, no other response would have been logical, for they considered Him to be their Lord and Savior: "They came and held Him by the feet and *worshiped* Him" (Matthew 28:9). Afterward, the apostles went away into Galilee, and again, "when they saw Him, they worshiped Him" (Matthew 28:17, NKJV).

Some have suggested that all of these people were merely giving Jesus Christ homage, as one pays respect to a king. Is it true that they were simply paying Him special respect as a man? While "homage" can be one meaning of the Greek word that is employed, the *basic* meaning of the word is "worship." In fact, this is the word that the writers of the New Testament used to express that meaning—"worship." And this is the very Greek term that Jesus spoke when He warned: "You shall worship the Lord your *God*; and Him only shall you serve" (Luke 4:8).

So we must face the obvious fact. *Unless* Jesus Christ Himself was the Lord God, then He was teaching the people idolatry, for He did not rebuke others for worshiping Him. When we read the Book of Acts, we observe that the apostles rebuked others for worshiping *them*. Peter rebuked Cornelius after the latter attempted to pay him undue respect—respect that should only go to God. (See Acts 10:25-26.) Paul rebuked others when they attempted to worship *him* as God. (See Acts 14:11-18.)

John recorded that, on more than one occasion, he fell to worship at the feet of an angel who showed him visions from God. But the angel kept telling him:

"You must not do *that! I am a fellow servant with you. . . .* Worship God" *(Revelation 19:10.) (See also Revelation 22:8-9.)*

Jesus Christ was not merely an angel. *He* did not say, "You must not *do* that!" On the contrary, Jesus always blessed His worshipers—healing them or their loved ones and forgiving their sins. When the risen Lord stood before the doubting Thomas, He said to His disciple:

"'Put your finger here, and see My hands. Put out your hand, and place it in My side. Do not be faithless, but believe.' Thomas answered Him, *'My Lord and my God!' Jesus said to him, 'Have you believed because you have seen Me? Blessed are those who have not seen and yet believe'" (John 20:27-29).*

We should be impressed that the inspired narrative has Thomas calling Jesus "my Lord and my God!" But we also should be impressed with the response of *Jesus*—which shows that He fully accepted Thomas's worship.

In his strange book, *The Passover Plot*, even Hugh Schonfield pictured Jesus as a good and sincere man. But for some reason, Dr. Schonfield did not explain why a "good man" would accept the worship of others, when he wrote:

> He was no charlatan, willfully and deliberately misleading his people, well knowing that his posing as the Messiah was fraudulent. There is not the slightest suspicion of pretence on his part. On the contrary, no one could be more sure of his vocation than was Jesus, and not even the threat of imminent death by the horrible torture of crucifixion could make him deny his messiahship. We have to accept the absolute sincerity of Jesus.[6]

Schonfield accepted the obvious fact that Jesus of Nazareth was a dedicated, sincere man, but he refused to believe that Jesus was the divine Messiah. However, we have a real problem with this kind of logic. The Cambridge professor C. S. Lewis analyzed this reasoning well:

I am trying here to prevent anyone [from] saying the really foolish thing that people often say about Him: "I'm ready to accept Jesus as a great moral teacher, but I don't accept His claim to be God." That is the one thing we must not say. A man who was merely a man and said the sort of things Jesus said would not be a great moral teacher. He would either be a lunatic—on a level with the man who says that he is a poached egg—or else he would be the Devil of Hell. You must make your choice. . . . You can shut Him up for a fool, you can spit at Him and kill Him as a demon; or you can fall at His feet and call Him Lord and God. But let us not come with any patronising nonsense about His being a great human teacher. He has not left that open to us. He did not intend to.[7]

Why did Jesus Christ accept the worship of others? The answer is inescapable: He claimed to be deity in the *tabernacle* of flesh.

In the Tabernacle of ancient Israel, the curtain that separated the Holy Place from the Most Holy Place was the "veil." (See Exodus 26:31-35.) The Bible teaches that the presence of God was in the Most Holy Place behind that veil. According to the Book of Hebrews, that veil is a type of the very flesh of Jesus of Nazareth—wrapped around the holy presence of deity:

"Therefore, brethren, having boldness to enter the Holiest by the blood of Jesus, by a new and living way which He consecrated for us, through the veil, that is, His flesh, . . . let us hold fast the confession of our hope without wavering, for He who promised is faithful"

(Hebrews 10:19-20, 23, NKJV). (See also John 1:1, 14; Colossians 1:19-20; Colossians 2:9.)

Jesus did not deserve to be worshiped if He was only a man—no matter how great or how good He was. According to the above passage from Hebrews, Jesus Christ was worshiped because His flesh merely *veiled* His Godhead. Dr. William Barclay has properly stated: "Now Jesus' flesh is that which veiled His godhead. Charles Wesley in his great hymn appealed to men, 'Veiled in flesh the godhead see.'"[8]

"Veiled in flesh the Godhead see"! Is this not what Hebrews 10:19-20 teaches us? Is this not what John 1:1, 14 teaches us? Is this not what Colossians 1:19-20 teaches us? Is this not what John 20:28-29 teaches us?

The King Eternal

When Isaiah saw a vision of Yahweh, he saw Him on a *throne*, and he exclaimed: "My eyes have seen the King, Yahweh of hosts!" (Isaiah 6:5). David, who himself was a king, exalted Yahweh God as *his* king: "Give heed to the voice of my cry, my King and my God, for to You I will pray" (Psalm 5:2, NKJV). David was a king over all Israel, but he knew that "God is the King over all the earth" (Psalm 47:7). David's own physical kingship lasted only for forty years, but he acknowledged that the kingship of God will never end: "Yahweh is King forever and ever" (Psalm 10:16).

If Yahweh is to be King forever, what did He mean when He Himself predicted through His prophets that the days would come when the "Branch" would rise up to rule? According to Zechariah: "The Branch . . . shall sit and rule upon His throne" (Zechariah 6:12-13). As we turn to Jeremiah, we find that He will be a "Righteous Branch" who shall "reign as King and deal wisely, and execute justice and righteousness in the land" (Jeremiah 23:5).

We learn who the "Branch" is when we read the next verse: "This is the name by which He will be called: *Yahweh, Our Righteousness*" (Jeremiah 23:6). Thus Yahweh's name is stamped upon the Branch so that He can be identified for whom and for what he is: "Yahweh, our Righteousness."

When we turn to the Book of Matthew, we find that Jesus came to dwell in Nazareth so that "it might be fulfilled which was spoken by the prophets, 'He shall be called a Nazarene'" (Matthew 2:23, NKJV).

This verse reminds me of the first time I lived in Israel. I had the opportunity of living on a kibbutz where I studied modern Hebrew in an *ulpan* (school of intensive training) and taught English in a special program for Israeli members of the kibbutz. In the English program, I taught under the personal supervision of a senior teacher named Sarah Rehabi, who happened to be the daughter of Prime Minister Golda Meir. The prime minister would periodically visit the kibbutz to see her daughter, son-in-law, and grandchildren. During my time on the kibbutz, I also had the opportunity to visit Sarah Rehabi's family— visits that I always cherished.

Life on the kibbutz was a stimulating experience in general, and in the following year it led to the water baptism in Jesus' name of my Jewish roommate from New York City. In addition, I became acquainted with both Israelis and Jewish young people from different countries. One day a former Jewish Peace Corps worker named Barry challenged me about Matthew 2:23. Barry contended that Matthew 2:23 was wrong since there did not seem to be any Old Testament prophecies that foretold the city of Nazareth and a coming Nazarene.

Skeptics have often misinterpreted this verse, claiming that nowhere does the Old Testament predict that the Messiah would be called a Nazarene. But the skeptics are wrong, because the Hebraic root of the words *Nazareth* and *Nazarene* actually means "Branch"! (See Isaiah 11:1.) Matthew 2:23 undoubtedly refers to the Hebrew Scriptures which had predicted that Yahweh Himself would rise up as the "Branch."

According to Jeremiah, the Branch would have Yahweh's *name* stamped upon Him. In this regard, we should remember that the name *Jesus* does mean "Yahweh-Savior." As we have already seen, Jeremiah stated that the Branch would be called "Yahweh, our Righteousness." The apostle Paul recorded that Jesus Christ *became* our "righteousness" (I Corinthians 1:30).

To quote Matthew again, this time from *The Amplified Bible*: "He went and dwelt in a town called Nazareth, so that what was spoken through the prophets might be fulfilled, 'He shall be called a Nazarene' (meaning Branch, Separated One)" (Matthew 2:23).

All this, of course, is just one of the many amazing prophecies of the Hebrew Old Testament that find their fulfillment in Jesus of Nazareth. "The Root and the Offspring of David" (Revelation 22:16) rose up as the "Branch" (Nazarene) eventually to *rule* as the divine Messiah.

The Nazarene predicted: "When the Son of Man comes in *His* glory, and all the holy angels with Him, then

He will sit on the throne of His glory" (Matthew 25:31, NKJV). In the same context, Jesus called Himself *"the King"* (Matthew 25:34).

The Kingship of the Christ will never end. In writing about Jesus, the author of Hebrews recorded: "Your throne, O God, is forever and ever" (Hebrews 1:8) (Notice the context, verses 1-8.)

We discussed an inspiring passage in Revelation 19 when we dealt with the Lordship of Jesus Christ. But may we notice that He who is "Lord of lords" is also "King of kings" (Revelation 19:16). Even though John described Jesus as "clothed with a robe dipped in *blood*" (Revelation 19:13), He will not return simply as a sacrificial lamb to atone for our sins. Rather, Jesus will come back as Lord and King (Revelation 19:11-16). Once again, we can read with reverence Paul's testimony as he referred to Jesus as Lord of lords and King of kings:

"I urge you in the sight of God . . . that you keep this commandment without spot, blameless until our Lord Jesus Christ's appearing, which He will manifest in His own time, He who is the blessed and only Potentate, the King of kings and Lord of lords, who alone has immortality" (I Timothy 6:13-16, NKJV).

Here we see that "our Lord Jesus Christ . . . will manifest in *His* own time" the appearance of His second coming. This statement is a parallel to Jesus' words that only the *Father* knows the day and hour of the coming of the Son of Man (Matthew 24:36-37). It also parallels the statement of the risen Christ when He told His apostles that it was not for them to know the "times or seasons" that the Father has put in "His own authority" (Acts 1:7).

According to I Timothy 6:13-16, Jesus *Himself* determines the time of His second coming; and He does so in the role of God the Father, the Lord of lords, and the King of kings. Consequently, Jesus is the same eternal King whom Paul discussed in the first chapter of this epistle:

"Now to the King eternal, immortal, invisible, to God who alone is wise, be honor and glory forever and ever. Amen" (I Timothy 1:17, NKJV).

We can know that Jesus is the subject of Paul's discussion in this verse, for the apostle referred to Him in the preceding verses 12-16. Verse 16 specifically mentions "Jesus Christ" and encourages us to "believe in *Him* for eternal life." We are to believe in Jesus for "eternal life" simply because Jesus is "the King eternal . . . the *only* wise God" (I Timothy 1:17, KJV).

The Alpha and the Omega

God, the "King eternal," also identifies Himself as "the First and the Last." Yahweh proclaimed through His prophet: "I am He! I am the First and I am the Last!" (Isaiah 48:12). "Thus says Yahweh, the King of Israel . . . I am the First and I am the Last. Beside me there is no God" (Isaiah 44:6).

Several hundred years later Yahweh appeared to John on the island of Patmos. It is not surprising that at Patmos God again called Himself "the First and the Last." But what is significant is that here "the First and The Last" made Himself known to John as Jesus—the One who died and rose again. John related:

"When I saw Him, I fell at His feet as though dead. But He laid His right hand upon me, saying, 'Fear not, I am the First and the Last, and the Living One. I died, and behold I am alive for evermore; and I have the keys of death and Hades'" (Revelation 1:17-18).

The One who calls Himself "the First and the Last" in Isaiah 44:6 claimed, "Beside *Me* there is no God." Then, from Revelation 1:17-18 we see that "the First and the Last" is Jesus Himself—the One who died and is alive forevermore. Jesus, as a man, died on the cross, but the eternal Spirit that was in Jesus could not and would not die. Therefore, three days later the Spirit of God lifted the physical body of the Nazarene—transforming that body with the mighty power of His own presence.

Some may not want to believe it, but the Bible *does* teach that Jesus Christ Himself is God—"the First and the Last." In addition, the Bible teaches us that Jesus—as God—is similarly "the Beginning and the End" and "the Alpha and the Omega." We all know what "the Beginning and the End" means—that *this* One is the eternal One— Yahweh—the "I Am."

The first and last letters of the Greek alphabet are *alpha* and *omega*. So Jesus is "the A and the Z." He declared to His servant John:

"Behold, I am coming quickly, and My reward is with Me, to give to every one according to his work. I am the Alpha and the Omega, the Beginning and the End, the First and the Last. . . . I, Jesus, have sent My angel to testify to you these things in the churches" (Revelation 22:12-13, 16, NKJV).

This is a testimony for the churches (verse 16), the congregations of God's people. And this is Jesus Christ speaking to us. May we listen to Him, for He identifies Himself as the First and the Last, the Beginning and the End, the Alpha and the Omega. Could there be a higher claim to deity than this? Hardly.

Therefore, it should not astound us that in Revelation 21 Jesus—the Alpha and the Omega—specifically *called* Himself God. Jesus proclaims to us today:

"I am the Alpha and the Omega, the Beginning and the End. . . . He who conquers shall have this heritage. And I will be his God, and he shall be My son" *(Revelation 21:6-7).*

In Revelation 22:13, 16 the Alpha and the Omega is *Jesus.* In Revelation 21:6-7 the Alpha and the Omega is *God.* And in both passages the Alpha and the Omega is the One speaking. This is Jesus Christ speaking. This is God speaking. This is God the Father speaking, who wants to treat us as "sons" (Revelation 21:7).

Furthermore, the Alpha and the Omega identifies Himself as "the Lord God . . . the Almighty":

"I am the Alpha and the Omega, says the Lord God, who is and who was, even the coming One [literal Greek] . . . The Almighty" *(Revelation 1:8).*

Who is the Alpha and the Omega? In the Book of Revelation the Alpha and the Omega declares that He is the First and the Last, the Beginning and the End, the coming One, Jesus, God, the Lord God, the Almighty. (See

Revelation 1:8; 21:6-7; 22:13, 16.) So Jesus—as the Alpha and the Omega—categorically identified Himself to be all these. And just as John quoted Jesus Christ as using the Greek emphatic pronoun—"I Myself"—when He declared Himself to be both the "Root" *and* the "Offspring" of David, likewise here, Jesus consistently used the same emphatic pronoun so as to leave us with no doubts concerning His identity. Let us once more look at the Alpha and Omega passages, translating the inspired Greek correctly. Jesus is speaking:

"I Myself [literal Greek] am the Alpha and the Omega, the First and the Last, the Beginning and the End. . . . I Myself [literal Greek], Jesus, have sent My angel to you with this testimony for the churches" *(Revelation 22:13, 16).*

"I Myself [literal Greek] am the Alpha and the Omega, the Beginning and the End! I Myself [literal Greek] will give water without price to the one who is thirsty—out of the fountain of the water of life freely. . . . And I will be his God, and he shall be My son" *(Revelation 21:6-7).*

"I myself [literal Greek] am the Alpha and the Omega, says the Lord God, who is and who was, even the coming One [literal Greek] . . . the Almighty" *(Revelation 1:8).*

Jesus did not *have* to utilize the emphatic pronoun—"I Myself"—to show us that He is the Alpha and the Omega, the First and the Last, the Beginning and the End, God, Lord God, the Almighty. Even without the use of the emphatic, an honest examination of the verses involved would substantiate that Jesus Christ is the *All*. As far as the Bible is concerned, this is Jesus' last word, and we would certainly do well to take that word seriously; for Christ warned us that if we deny the truth that He has revealed to us in the Book of Revelation, then we will suffer the consequences. In Jesus' own words: "If anyone takes away from the words of the Book of this prophecy, God will take away his share in the tree of life and in the holy city, which are described in this book" (Revelation 22:19).

The Judgment Seat of Christ

The foregoing declaration by Jesus indicates a coming judgment; and the Bible tells us all that "just as it is appointed for men to die once, after this comes judgment" (Hebrews 9:27).

It is obvious that we will not live forever in our mortal flesh. We are born to die. And we all do die, although some may not like to think about it. As this revised edition was being written, Diana, Princess of Wales, was tragically killed in a violent car accident in Paris, France. Millions around the world were in a state of grief and shock. It was another lesson as to how precious and uncertain life is and how none of us are immune to death, which can come to us at any time. Since others are dying all around us, it should make us think about *our* life, about *our* death—and the judgment that is sure to follow. We should think about it because our Judge will be our Creator—God Himself:

"Our God shall come and shall not keep silent. Before Him shall be a devouring fire and round about

*Him a mighty tempest. He calls to the heavens above
and to the earth, that He may judge His people . . . for
God Himself is Judge" (Psalm 50:3-4, 6).*

Let us contemplate Solomon's advice: "The end of the
matter; all has been heard. Fear God and keep His commandments. For this is the whole duty of man. For God
will bring *every* deed into judgment, with *every* secret
thing, whether good or evil" (Ecclesiastes 12:13-14).

Some prefer only to think of our Creator as a God of
love and mercy. And the Bible does depict God as possessing these characteristics. But the God of two
Testaments is also a "God of justice" (Isaiah 30:18, NKJV
and NIV)—a "God of judgment" (KJV).

As I was writing these words, outside my window just
a few feet away hail began to fall from a violent thunder-
storm. Where did the hail come from? Where did the
thunder and the lightning come from? Where did the
storm clouds come from? Just a few moments earlier
there was not a cloud in the sky. The God who blesses us
with the sunshine is also the One who can send lightning
and hail at His command. The God who has given us temporary life is also the One who has the right to take that
life away at any time. The God who has offered us the
choice of *either* eternal life with Him *or* the judgment of
hell has the right to judge us—indeed, to cast us into the
lake of fire if we reject Him. *He* has that right. *He* is the
Creator. We are the created.

When the prophet called Yahweh "our King" and "our
Lawgiver," he also referred to Him as "our Judge"—in the
same verse. And may we consider which title Isaiah put
before the others:

*"Yahweh is our Judge. Yahweh is our Lawgiver.
Yahweh is our King" (Isaiah 33:22).*

The same Judge who will judge all of us who are now
living will also judge all who have ever lived in the past
and all who will ever live in the future, even the powerful
men and women of history—pharaohs, Roman emperors,
Eastern potentates, European kings and queens,
American presidents, and all dictators, past, present and
future. Consequently, it is appropriate that the Bible
should designate this One who judges us as "God, the
Judge of all" (Hebrews 12:23).

Time and time again the Nazarene warned that *He*
would return at the end of the age to personally judge
humanity. He said, "As I hear, I judge. And My judgment is
just" (John 5:30). "My judgment is true" (John 8:16).

Do we completely appreciate the ramifications of this
claim? Certainly, a respected minister put Jesus' claim
into proper perspective:

> This is perhaps the most fantastic of all His state-
> ments. . . . It is hard to exaggerate the magnitude of
> this claim. Imagine a minister addressing his congre-
> gation in these terms today: "Listen attentively to my
> words. Your eternal destiny depends on it. I shall
> return at the end of the world to judge you, and your
> fate will be settled according to your obedience to
> me." Such a preacher would not long escape the
> attentions of the police or the psychiatrists.[9]

And yet, Jesus Christ made this claim. In obvious reference to Himself, He declared:

*"When the Son of Man comes in His glory, and all
the holy angels with Him, then He will sit on the
throne of His glory. All the nations will be gathered
before Him, and He will separate them one from
another, as a shepherd divides his sheep from the
goats. And He will set the sheep on His right hand, but
the goats on the left" (Matthew 25:31-33, NKJV). (See
also verses 34-46.)*

In this passage the "Son of Man" is King and Judge,
and all the nations will stand before Him—for judgment.
Before this Judge will stand Russians, Chinese,
Americans, Cubans, Canadians, Israelis, Egyptians—all
the nations—past, present, future. Down through the
ages many have ridiculed and blasphemed the name of
Jesus. What will they say when they stand before Him
then? What will *we* say?

The Bible has not left us without witness. Throughout
its pages we find the same proclamation: Jesus is Judge.
Paul wrote, "He who judges me is the Lord. Therefore,
judge nothing before the time, until the Lord comes, who
will both bring to light the hidden things of darkness and
reveal the counsels of the hearts; and then each one's
praise will come from God" (I Corinthians 4:4-5, NKJV).
He also recorded:

"The Lord Jesus *[will be] revealed from heaven
with His mighty angels, in flaming fire taking
vengeance on those who do not know God, and on those
who do not obey the gospel of our Lord Jesus Christ.
These shall be punished with everlasting destruction
from the presence of the Lord and from the glory of His*

power, when He comes in that Day, to be glorified in His saints" (II Thessalonians 1:7-10, NKJV).

Paul once admonished: "I charge you therefore before God and ["even," *kai*] the Lord Jesus Christ, who [*singular* relative pronoun!] will judge the living and the dead at *His* appearing and *His* kingdom . . ." (II Timothy 4:1, NKJV).

At the close of the age, all will recognize Jesus Christ as the Judge: "For we must *all* appear before the judgment seat of Christ, that each one may receive the things done in the body, according to what he has done, whether good or bad. Knowing therefore, the terror of the Lord, we persuade men" (II Corinthians 5:10-11, NKJV).

Furthermore, James warned us, "There is *one* Lawgiver, who is able to save and to destroy. Who are *you* to judge another?" (James 4:12, NKJV). In the next chapter James associated the judgment with the coming of the Lord: "Therefore be patient, brethren, until the coming of the Lord. . . . Behold, the *Judge* is standing at the door!" (James 5:7, 9, NKJV).

Similarly, the apostle Peter wrote of this Judge and of our responsibility to Him. People may now scoff at the judgment of which the Bible testifies: "But they will give account to the *One* who is ready to judge the living and the dead" (I Peter 4:5). And in his second epistle Peter spoke of "the day of judgment" in the same context as "the day of the Lord" and "the day of God." (See II Peter 3:7, 10, 12.)

John had a vision of this coming Judge:

"Then I saw heaven opened, and behold, a white

horse. And He who sat upon it is called the Faithful One and the True One, and in righteousness He judges and makes war. His eyes are like a flame of fire, and on His head are many diadems. And He has a name inscribed which no one knows but He Himself. He is clad in a robe dipped in blood, and the name by which He is called is the Word of God. And the armies of heaven, arrayed in fine linen, white and pure, followed Him on white horses. From His mouth issues a sharp sword with which to smite the nations; and He will rule them with a rod of iron. He will tread the wine press of the fury of the wrath of God the Almighty. And on His robe and on His thigh He has a name inscribed, King of kings and Lord of lords" (Revelation 19:11-16).

This passage is truly a scene of Jesus, the King of kings and Lord of lords, who will return as the Judge of all the earth.

Emmanuel: God with Us

"And without controversy great is the mystery of godliness: God was manifest in the flesh, justified in the Spirit, seen of angels, preached unto the Gentiles, believed on in the world, received up into glory" (I Timothy 3:16, KJV).

Without controversy, stated Paul, *this* is the mystery of godliness; and it is great. The Bible does not tell us to comprehend God, but it asks us to believe Him—and to believe what He has done in Jesus. Why is it the "mystery" of godliness? Let us consider Jesus of Nazareth for a moment:

> As a man He was born in humility, but as God He was worshiped by men and angels. As a man He was tempted in all points as we are, but as God He defeated every power of the Devil. As a man He sat down on a mountain and spoke to the people, but as God He brought peace and comfort to every troubled life. As a man He prayed and taught other men, but as God He forgave their sins. As a man He grew weary, but as God He had all power in heaven and on earth. As a man He walked the paths of men, but as God He walked upon the waves of the sea. As a man He slept on a pillow in a ship, but as God He rebuked the wind and the sea into obeying Him. As a man He became hungry, but as God He caused bread to grow and multiply at His command. As a man He wept at the tomb of Lazarus, but as God He called Lazarus from the dead. As a man He talked with the blind and lame, but as God He opened their eyes and made their feet to walk. As a man He was scorned by men, but as God He was obeyed by demons. As a man He suffered and died, but as God He arose from the dead. As a man He was laid in a tomb, but as God He came forth conquering.[10]

This, according to Paul, is the mystery of godliness. In I Timothy 3:16 some Greek manuscripts do not have the reading that "God" was manifested in the flesh. Instead, they have a very awkward Greek construction, "He who" was manifested in the flesh—a most unlikely construction by Paul, who wrote a literary Greek.

By having "God" begin the sentence instead of the relative pronoun "He who," the King James Version and the New King James Version have the more probable reading. First of all, relative pronouns do not normally begin sentences. Second, in contrast to the previous statement, it would be natural for the sentence to begin with the nominative (subject) case of a proper noun, such as "God."

A third reason why the divine title "God" is most likely the correct rendering is because of the immediate context of verse 16. Every declaration of I Timothy 3:16 points to a God who became incarnate in the flesh of the Nazarene and who was glorified after accomplishing His divine mission. According to this verse, He was (1) manifested in the *flesh*, (2) justified in the *Spirit*, (3) seen by *angels*, (4) *preached* among the Gentiles, (5) *believed on* in the world, and (6) *received up* into *glory*. In this exalted statement the apostle Paul obviously wrote about our God, who became flesh in the form of the Nazarene.

A fourth reason why "God" is undoubtedly the correct reading is because of the strong, consistent evidence of the Byzantine family of manuscripts. As we have already pointed out, the King James Version and the New King James Version have normally followed the Byzantine text, and these two translations have done so in this verse with justification. It is significant that the rendering of the numerous Byzantine manuscripts is supported in a dramatic way by (1) the normal employment of Greek grammar and (2) the august pronouncements in the verse itself. I Timothy 3:16 clearly glorifies our Lord God.

The New King James Version translates this majestic verse of Scripture very much like the King James Version:

"And without controversy great is the mystery of godliness: God was manifested in the flesh, justified in the Spirit, seen by angels, preached among the Gentiles, believed on in the world, received up in glory" (I Timothy 3:16, NKJV).

Even if the considerable evidence were lacking for the divine title "God" in this verse, the relative pronoun "He who" could refer to no one else other than God anyway, for several reasons: (1) the content of the verse itself, as we have already demonstrated; (2) the many Messianic prophecies in the Old Testament (Isaiah 9:6-7; Micah 5:2; Zechariah 12:10, etc.) which predicted that the coming Messiah was to *be* God; (3) the way in which New Testament writers repeatedly identified Jesus as Yahweh, the God of the Old Testament (compare Matthew 3:3 and Luke 1:76 with Isaiah 40:3, and compare Philippians 2:10-11 with Isaiah 45:23, etc.); and (4) the manner in which the New Testament authors from Matthew to Revelation consistently portrayed Jesus Christ as deity in unmistakable language (John 1:1, 14; 20:27-29; Colossians 1:19, 2:9; Titus 2:13-14, etc.).

Consequently, the fact that God became a Son in order to redeem His creation for Himself is supported by hundreds of verses throughout the Old Testament and New Testament Scriptures. And I Timothy 3:16 is only one of many Biblical passages that glorify and exalt our majestic God because of what He did as the Man from Nazareth.

In addition to I Timothy 3:16, other verses of Scripture teach us that God was manifested in the flesh. The Bible clearly states that "the grace of God has appeared for the salvation of all men" (Titus 2:11). Because of this, we should be "awaiting our blessed hope, the appearing of the glory of our great God and Savior, *Jesus Christ,* who gave Himself for us to redeem us from all iniquity and to purify for Himself a people of His own who are zealous for good deeds" (Titus 2:13-14).

The apostle wrote that "our great God" gave Himself for us in order to redeem for Himself a people. In so doing, God was manifested in the flesh. The following verses of Scripture teach the same thing:

- *"God was in Christ, reconciling the world to Himself" (II Corinthians 5:19).*
- *"For in Him all the fullness of God was pleased to dwell" (Colossians 1:19).*
- *"In the beginning was the Word . . . and the Word was God. . . . And the Word became flesh and dwelt among us, . . . full of grace and truth" (John 1:1, 14).*
- *"For you know the grace of our Lord Jesus Christ, that though He was rich, yet for your sake He became poor, so that by His poverty you might become rich" (II Corinthians 8:9).*

It was for *our* sake that God was manifested in the flesh. It was for our sake that the Lord of glory became as one of us. It was for our sake that He suffered and sacrificed Himself to redeem a people. It was for our sake that He died and rose from the dead to become our Lord and Savior.

The Bible proclaims that in Jesus Christ, God was with us. The first book of the New Testament records:

"All this took place to fulfill what the Lord had spoken by the prophet, 'Behold a virgin shall conceive and bear a son; and His name shall be called Emmanuel,' which means 'God with us'" (Matthew 1:22-23). (See Isaiah 7:14.)

Emmanuel is a Hebrew name, and the last syllable of this name is *El*, the Mighty God of the Old Testament. Thus *Emmanu-El* signifies by its very name that the God of the Hebrew Scriptures became the Messiah. Because *Emmanuel* is a Hebrew word, Matthew, by inspiration, translated it into the Greek—as we see from his clause "which means, 'God with us.'" What is particularly interesting is that in the Greek translation, Matthew used the definite article "the" before the word "God." The Bible often employs the term "God" without the definite article, since it designated the one and only true God. However, sometimes the New Testament authors used the article, and Matthew 1:23 is such an example. Here, the inspired writer made it impossible for us to misunderstand. In Matthew's own words, Jesus Christ as Emmanuel was *"the* God with us" (Matthew 1:23).

We are not discussing a Christian invention. The Old Testament prophets had predicted that the coming Messiah would *be* God Himself. Isaiah predicted seven hundred years before the Christian era:

"For to us a child is born; to us a son is given. And the government will be upon His shoulder. And His name will be called Wonderful, Counselor, Mighty God, Eternal Father, Prince of Peace" (Isaiah 9:6).

The context of this verse shows that it is a messianic prophecy; and the verse speaks for itself in calling the Messiah the "Mighty God." This is not simply a Christian interpretation. Albert Barnes reminds us that ancient *Jewish* scholarship considered Isaiah 9:6 to be a proof-text that the Messiah would be God. Concerning this verse, Barnes's statement of one hundred years ago is still appropriate:

> The ancient Jews incontestably referred it to the Messiah. Thus the Targum of Jonathan renders it, "His name shall be called God of wonderful counsel, man abiding forever, *The Messiah*. . . ." Rabbi Jose, of Galilee, says, "The name of the Messiah is . . . *Shalom*, as it said in Isaiah ix.6, 'Father of Eternity, Prince of Peace.'" Ben Sira . . . numbers among the eight names of the Messiah those also taken from this passage, "Wonderful, Counsellor, Mighty God, Prince of Peace." The later Jews, however, have rejected this interpretation, because the Messiah is here described as God.[11]

It does appear obvious that Isaiah 9:6 is a reference to a divine Messiah. When the prophet called the coming Messiah "Mighty God," he used the Hebrew word *El*, the appellation that was stamped upon Jesus seven hundred years later in *Emmanu-El:* "Mighty God with us."

Let us quote once again two passages:

"In those days John the Baptist came preaching in the wilderness of Judea, and saying, 'Repent, for the kingdom of heaven is at hand!' For this is He who was

spoken of by the prophet Isaiah, saying: 'The voice of one crying in the wilderness: "Prepare the way of the Lord, make His paths straight"'" (Matthew 3:1-3, NKJV).

"The voice of one crying in the wilderness: 'Prepare the way of the Lord; make straight in the desert a highway for our God'" (Isaiah 40:3, NKJV).

From the New Testament we find that John prepared the way of "the Lord." But the New Testament accounts are actually direct references from Isaiah 40:3. The prophet Isaiah had, in fact, predicted that the messenger would prepare the way of the Lord; but Isaiah *identified* the Lord as "Yahweh" and "our God." In addition, the prophet's word for "God" here is *Elohim*. So according to this inspired Hebrew prophet, when John was to prepare the way for the Messiah, he would actually prepare the way for Yahweh—even Elohim. All of this means that the Messiah—Jesus Christ—is specifically both *Yahweh* and *Elohim*!

As this study has already shown, the Gospels' application of Isaiah 40:3 to Jesus is not the only instance in which Christ is identified with the God of the Hebrew Scriptures. For example, we read: "But concerning the Son, 'Your throne, O God, is forever and ever'" (Hebrews 1:8). The entire passage in Hebrews from which this verse comes, is a quotation from Psalm 45:6-7—where David wrote: "Your throne, O *Elohim*, is forever and ever!" (Psalm 45:6). So again, we see that Jesus is specifically Elohim, "Mighty God."

When the Nazarene made His well-known entry into Jerusalem before His betrayal, it appears that the people were capable of catching—at least to some extent—the glory of His presence: "Then the multitudes who went before and those who followed cried out, saying: 'Hosanna to the Son of David! "Blessed is He who comes in the name of the LORD!" Hosanna in the highest!' And when He had come into Jerusalem, all the city was *moved*, saying, 'Who is this?'" (Matthew 21:9-10, *NKJV*). (The Greek verb for "moved" means "as shaken by an earthquake.")

At that time, even the children in the Temple were inspired to cry out to Jesus: "Hosanna!" "And the blind and the lame came to Him in the temple, and He healed them. But when the chief priests and the scribes saw the wonderful things that He did, and the children crying in the temple, 'Hosanna to the Son of David!' they were indignant" (Matthew 21:14-15).

Why were the chief priests and scribes so enraged? Jealousy? Perhaps. But very likely part of the answer lies in the acclamation "Hosanna." For *Hosanna* was a Hebrew invocation that was addressed to *God*. It means literally: "O save!"[12]

An example of this invocation is in the Psalms, where David exclaimed: "Save us [*Hosanna*], we beseech You, O Yahweh" (Psalm 118:25). Small wonder that the scribes were indignant, for the multitudes were beseeching Jesus Christ as *God* to save them!

From Luke's account we learn that "some of the Pharisees in the multitude said to Him, 'Teacher, rebuke your disciples'" (Luke 19:39). But the Christ replied: "I tell you, if these were silent, the very stones would cry out" (Luke 19:40).

In Chapter 4 we pointed out that, on occasion, a heavenly voice was heard as a testimony for the people. That voice was heard at the baptism of Jesus. It was heard again at His transfiguration. And now here, Christ stated that the very stones would cry out in praise if the people themselves *had* been silent.

Were those people not witnessing a visitation from God? Shortly after this scene, Jesus looked upon the city of Jerusalem, and He wept. He knew what the future held for that city—its rejection of its Messiah and its own eventual destruction by the legions of Rome. Thus Jesus reflected: "You did not know the time of your visitation" (Luke 19:44).

Certainly, the Christ here referred to Himself and His *own* visitation upon that people. But we should realize that this is the kind of language that is reserved for deity. Several of the English translations have brought this point out when they consider the "visitation" mentioned in Luke 19:44 as being no less than the visitation of God. According to William Barclay's translation of this verse: "You did not recognize the day when God visited you."[13] *The Amplified Bible* renders the verse: "You did not come progressively to recognize and know and understand [from observation and experience] the time of your visitation [that is, when God was visiting you]" (brackets in original).[14] J. B. Phillips's translation states: "All because you did not know when God Himself was visiting you!"[15]

These translations have a valid foundation for such renderings because the Bible in several places speaks of God "visiting" His people. For example, Zacharias, filled with the Holy Spirit, prophesied of the Messiah: "Blessed be the Lord God of Israel, for He has visited and redeemed His people!" (Luke 1:68). (See also verses 67-79.) After Jesus raised a man from the dead in the village of Nain, fear seized the people. They cried out, "*God* has visited His people!" (Luke 7:16). In writing of the second coming of Jesus, Peter predicted that we will "glorify God on the day of visitation" (I Peter 2:12).

And long after His incarnation, death, and resurrection, our Lord is still visiting us through His eternal Spirit.

Jesus Christ truly made a startling claim when He once promised His disciples: "Where two or three are gathered together in My name, I am there in the midst of them" (Matthew 18:20). This is definitely a claim for deity. In an interesting admission, the liberal Jewish scholar Dr. Hugh Schonfield stated:

> The quotation relates to the presence of God. The exact source is unknown, but cp. Exodus xx.24 and I Chronicles vii.14-16. The Jewish authorities express the same view (*Aboth*, iii.2-6) where Malachi iii.16 is cited to show that God's presence is with two, and Exodus xx.24 to show that he is even with one person.[16]

When Jesus made the promise that He would be present when two or three gather together in His name, He made a promise that, of course, He could *only* carry out as God.

According to the New Testament record, Jesus Christ did not act or speak like an ordinary man. He did act and speak like deity in the flesh—"God with us." And we can thoughtfully consider the appropriate comment by Carl Henry in this regard:

Some years ago a brilliant professor of law at Harvard University studied the evidence and concluded that Jesus must certainly be found guilty of the claim to deity and that any impartial jury in the world would find Him guilty of that charge. (The essay may be found in the appendix to Greenleaf's *The Testimony of the Evangelists*.) The all-important question, then, was whether He rightly or wrongly made the claim—whether He should be sentenced to death as a blasphemer or acknowledged as the Lord of life and death.[17]

"Our Great God and Savior"

There is a fundamental principle of Greek grammar that has a direct bearing upon this study. It is called "Sharp's rule." And since it has been discussed ably by Dr. Bruce Metzger in an article concerning the Jehovah's Witnesses, the following is a portion of that article. Professor Metzger discussed certain mistranslations of the Bible made by the sect:

> In still another crucial verse the New World Translation has garbled the meaning of the original so as to avoid referring to Jesus Christ as God. In Titus 2:13 it reads, "We wait for the happy hope and glorious manifestation of the great God and of our Savior Christ Jesus." This rendering, by separating "the great God" from "our Savior Christ Jesus," overlooks a principle of Greek grammar which was detected and formulated in a rule by Granville Sharp in 1798. This rule, in brief, is that when the copulative *KAI* connects two nouns of the same case, if the article precedes the first

noun and is not repeated before the second noun, the latter always refers to the same person that is expressed or described by the first noun. This verse in Titus, therefore, must be translated, as in fact the Revised Standard Version (1952) renders it, "Awaiting our blessed hope, the appearing of our great God and Savior Jesus Christ."

In support of this translation there may be quoted such eminent grammarians of the Greek New Testament as P. W. Schmiedel, J. H. Moulton, A. T. Robertson, and Blass-Debrunner. All of these scholars concur in the judgment that only one person is referred to in Titus 2:13 and that therefore it must be rendered, "Our Great God and Savior Jesus Christ."[18]

The translators of the King James Version lived long before the rule was formulated. Likewise, the Protestant Reformers of Europe had the same disadvantage. If the Christian scholars and Bible translators of the sixteenth and seventeenth centuries had known about what Granville Sharp later discovered, they undoubtedly would have translated Titus 2:13 like the Revised Standard Version, the New International Version, the New King James Version, and other modern translations of our time.

Even so, the King James Version and other early translations still present the truth that our Lord Jesus is our great God whom Paul discussed. While the KJV and other early versions may not present Titus 2:13 as clearly as the Greek and as many modern versions, the truth is still there for us to appreciate if we read the earlier translations carefully and honestly.

At any rate, contemporary Greek scholarship unanimously affirms with a clear voice that the Greek construction in Titus 2:13 makes it certain that the apostle was designating Jesus Christ as "our great God." And Granville Sharp's rule is so fundamental that students of Greek are often introduced to it no later than in the second year's study of the language.

In my possession is more than one Greek grammar that gives Titus 2:13 as the classic example of this rule. One such grammar is that standard work by Dana and Mantey; and in line with other scholars, these Baptists state that the Greek of Titus 2:13 definitely "asserts that Jesus is the great God and Saviour."[19]

Like other scholars, Dana and Mantey recognize that we must also apply Sharp's rule to similar passages of Scripture in order to have an accurate rendering. One example is II Peter 1:1, where the grammarians freely acknowledge that Peter likewise "means that Jesus is our God and Saviour."[20] Other New Testament examples concerning Jesus in which we see Granville Sharp's rule are II Peter 1:11; 2:20; 3:2, 18; I John 5:20; and Jude 4. We will discuss the reference in Jude later in this chapter.

As far as Greek scholarship is concerned, it is an open-and-shut case. In a comment concerning Titus 2:13, Dr. A. T. Robertson pointed out that Dr. Moulton found "most pertinently papyri examples. . . , which show that among Greek-speaking Christians 'our great God and Saviour' was a current form of speech. . . . Moulton's conclusion is clear enough to close the matter."[21] This quotation is from Robertson's voluminous grammar of 1454 pages—the standard work on New Testament Greek.

The scholars of Greek inform us that Sharp's rule in

Titus identifies Jesus Himself to be "our great God and Savior." But in spite of the unanimous verdict of the Greek grammarians, Hugh Schonfield, the author of *The Passover Plot*, has written in another strange book, *Those Incredible Christians*: "Never anywhere does Paul identify Christ with God."[22]

One should consider *that* an incredible statement by Dr. Schonfield. We have just seen that Paul specifically called Jesus Christ "our great God." In addition to Titus 2:13, that apostle identified Christ with God in II Corinthians 5:19; Romans 9:5; I Thessalonians 3:11 (literal Greek); II Thessalonians 2:16-17 (literal Greek); Colossians 1:19; 2:9; I Timothy 1:16-17—not to mention the many Yahweh passages that Paul identified with Jesus throughout his epistles! There can be no doubt that Paul most certainly *did* "identify Christ with God"—on many occasions. And in so doing, he was simply in agreement with the other inspired writers of the New Testament.

In his electrifying book, *Set Forth Your Case*, Dr. Clark Pinnock wrote:

> All the evidence of the New Testament points in the same direction—to a Messiah who is both human and divine, and to whom men owe all their allegiance. It matters not whether we read Matthew, Luke or John, Peter, Paul, James or Jude, the message is the same. The only understanding of Christ which is *not* based upon a speculative reconstruction of the historical materials is one of worship and praise, "My Lord and my God!" The divine Christ is the only Christ which any document in the New Testament has any knowledge.[23]

Pinnock is right. If we claim that we believe the Biblical record, we must take seriously the New Testament's claim—a claim for the full deity of Jesus Christ:

"For in Him all the fullness was pleased to dwell" (Colossians 1:19, literal Greek).

Colossians 1:19 does not have either "the Father" or "God" in the Greek, which some English translations have. What did Paul mean when he said "the fullness"? The fullness of what? Just a few verses later, the apostle explained that it is "the fullness of *the Godhead*":

"For in Him dwells all the fullness of the Godhead bodily" (Colossians 2:9, NKJV).

Both Colossians 1:9 and 2:9 are challenging verses of Scripture. They do not simply say "fullness." They do not simply say "*the* fullness." What they do tell us is that "all" the fullness of the Godhead was pleased to dwell in Jesus Christ! This makes the deity of Jesus truly complete, for He has *all* of the fullness of the Godhead, not just part of the Godhead.

Because of the context of Colossians 1:19 itself and because Colossians 2:9 reveals it to be the fullness of "the Godhead," several English versions bring out the complete deity of Jesus in their translation of Colossians 1:19: "It was in him that the full nature of God chose to live" (Colossians 1:19, J. B. Phillips's translation). "For in him the complete being of God, by God's own choice, came to dwell" (Colossians 1:19 New English Bible).

Similarly, the New English Bible properly translates the related verse, Colossians 2:9, as: "For it is in Christ that the complete being of the Godhead dwells embodied" (Colossians 2:9). In commenting on this verse, a Biblical scholar has accurately stated:

> It means that everything without exception which goes to make up the godhead . . . dwells or resides in Jesus Christ bodily. . . . It is to be noticed also that Paul uses the present tense of the verb, "dwells." He does not say that the fullness of the divine quality "has dwelt" or "will dwell" in Jesus Christ, but that it dwells there.[24]

An additional word might be said concerning Paul's verb "dwells." In both Colossians 1:19 and Colossians 2:9 the same Greek verb appears, and it means to "settle down"—not simply to "dwell." To be even more exact, the verb in the Greek means to "dwell permanently."

This verb occurs also in Matthew 2:23. When we consult the translation of Charles B. Williams, we see that he included a footnote to the verb in Matthew. In the words of Dr. Williams: "This vb. means *to dwell permanently*" (emphasis his).[25]

The Greek lexicons agree. Thus we have an inspired apostle of God who noted *twice* (Colossians 1:19, 2:9) that all the fullness of the Godhead "dwells permanently" in Jesus. The editors of *The Oxford Annotated Bible* of the Revised Standard Version have suggested that the whole being of the Godhead will dwell "eternally" in the Messiah.[26] Indeed, the verse appears to have this meaning.

In the previous chapter concerning the Lord, we demonstrated that Jude 4 and many other verses of Scripture magnify Jesus as the only Lord God whom we are to worship. Jude 4 does exalt Jesus as Lord and God in clear, unambiguous language. The writer not only used the divine title "God" (according to the reliable Byzantine manuscripts and other ancient sources), but he also used two different Greek words for "Lord" that refer to the true God in other Biblical passages.

We saw earlier that because Jude 4 discusses "the *only* Lord God" in the same context as "*our* Lord Jesus Christ," it would be appropriate to translate *kai* as "even" in the phrase "the only Lord God, *even* [*kai*] our Lord Jesus Christ."

However, another interesting point about this verse is that it utilizes Granville Sharp's rule in its exaltation of Jesus as our Lord and God. In the last part of the verse, the writer used only one definite article before two nouns that are separated by *kai*, and it is before the first noun, "Lord" (*Despotes*). According to Sharp's rule, Jude referred to only one Lord God who is our Lord Jesus Christ. What is particularly interesting about Jude 4 is that even without the application of Granville Sharp's rule, it is obvious that Jesus is the only Lord God discussed by the inspired author. Sharp's rule, as a principle of Greek syntax, simply *emphasizes* the truth of Jesus' Lordship and deity that is so clearly expressed.

Jude 4 can be correctly translated various ways into the English. The important point is that any translation should be faithful to the syntax (grammar) and vocabulary in bringing across Jude's message—that our only Lord God is Jesus. If we take Sharp's rule into consideration, then we can translate *kai* as "and" and the exalted phrase as: "our only Master God and Lord, Jesus Christ." As we have already noted, the verse has two different titles for "Lord" in the Greek, *Despotes* and *Kurios*, and other New Testament passages apply both titles to Jesus. We have already pointed out that the New Testament uses *Kurios* not only as an exalted, divine title for God but also for Jesus, simply because He *is* our Lord God. Acts 4:24 uses *Despotes* for God, and in like manner the word refers to Jesus in II Peter 2:1. Of course, as we have seen, in Jude 4 *both* divine titles refer to Jesus, who is glorified as "the only Lord God" and "our Lord."

At this time, it is relevant to remember what we said about *kai* and Jude 4 in chapter 6. There, we learned that often we can translate *kai* in the Greek New Testament not only as "and" but also as "even" or "that is." The content of the verse in Jude shows that only one Lord is being honored and that He is Jesus. Because of this, it is evident that "even" is a natural English translation of *kai* in Jude 4. If we render *kai* as "even" instead of "and," then an accurate, literal translation of the last portion of the verse would be: "the *only* Lord [or "Master"] God, even [*kai*] *our* Lord Jesus Christ." And we reiterate what we stated in the previous chapter: because of the context of the verse itself, "even" is actually a more appropriate English translation of *kai* than "and."

In view of this, we should note that use of the English word "even" (instead of "and") does not conflict with the application of Sharp's rule at all. That principle of Greek is in force throughout Hellenistic Greek literature whether one translates *kai* as "and" or "even." Granville Sharp's rule establishes that only *one* place, thing, person, or supernatural being is described by the use of two nouns, *kai*, and one definite article. It is important to realize that this Greek grammatical rule has never been shown to have any exceptions. Because it is a valuable, consistent principle of ancient Greek syntax, its importance to the Greek New Testament in general, and to the study of the nature of God in particular, is obvious.

What is also interesting about Jude 4 is that, by having the two titles for "Lord," it may well be yet another verse that points to the two important roles of one God as Father and Son. It is significant that both divine titles here for "Lord" clearly refer to Jesus Christ, as shown by (1) the precision of Greek grammar and (2) the message of the verse itself.

It is undoubtedly true that one reason why God chose Greek to be the inspired, original language of the New Testament is because of the unusual exactness of Greek grammar, and we can marvel in this fact. However, we can also appreciate the fact that our Lord God has seen to it that His glorious, basic truths (1) are taught consistently throughout His Scriptures and (2) shine forth in the different translations down through the centuries. Even without a knowledge of Greek in general and Granville Sharp's rule in particular, the truth of God's Word can be seen by those who love God (I Corinthians 2:9) and who receive revelation from Him through His Spirit (I Corinthians 2:10-11) and His Word (II Timothy 3:16-17).

Some modern English translations (e.g., NIV, RSV) do not have the word "God" in Jude 4. However, under the Lord's providential hand, Jude 4 is so plain that one can recognize even in the different translations that Jesus Christ is the only Lord in whom we are to place our faith.

And for almost four hundred years, those able to read English have seen in the King James Version, and now in the New King James Version, that Jude 4 identifies Jesus not simply as "our only Lord," but correctly as "our only Lord *God*."

We can observe God's providential care of His Word in other languages as well. For example, I have a popular modern Hebrew translation of the Greek New Testament, which I purchased in Jerusalem. Israelis are reading the New Testament in Hebrew, as well as in other languages, and some of these Israelis are Hebrew Christians—believers in Jesus as their Lord God and Messiah (Christ). It is interesting that this Hebrew edition of the New Testament agrees with the KJV and NKJV in having "God" (as "Elohim") in Jude 4, thus correctly identifying Jesus as our "only Lord God." So we see that God in His wisdom and grace continues to permit the truths of His Word to be faithfully translated, published, and distributed, despite the frailties of the flesh and the weakness of humanity.

"The True God"

The Jehovah's Witnesses' *New World Translation* of the Bible renders a portion of the first verse of John as: "And the Word was a god" (John 1:1). Quite frankly, if the Watch Tower Society is serious about this rendering, then they are none other than polytheists—and certainly not worshipers of the one and only true God of which the Holy Scriptures testify.

The Jehovah's Witnesses translate the Greek in John 1:1 as "a god," supposedly because there is no definite article before the noun. However, Greek grammar simply will not allow such a rendering, for the noun "God" in this verse is a predicate nominative, and it is placed *before* the verb. When this is the case, the Greek definite article is not utilized in order to have the definite idea present. In the words of a leading grammarian: "When the predicate nominative *precedes* the verb in Greek, it generally does *not* have the article. Since this is true, it is frequently necessary to supply a definite article in English, even though there is none in Greek."[27]

Some years ago, Dr. Ernest Colwell of the University of Chicago pointed out in a study of the Greek definite article: "A *definite* predicate nominative has the article where it follows the verb; it does not have the article when it precedes the verb."[28]

That rule still stands. John 1:1 does have the predicate nominative "God" before the verb—thus "God" here is a "*definite* predicate nominative" even though the definite article is not present. In this circumstance, the Greek article simply is not necessary in the idiom of the language.

The Watch Tower Society views Jesus as "a god" and completely distinct from "the God." But many times the Greek New Testament refers to God the Father *without* the use of the definite article. In John 1 itself, this is the case in several verses (verses 6, 12, 13, 18). Do the Jehovah's Witnesses translate these instances as "a god" also? No, they do not. *The New World Translation* is not consistent in its mistranslations—even within the same chapter in which John 1:1 appears.

In addition, we should also keep in mind that the Bible treats the word "God" as a proper noun. Even in English, we capitalize proper nouns and consider them as specific entities—*without* the necessity of a definite article. A person's name or title is a proper noun in English, and in both English and Greek a proper noun does not need the definite article in order to express the definite sense. And so it is in the Bible; whether it speaks of Him as "the God" or simply "God," the inspired writers considered Him always to be "God"—and *never* "a god." In Paul's words, "There is no other God but one" (I Corinthians 8:4).

"What think ye of the Christ?" (Matthew 22:42). According to the Biblical testimony, it is not enough for us to call Jesus "a god." It is not enough for us to say that Jesus Christ is "divine"—and let it go at that. If Jesus is divine, He is deity—complete deity. We saw earlier that the Bible speaks of Jesus as *the* God—"the God with us" (Matthew 1:23). Furthermore, when an apostle called Jesus Christ "my Lord and my God," the inspired literal Greek has Thomas exclaiming: *"the* Lord of me and *the* God of me!" One simply cannot be more specific than this. Jesus was the only Lord and God that Thomas knew.

It may come as a surprise to some, but the Greek in John 1:1-2 does not exactly say that "the Word was *with* God." First of all, the context does not allow us to take the Greek preposition in that sense, for the inspired writer went on to inform us in verse 1 that this Word "was" God! Obviously, if the Word *was* God, He was not separate from God. Second, the meaning of the preposition in question means basically "toward" or "pertaining to," not "with." As a matter of fact, the exact Greek phrase (with the same preposition) occurs not once but twice in the Book of Hebrews (2:17; 5:10). And here the King James Version correctly renders the phrase as "pertaining to God." Similarly, in using the same preposition, *pros*, John

1:1-2 appears to affirm that the Word "pertains to God," especially since the writer also proclaimed that God Himself *is* the Word.

We pointed out earlier that "God" in John 1:1 is definite because (1) the Bible uses the divine title as a proper noun for the one and only true God, and (2) "God" in this verse is a predicate nominative that *precedes* the verb. The exact order of the words in the Greek is as follows: "In the beginning was the Word, and the Word was with [*pros*] God, and *God* was the Word" (John 1:1). It is instructive to see how different English versions have translated the last part of the verse:

- *"He has always been alive and is* himself *God"* *(John 1:1, Living Bible).*
- *"The Word was God* Himself" *(John 1:1, Amplified Bible).*
- *"Yea, the Word was God* Himself" *(John 1:1, Charles B. Williams).*

These versions very likely translate John 1:1 by putting "God" in the emphatic sense of "God Himself" because the predicate nominative, "God," appears *before* the verb, while the subject of the sentence, "the Word," appears after it. Another justifiable reason for a translation of emphasis is that the Greek text emphasizes "God" by repeating the Word in the verse. "God Himself" is the accurate rendering according to Greek syntax.

We saw in a previous section of this chapter that Jesus, as the Alpha and the Omega, identified Himself to be "the Lord" and "the Almighty" (Revelation 1:8). Later, John identified Jesus as "the Lord *God* Almighty"

(Revelation 15:3) and there also referred to Him as "the Lamb." Similarly, Revelation 21 specifically identifies the Lamb *as* the Lord God Almighty:

"And I saw no temple in it. For the Lord God Almighty is its temple, even the Lamb" (Revelation 21:22).

The Greek verb is singular—"is"—and most certainly is not the plural. Till now, it has been common for English versions to translate the verse by incorrectly rendering the Greek verb as "are." Consequently, they falsely leave the impression that "the Lord God Almighty and the Lamb *are* the temple of it" (Revelation 21:22). This is simply not a correct translation. The Greek verb in the verse is *estin*, the *singular* form—as any first-year student of New Testament Greek quickly learns! So John said, according to the inspired Greek language: "The Lord God Almighty, even [*kai*] the Lamb, is [*estin*] the temple of it (Revelation 21:22). The RSV correctly translates *estin* as "is," although it inaccurately makes "temple" the subject of the sentence instead "Lord." (Compare "the Almighty" in this verse with Revelation 1:8 and 15:3.)

In short, we can be certain that *kai* in this verse is to be translated as "even" and not simply as "and," because (1) the Greek singular verb, *estin*, requires it, and (2) the Lamb Himself is the Lord God Almighty, as we saw earlier. (Besides Revelation 1:8 and 15:3, see also Revelation 19:6-7, 13-15.)

Naturally, the Lord God Almighty is "God *over* all," and the apostle Paul exalted Jesus Christ with this very phrase in the Book of Romans:

"Christ came, who is God over all, blessed forever" *(Romans 9:5, literal Greek).*

The NIV says, "Christ, who is God over all, forever praised! Amen." (See also the KJV and NKJV). Some English versions have added an unwarranted period between "Christ" and the phrase "God over all." However, such a separation is completely without justification. In the words of Dr. Oscar Cullmann, "it is hardly the one suggested by a philological and material consideration of the context."[29]

Concerning Christ as "God over all" in Romans 9:5, the inspired writer said essentially the same thing only a few verses earlier when he praised Jesus in the latter part of the previous chapter (Romans 8:35-39). In verse 35 he asked, "Who shall separate us from the love of Christ?" He then answered his own question just a few verses later: "For I am persuaded that neither death nor life, nor angels nor principalities nor powers, nor things present nor things to come, nor height nor depth, nor any other created thing, shall be able to separate us from the love of God which is *in* Christ Jesus our Lord" (Romans 8:38-39, NKJV).

The same apostle continued to exalt the risen Christ in the chapter *following* Romans 9:5 when he proclaimed: "For there is no distinction between Jew and Greek, for the *same Lord over all* is rich to all who call upon Him. For 'whoever calls upon the name of the Lord shall be saved'" (Romans 10:12-13, NKJV). (See Joel 2:32.)

This passage is another of the many Yahweh passages from the Old Testament that the New Testament writers specifically identified with Jesus. So we see that "Christ,

God over all" of Romans 9:5 is "the same Lord over all" of Romans 10:12. And of course, He is also the same "Lord *of* all" who is honored in Acts 10:36.

Some Bible translators and other liberal scholars often display an antisupernatural bias regarding Jesus in verses like Romans 9:5; Revelation 21:22; I Timothy 3:16. However, the Biblical evidence is indisputable in these and many other passages, saying in the most absolute language that our Lord Jesus is the one and only true God. In conclusion, according to the inspired record, Jesus Himself is:

1. The Alpha and the Omega (Revelation 1:7-8, 11-13; 22:13, 16).

2. The Beginning and the End (Revelation 1:7-8; 22:13, 16).

3. The First and the Last (Revelation 1:11-13; 22:13, 16).

4. The Root and the Offspring of David (Revelation 22:16).

5. The King of kings (Revelation 19:13, 16; I Timothy 6:14-15).

6. The King eternal (I Timothy 1:16-17).

7. The one Lord (I Corinthians 8:6).

8. The Lord of lords (Revelation 19:13, 16; I Timothy 6:14-15).

9. The Lord of all (Acts 10:36).

10. The Judge of all (II Corinthians 5:10; Matthew 25:31-46).

11. The Great *I Am* (John 8:58; Exodus 3:14-15).

12. Yahweh (compare Isaiah 40:3 with Matthew 3:3; Mark 1:3; Luke 3:4; John 1:23).

13. Yahweh-Savior (the Hebrew meaning of the name *Jesus*)

14. Eternal Father (Isaiah 9:6; John 14:7-9; I John 3:1).

15. The Holy Spirit (II Corinthians 3:14-17; Romans 8:9-10).

16. The Author of life (John 1:3-4; Acts 3:15; Colossians 1:15-18).

17. Elohim (Psalm 45:6; Hebrews 1:8).

18. Mighty God (Isaiah 9:6).

19. The Lord God Almighty (Revelation 15:3; 19:6-7; 19:13, 15; 21:22, literal Greek).

20. Our Great God (Titus 2:13, literal Greek).

21. Emmanu-El: God with us (Matthew 1:23; Isaiah 7:14).

22. *The* God (Matthew 1:23; John 20:18, literal Greek).

23. God Himself (John 1:1; see *Amplified Bible* and other modern translations; also compare Revelation 19:7-9 with Revelation 21:2-3).

24. The only God (I Timothy 1:16-17).

25. The only Lord God (Jude 4).

26. God over all (Romans 9:5).

27. The same Lord over all (Romans 10:12).

28. The same Lord (I Corinthians 12:3, 5).

29. The same Spirit (I Corinthians 12:4).

30. The same God (I Corinthians 12:6).

31. The eternally blessed God (Romans 9:5, NKJV; see also KJV).

32. The true God (I John 5:20).

Some ask, "Who is Jesus?" An honest examination of

the two Testaments—the Bible—makes it plain. And the *God* of the Bible challenges us to put away our idols and false gods—and not only of metal and stone. For we are called upon to put away the idols and the false gods of imagination and tradition as well. Who is Jesus? The Bible declares:

"*We are in Him who is true,* in His Son *Jesus Christ.* This *is the true God. . . . Little children, keep yourselves from idols*" (I John 5:20-21, NKJV).

Chapter 8

No Other Name

Sharp's Rule in Reverse?

In the previous chapter we learned Granville Sharp's rule: when two nouns (of the same case) are connected by "and," the nouns always refer to *one* person, place, or thing if only the first noun has the Greek definite article before it. Further, we observed that the rule is relevant to our discussion because it is yet another pillar which substantiates just that much more (1) the oneness of the Christian God and (2) the complete deity of Jesus Christ.

It is unfortunate that an unjustifiable attempt has been made to use Sharp's principle "in reverse" in order to try to prove the existence of more than one person in the Godhead. Let us consider the following comment concerning Matthew 28:19, for it is a classic example of

Sharp's rule being misapplied:

> The Bible says, "Go ye therefore and make disci-
> ples of all nations, baptizing them into the name of
> the Father and of the Son and of the Holy Spirit." Now
> look carefully at the verse. We have three things
> joined together by the conjunction "and." The Father
> and the Son and the Holy Spirit. Now there is a rule in
> the grammar of the NT which states that when nouns
> of the same case are joined together by the conjunc-
> tion "and," they may or may not refer to the same per-
> son or thing. Here before me is a copy of *A Manual
> Grammar of the Greek NT* by Dana and Mantey. . . .
> I have the rule marked on page 147. . . . Now the rule
> essentially is this: when these nouns of the same case
> are joined together by the conjunction "and," if there
> is not an article preceding each one, then they simply
> refer to three manifestations of the same thing.
> However, if each one of the three nouns is preceded
> by the definite article, they must refer to three sepa-
> rate persons. Notice the situation before us. The
> record does not say, "baptizing them into the name of
> the Father, Son and Holy Spirit. . . ." But note that
> there is an article before Father, an article before Son,
> and an article before Holy Spirit. Hence, they do not
> refer to three manifestations of one person, but rather
> they refer to three separate, distinct, individual per-
> sons. This is known as Granville Sharp's rule.[1]

The conclusions drawn in this unfortunate quotation
are completely false. Neither Dana and Mantey nor any
other Greek grammarian would explain Granville Sharp's

rule in this way. No explanation of Sharp's rule in any Greek grammar has ever claimed that "if each one of the three nouns is preceded by the definite article, they must refer to three separate persons."

On the contrary, in all honesty we must categorically reject the last statement of the above quotation. For this explanation is not known as Granville Sharp's rule. It is sad that a minister would make the completely false claims in the foregoing comments, even if he may have been simply mistaken. It is particularly disturbing that he stated that he had the rule "marked on page 147" of Dana and Mantey's grammar. If he had the rule marked, he might have acknowledged that Dana and Mantey did *not* give Matthew 28:19 as an example of it. If he had the rule marked, he might have acknowledged that these grammarians did give Titus 2:13 as an example and that they said Sharp's rule in the latter verse illustrates that Jesus Christ Himself is "our Great God."

As we observed earlier, we can apply the grammatical principle known as Sharp's rule only when there is one definite article. And the rule applies only when the one article occurs before the first of a series of nouns connected by "and." In this circumstance, the use of the one article demands that all the nouns refer to one person, not two or three. Since Titus 2:13 uses only one article, we know that the inspired writer definitely referred to Jesus as his "great God and Savior." Since II Peter 1:1 uses only one article, we know that this writer considered Jesus Christ to be *his* God and Savior.

The author of the forgoing lengthy quotation attempted to use Sharp's rule in reverse. He claimed that the rule allows that any nouns in question "may or may not refer to the same person or thing." As a matter of fact, Granville Sharp's rule *always* demands that only one person or thing is indicated.

It is ironic that anyone would use this grammatical principle to try to establish exactly the opposite of what it does establish. But our confused minister did just that when he added: "If each one of the three nouns is preceded by the definite article, they must refer to three separate persons." Finally he incorrectly concluded, "This is known as Granville Sharp's rule."

We feel compelled to reiterate that we cannot even consider this rule in Matthew 28:19 since more than one article is present in this verse. Because the verse has three articles, we might consider other principles of Greek grammar, but not Granville Sharp's rule.

In Matthew 28:19 we find the same situation that we have in Revelation 1:17-18. The latter reference says that Jesus is "the First, and the Last, and the Living One." Here are three definite articles, as in Matthew 28:19. Yet surely no one will insist that the presence of three articles in Revelation 1:17-18 proves three distinct persons! Whether we consider "the Father, and the Son, and the Holy Spirit" from the Book of Matthew or "the First, and the Last, and the Living One" from the Book of Revelation, the use of three articles does not signify three persons.

The distinguished Dr. A. T. Robertson enlightens us in this very regard: "When a second article does occur, it accents sharply a different aspect of the person or phase of the subject. So in Revelation 1:17 . . . one article would have been sufficient, but would have obscured the separate affirmations here made."[2]

There are many other similar examples that make the

same point, and they also speak about Jesus. In Revelation 1:8 Jesus Christ said that He *Himself* [literal Greek] is "the Alpha and the Omega." Both nouns, "Alpha" and "Omega," have a definite article, and yet both nouns refer to Jesus and Him alone. In Revelation 1:11, Jesus said that He *Himself* [literal Greek] is "the Alpha and the Omega, the First and the Last." Here, all *four* nouns have a definite article, and yet they all refer to Jesus and Him alone. And finally, in Revelation 22:13 Jesus said that He *Himself* [literal Greek] is "the Alpha and the Omega, the Beginning and the End, the First and the Last." In this verse all *six* nouns have a definite article, and yet they all refer to Jesus and Him alone.

We simply cannot ignore the clear, exalted language of Scripture. Clever arguments and presumptuous attitudes will not make it go away. The inspired literature of the Bible repeatedly honors and glorifies Jesus as the living God of two Testaments.

Matthew 28:19

What does this verse of Scripture really mean? In considering the verse, this question should be foremost in our minds. For it is a verse that refers to the Christian God by the titles of Father, Son, and Holy Spirit. What did Jesus mean when He told His disciples to baptize others in the *name* of the Father, and the Son, and the Holy Spirit?

Before we examine Matthew 28:19 in detail, it is appropriate for us to consider the three titles at this time because this study established earlier that Jesus Christ, being *Emmanuel—God with us*—cannot really be separate from the Father, Son, or Holy Spirit. Since we treated this point in depth in chapters 3, 4, and 5, the reader is encouraged to turn back and review that portion of our discussion. The treatment that follows will only present a few high points of what we have already established.

The Father

At this time, it is important to review who the Father really is, because many people are sincerely confused about Matthew 28:19. Very possibly this confusion is the result of a few verses like Matthew 28:19 being misinterpreted and misapplied for so long. Whether Matthew 28:19 or any other verse of Scripture is involved, it is essential that we keep in mind the clarity of the Biblical evidence that identifies Jesus as God the Father manifested in the flesh. If we hold in our heart the great foundation of truth that the eternal Spirit of God was, indeed, *in* Jesus of Nazareth, then the related truths of the Son and the Holy Spirit will naturally fall into place.

Actually, whether we search for the identity of the Father, the Son, or the Holy Spirit, the Biblical record always leads us to Jesus. This is the wonderful reality of the matter. In the grandeur of the Word of God, the many passages about the Father, the Son, and the Holy Spirit are profoundly interrelated, all pointing to the majestic truth of the oneness of our God who has revealed Himself to us in Jesus Christ. We should be humbly grateful that the Biblical testimony of an eternal, indivisible God is *consistently* undergirded by what He reveals in His Word about His different roles and manifestations—the Father, the Son, and the Holy Spirit.

We saw in chapter 4 that Jesus Christ is the Light of the world (John 8:12). And being the Light that came into the world to enlighten every person, Jesus told others: "A little while longer the light is with you. . . . While you have the light, believe in the light, that you may become *sons* of light (John 12:35-36, NKJV).

In obvious reference to Himself as the Light, Jesus called His disciples "sons of *the* Light" (Luke 16:8). Later, Paul reminded his fellow Christians, "You are *all* sons of light" (I Thessalonians 5:5, NKJV). In a related passage, this apostle stated that *because* we are "light in the Lord," we are to *walk* as "children of light" (Ephesians 5:8, NKJV). If Jesus is the Light of the world, and if we are the children of the Light, then Jesus is our Father, and we are His children.

To pose a question we asked in chapter 4: Is it strange to think of the Lord Jesus Christ as our heavenly Father? If Jesus, the Lord of the New Testament, is also the Lord of the Old Testament—and He is—then He most certainly is our heavenly Father. And if Jesus is "our great God and Savior"—and He is (Titus 2:13)—then he most definitely is God the Father. In writing of the second coming of Christ, John said:

"And now, little children, abide in Him, so that when He appears we may not shrink from Him at His coming. If you know that He is righteous, you may be sure that everyone who does right is born of Him" (I John 2:28-29).

If we are born of Jesus, we are His children. And again, if we are *His* children, then He is our Father. And this is precisely what John called Jesus in the very next verse:

"See what love the Father *has given us, that we*

should be called children of God; and so we are. The reason why the world does not know us is that it did not know Him" (I John 3:1).

The "Him" of the latter portion of the verse is the "Father" of the earlier portion. It is because the world "did not know Him," did not recognize Him for who He was, that the world rejected Him and crucified Him on a cruel cross. Do we know Him? Do we recognize Him as our heavenly Father? Do we *accept* Him and *honor* Him as our heavenly Father?

We have already studied many Biblical passages which reveal that the resident deity in Jesus was God the Father. It is true that the Scriptures sometimes make a distinction between the manifestations or roles of God. It is also true that Jesus Christ Himself spoke about the Father in figurative language. In His own words: "Until now you have asked *nothing* in My name. Ask, and you will receive, that your joy may be full. These things I have spoken to you in figurative language; but the time is coming when I will no longer speak to you in figurative language, but I will tell you *plainly* about the Father. In that day you will ask in *My* name, and I do not say to you that I shall pray to the Father for you" (John 16:24-26).

Jesus then went on to say that He "came forth from God" (verse 27) and that He "came forth from the Father" (verse 28). The Greek verb in verses 27 and 28 literally means "came *out of*," not simply "came *from*." Christ continued by stating that He was going to leave the world and "go to the Father" (verse 28). It was at this point that Jesus' disciples responded by exclaiming: "See now You are speaking plainly, and using no figure of speech! Now we are sure that *You know all things.* . . . By this we believe that You came *forth* [*ex*, "out of"] from God" (John 16:29-30, NKJV).

Jesus replied by simply asking, "Do you now believe?" (verse 31).

Why did the disciples realize that Jesus knew all things? Certainly, they grasped that the divine *Mind* in Jesus cannot be separated from God the Father who was in Him. For the Nazarene told them that He had come "out of" God (as the perfect, human Son) and that He was going to put off mortality and go back to God. Jesus also made it clear to His disciples that the day would come when His disciples would pray in *His* name and that He, Jesus, would not have to "pray to the Father" for them (John 16:26). It is rather apparent that Christ was looking ahead to His resurrection and glorification when He would no longer be in mortal flesh. At that time, His disciple could pray to *Him* in *His* name as the Father!

This is why the New Testament instructs Christians to pray to God the Father *in the name of Jesus Christ*. The incarnation of God in Jesus of Nazareth and His atoning death allow us to approach a holy God in the name of Jesus (Philippians 2:5-11). Therefore, we are to pray by "giving thanks always for *all* things to God the Father in the *name* of our Lord Jesus Christ" (Ephesians 5:20).

We saw in chapter 4 that the precision of a singular Greek verb in I Thessalonians establishes conclusively that the apostle Paul identified "our Lord Jesus Christ" as "our God and Father" (I Thessalonians 3:11). We also learned that in II Thessalonians Paul used no less than *four* singular Greek verbs in the exactness of the Greek language when he *again* identified "our Lord Jesus Christ

Himself" as none other than "God our Father" (II Thessalonians 2:16-17)!

We should never forget a wonderful passage in the
Gospel of John. A frustrated Thomas once told Jesus that
he and the other disciples did not know *where* Jesus was
going and that they did not know the way (John 14:5).
This is when Jesus made it *very plain* to His disciples
who He really was:

"If you had known *Me, you would have known* My
Father also; *and from now on* you know Him and have
seen Him" *(John 14:7, NKJV).*

After these words by Jesus, Philip was *still* confused.
He told Christ that if He would show them the Father,
then they would be satisfied (John 14:8). At this point,
Jesus gave a response that we cannot possibly misunderstand:

*"Have I been with you so long, and yet you have
not known Me, Philip?* He who has seen Me has seen the
Father; *so how can you say, 'Show us the Father'?"*
(John 14:9, NKJV).

Thus John 14:7-9 is yet another marvelous passage of
Scripture that reveals to us in unmistakable language that
Jesus Christ Himself was, indeed, the heavenly Father!

Jesus of Nazareth made a personal promise to His
disciples: "I will not leave you as orphans; I will come to
you" (John 14:18). Even today, Jesus does not wish to
leave us as orphans. His desire is to come to us, to adopt
us as His spiritual children; His desire is to be our Father.

The Christ was quite explicit in His claim that the Father was *in* Him and thus was not to be set apart from Him (John 10:38). Unlike John the Baptist and other prophets, Jesus could claim that the Father was in Him, and not only with Him.

All of the preceding passages of Scripture, as well as others, proclaim the same wonderful truth: "the Father" of whom Jesus Christ spoke in Matthew 28:19 was the selfsame Father who was dwelling in Him.

The Son

Chapter 3 of this book described how the Hebrew God *became* a Son in order to reconcile His creation to Himself. In Jesus' words: "For as the Father has life in Himself, so He has given the Son to have life in Himself" (John 5:26). If God the Father "has given" the Son to have life in Himself, then there was a time when the Son did not have this life. It is true that Micah 5:2 speaks of the *eternity* of the Messiah—but as God, not as a Son. God is an eternal Father, but a Father who was willing to *become* a Son, as Isaiah prophesied would happen:

"For to us a child is born; to us a Son is given. . . . And His name will be called Wonderful, Counselor, Mighty God, Eternal Father, Prince of Peace" (Isaiah 9:6).

This is "the Son" of whom Jesus spoke in Matthew 28:19, the One who was called *both* "Son" and "Eternal Father" by the prophet Isaiah in approximately 700 B.C.

It is important to remember that the Bible nowhere

teaches a doctrine of "an eternal Son." Those who advocate a trinity of three persons in the Godhead have sometimes spoken and written about a Son who is "eternally begotten" by the Father. In fact, this is a self-contradictory doctrine, and it evolved in the Roman Catholic Church centuries after the New Testament was completed. The Son obviously cannot be *both* eternal *and* begotten. The two concepts are a contradiction in terms! And as far as both the Old Testament and the New Testament are concerned, the Sonship of God occurred at a particular time in human history. As far as the Bible is concerned, the Son was begotten on a certain *day* (Hebrews 1:5; Psalm 2:7), when He came into the world as a firstborn (Hebrews 1:6).

The Gospel of Luke explains in vivid detail that it would happen when the "Holy Spirit" would come upon the virgin Mary and the power of "the Highest" would overshadow her. Because of this, the angel said, "That Holy One who is to be born will be called the Son of God" (Luke 1:35, NKJV). Earlier, the angel had told Mary that she was to call the Son's name "Jesus" and that He would also be called "the Son of the Highest" (Luke 1:31-32).

The Gospel of John states that the "only begotten" of the Father became flesh and dwelt among us, full of grace and truth (John 1:14). This "only begotten Son" is the One who "declares" or reveals to us the Father (John 1:18).

In addition to the title of "Son of God," the New Testament often calls Jesus Christ the "Son of Man." Because Jesus was supernaturally conceived in the virgin Mary from the Holy Spirit of God, He was born with a uniquely dual nature. Whereas the title "Son of God" points to Jesus' divine nature, His title "Son of Man" points to His human nature. Both titles, of course, are appropriate since Jesus was both fully God (because of His Spirit or Mind) and fully man (because of His flesh).

As the Son, Jesus Christ was "the *image* of the invisible God" (Colossians 1:15). In these last days, God has spoken to us "in a Son" [literal Greek], who is "the brightness of His glory" and "the express *image* of His person," and who upholds all things by "the word of His power" (Hebrews 1:1-3).

Although some English translations do have the word "person" in Hebrews 1:3, the Greek term *hupostasis* literally means "nature" or "being," not "person." Therefore, according to Hebrews 1:3, the Son is *the express image* of the nature or being of God.

The Son of God was "made" from a woman and "made" under the law (Galatians 4:4). In addition, He was "made" from the seed of David (Romans 1:3). The King James Version's rendering of "made" in these two passages is a proper translation of the Greek verb, *ginomai*. According to the Greek lexicons, *ginomai* means "made, be created, be born, become, or come into being." By using this Greek word in these verses, Paul confirmed the Biblical revelation of other passages—that the Sonship of God in Jesus had a beginning approximately two thousand years ago.

God loved the world *so much* that He "gave" His only begotten Son, that whoever believes in *Him* should not perish but have everlasting life (John 3:16). Elsewhere, the Bible explains that when God "gave" His only begotten Son, "our great God and Savior Jesus Christ" actually "*gave Himself*" (Titus 2:13-14)! He did this so that He might redeem us and purify "*for Himself*" His own special people (verse 14). The apostle Paul further explained that when the Lord God "sent" the Son into the world, God was actually *"sending a Son of Himself"* (Romans 8:3). By using the reflexive pronoun "of Himself" in this verse, Paul expressed exactly the same thing that he declared in Titus 2:13-14. God sent Himself into the world in the form of a Son of flesh and deity so that *He* could condemn sin "in the flesh" (Romans 8:3).

The Holy Spirit

We learned in chapter 5 that the Holy Spirit is only one of many descriptive titles for God in the Bible. The Scriptures reveal that God the Father Himself is the Holy Spirit, just as they reveal our risen Lord, Jesus, to be the Holy Spirit. According to the Biblical record, they are all the one Spirit-Being known as God. There is *one* Spirit of Almighty God (Ephesians 4:4), and this Spirit is an eternal Spirit (Hebrews 9:14). As early as Genesis, Yahweh referred to this Spirit as *His* Spirit (Genesis 6:3). Much later, this same Spirit is called "the Spirit of your Father" (Matthew 10:20). A parallel passage calls Him simply "the Holy Spirit" (Mark 13:11).

Romans 8:9-10 uses the phrase "Spirit of God" interchangeably with the phrase "the Spirit of *Christ*." In a touching scene, Christ promised His disciples that they would not be alone after His departure (John 14). First, Jesus said that they would receive a "Comforter" that would abide with them forever (verse 16). Then, He called this Comforter "the Spirit of truth" (verse 17). And finally, Jesus specifically identified this Comforter or Spirit of truth as none other than Himself:

"But you know *Him, for He dwells* with *you and*

will be in *you. I will not leave you [as] orphans; I will come to you" (John 14:17-18, NKJV).*

"The Spirit of truth" was already dwelling "with" the disciples in the physical form of the Nazarene. After His death on the cross and His resurrection from the dead, He Himself would not simply be with them; He would actually be "in" them (verse 17) in the form of the Holy Spirit of God. In I Corinthians 15:45 Paul identified Christ, "the last Adam," as the "life-giving Spirit" who saves us.

In II Peter 1:21 the apostle Peter wrote of "the Holy Spirit" that moved the prophets of old. In I Peter 1:10-11 the same writer called this Spirit behind the prophets "the Spirit of *Christ.*"

In the Book of Revelation, He who is repeatedly speaking calls Himself "the Spirit." In Revelation 2:7 "the Spirit" has a message for the churches. The next verse identifies Him as Jesus Christ, "the First and the Last, He who died and came to life" (Revelation 2:8). (The Son of Man died, not the eternal Spirit *in* Him.) According to Revelation 2:17, 25, 29, "the Spirit" is the One who exhorts us to hold fast *until He comes,* and in this context the Spirit specifically reveals Himself to be "the Son of God" (Revelation 2:18).

Throughout the Book of Revelation we find consistently that Jesus Himself is the Holy Spirit of God. In the last chapter of the book the Lord God again identified Himself as "Jesus . . . the Root and the Offspring of David, the Bright and Morning Star" (Revelation 22:16). Then the next verse refers to Him once again as the Spirit, when it gives the great invitation before the book closes:

"And the Spirit [Jesus] and the bride [the church] say, 'Come!' And let him who hears say, 'Come!' And let him who thirsts come. And whoever desires, let him take the water of life freely" (Revelation 22:17, NKJV).

The Book of Philippians refers to the Holy Spirit simply as "the Spirit" in Philippians 2:1 but as "the Spirit of Jesus Christ" in Philippians 1:19.

An angel from the Lord told the virgin Mary that the Holy Spirit would supernaturally come upon her and overshadow her so that she would conceive in her womb, bring forth a Son, and call His name *Jesus* (Luke 1:31, 35). After that happened, an angel of the Lord assured her husband, Joseph, that the baby who had been conceived in Mary was the result of supernatural activity of the Holy Spirit of God (Matthew 1:20).

These passages of Scripture confirm to us that the Holy Spirit was the Father of Mary's Son, Jesus of Nazareth. On many occasions, Jesus referred to God as His Father, and this is why the Jews tried to kill Him— because He said that God was His Father, "making Himself equal with God" (John 5:17-18). But regardless of what some people then thought, and what some now think, the only Father that Jesus had was the Holy Spirit of God—in other words, God Himself, who is a Spirit (John 4:24). Concerning this, it is important for us to remember that there is only "one God the Father" (Ephesians 4:6) because there is only "one Spirit" (Ephesians 4:4), who is also our "one Lord" (Ephesians 4:5)—Jesus. (See Ephesians 1:2-3, 15, 17; 3:11, 14; 5:20; 6:23-24.)

Christ is definitely the One of whom Paul wrote in II Corinthians 3. (Note verse 14.) So there should be no misunderstanding of Paul's reference to the Lord Jesus in verse 17: "The *Lord* is the Spirit." This is the Spirit of whom Jesus spoke in Matthew 28:19, the same Spirit that was dwelling in the Nazarene Himself.

The preceding review of the Father, the Son, and the Holy Spirit should leave no doubt that these three titles represent three manifestations, modes, and roles of one indivisible God. And it is enlightening that Scripture describes God's manifestations and roles by using many other titles as well: the Lord, I AM, Almighty God, Creator, Shepherd, King, Judge, the Word, the Alpha and the Omega, Savior, Servant, Lamb, etc.

This study has established that Holy Writ majestically identifies the three titles "Father," "Son," and "Holy Spirit" with our Savior and Lord, Jesus Christ. And it is interesting that Matthew 28:19 is the only verse in the entire Bible where these three titles appear together. Furthermore, what is particularly interesting is that the immediate context of Jesus' own words shows that the risen Christ was obviously exalting *Himself* by revealing Himself to *be* the Father, the Son, and the Holy Spirit. (See Matthew 28:16-20.) And this great truth is also supported by passages in the other Gospels that are parallel to Matthew 28.

When the risen, glorified Christ commanded His disciples to baptize in the *name* of the Father, and the Son, and the Holy Spirit, was He, in fact, commanding them to baptize in *His* own name—Jesus? He most certainly was, if we are to accept and believe the immediate context of Matthew 28:19 as well as the many other passages of Scripture that we have noted. As a matter of fact, Matthew 28:18-20 proclaims the complete deity of Jesus and the oneness of God in very clear and majestic language! The following section of this study discusses many additional passages of Scripture directly related to Matthew 28 that teach the same, great, marvelous truth—leaving us with a testimony of absolute clarity.

The Weight of the Evidence

Let us now examine the meaning of Matthew 28:19 itself. The Gospel of Matthew closes with these words by the risen Christ shortly before His ascension to heaven:

"Then Jesus came and spoke to them, saying, 'All authority has been given to Me in heaven and on earth. Go therefore and make disciples of all the nations, baptizing them in the name of the Father and of the Son and of the Holy Spirit, teaching them to observe all things that I have commanded you; and lo, I am with you always, even to the end of the age'" (Matthew 28:18-20, NKJV).

What is the real meaning of these words of Jesus? This should be our utmost concern. Like the salutations, this passage of Scripture has been blatantly misinterpreted for a long time because of trinitarian presuppositions. As a result, Christian believers have been told for many generations that Matthew 28:19 is a trinitarian baptismal formula. According to this interpretation, the verse is said to teach that God is a trinity of three distinct persons known as the Father, the Son, and the Holy Spirit.

Because Matthew 28:19 has been promoted as a trinitarian baptismal formula, many Christians have been misled, confused, and troubled. All of us should be concerned at this interpretation for at least two reasons: (1) the traditional, trinitarian interpretation of the verse completely contradicts many other related passages of Scripture, and (2) such an interpretation does not fit the context of the passage itself.

We can be grateful that the Biblical evidence is conclusive as to what the passage really teaches. The Lord God, in His wisdom and majesty, has left us a consistent, Biblical testimony regarding His being and nature, despite influential traditional interpretations.

It is enlightening that parallel passages in the other Gospels and the Book of Acts explain how the *apostles* and the *other* Christians of the New Testament age understood Jesus' words in Matthew 28:19 itself. We will soon look at these related passages in detail.

It is also interesting that there have always been Christians in church history—from the Book of Acts to the present day—who have understood that Matthew 28:19 is not a trinitarian formula. When we read verse 19 in the context of verses 16 to 20, we see that the emphasis is definitely upon the risen, glorified Christ, not a trinity of three persons. Verses 16 and 17 inform us that when Jesus appeared to His eleven disciples, "they worshiped Him."

Furthermore, when Jesus gave the great commission, He declared that He had "all authority." In His own words, this meant all authority "in heaven" and all authority "on earth" (verse 18). This is a significant declaration in that Jesus made it right before He told His disciples to baptize in the name that represents three divine titles. For if Jesus Himself has all authority, then the Father and the Holy

Spirit do not have any authority unless they and Jesus are all one and the same.

It is also noteworthy that Jesus used the important word "therefore" in verse 19, which is the English conjunction for the Greek word *oun*. The New Testament uses this Greek term many times to show that a logical conclusion follows. In other words, Jesus Christ said, "*Because* I have all authority in heaven and on earth, you are to baptize My new disciples in My name, 'Jesus'—the name of the Father, the Son, and the Holy Spirit." It is not logical to interpret Jesus' words any other way. It is not logical to understand these words as meaning that Jesus' disciples are to baptize in other persons' names after He had just informed them that He Himself is the One who has all authority both in heaven and on earth.

Several things about this passage are striking, and they all point in the same direction. Matthew 28:19 specifically mentions "name" in the *singular*—one name, not three names. It is also significant that "the Father, the Son, and the Holy Spirit" are three *titles* of God, not three names.

Every Christian believer knows that the name of "the Son" is "Jesus" (Matthew 1:21). There is no disagreement on this point. And the immediate context of Matthew 1:21 refers to *Emmanuel*, "God with us" (Matthew 1:22-23; Isaiah 7:14). *Emmanuel*, "God with us," was associated with the name "Jesus" even before His supernatural birth because God wanted to make it absolutely clear that the name "Jesus" was to be the name of *God*. This One coming into the world was to be known as *Emmanuel* because He was "God with us." And God, who came as a Son, was to have a particular name, *Jesus* ("Yahweh-

Savior"), which pointed to Yahweh coming into the world *as* a Savior.

If all agree that the name of the Son is "Jesus" because He *is* Yahweh our Savior, then it should not be difficult to understand why "Jesus" is also the name of the Father and the Holy Spirit, other titles of the same God who was known as Yahweh in the Old Testament. This is *why* the word "name" is in the singular in Matthew 28:19; it is one name that refers to three titles of one God. If we know the name of the *Son* in this verse (or in any other verse in the Bible), then we *know* the name of the Father and the Holy Spirit as well. This is the simple, wonderful truth of the matter.

What is at stake in Matthew 28:19 is not simply the wording of an oral baptismal formula. What is at stake is *who* we believe Jesus really was and *what* we believe God really did in the Nazarene. God makes it abundantly clear in His Word who Jesus was—and is. The Lord Jesus, as God, will deny us if we deny Him, but He will *not* deny Himself. In this regard, the apostle Paul declared about Jesus Christ: "This is a faithful saying: For if we died with Him, we shall also live with Him. If we endure, we shall also reign with Him. If we deny Him, He also will deny us. If we are faithless, He remains faithful; He cannot deny Himself" (II Timothy 2:11-13, NKJV).

The name "Jesus" is the name of God, for Christ Himself revealed that it is the name of the Father *and* the Son (John 17:11) (See the Greek, NIV, RSV, etc.). Matthew 28:19 is only one of many exalted Biblical passages that glorify Jesus for who He is and what He has accomplished in different divine roles. May we not be guilty of perverting Matthew 28:19 or any other verse that exalts Jesus in order to support an influential, man-made, tritheistic doctrine that evolved many years later in the Church of Rome. And may we not be guilty of misinterpreting Matthew 28:19 in order to cling to a doctrine that is non-Biblical, self-contradictory, confusing, and that does not properly honor Jesus with the complete deity that He possesses.

Immediately *following* our Lord's reference to the three divine titles, He then told His disciples to teach others:

"Observe all that I commanded you; and lo, I Myself *[literal Greek, not "We"] am with you always, even to the end of the age" (Matthew 28:20).*

Are we capable of comprehending the grandeur of this proclamation? In the same context in which Jesus commanded His followers to baptize in "the name" of the Father, Son, and Holy Spirit, He admonished them (and us) to keep *His* commandments. And then He comforted them (and us) by promising that He *Himself* [literal Greek] will be with them (and us) even until the end of the age!

Verse 20 is another verse in this majestic passage that gives Jesus Christ the full authority and glory He deserves. In this declaration that He Himself will be with us, Christ did not leave out "the Father" and "the Holy Spirit," for these titles, together with "the Son," are all identified with our Lord Jesus, since He is the eternal Spirit known as God. Hundreds of verses in this study have already established this truth, and we noted earlier that, indeed, "God *was* in Christ, reconciling the world to Himself" (II Corinthians 5:19).

Have we yet captured the tremendous magnitude of

this statement by the apostle Paul? Have we allowed our-selves to reflect soberly and thankfully upon these words, and many similar words in the Bible, to the extent of understanding and accepting what the incarnation of God in Jesus really signifies? In short, Jesus categorically identified Himself to *be* the Father, the Son, and the Holy Spirit in Matthew 28:19; and His statements in the verses before and after verse 19 consistently support this won-derful revelation.

In the parallel passages in the three other Gospels, we find further corroboration that this is the correct expla-nation of the great commission in Matthew. When the risen Christ sent out His disciples in Mark 16:14-18, as in Matthew He mentioned baptism. In this second Gospel, the Son of God promised that after His followers would believe and be baptized, they would be saved (Mark 16:16). Then Jesus declared, *"In My name,"* signs will follow those who believe (verse 17).

The Gospel of Luke also specifically refers to the name of Jesus. Christ sent out His disciples on the great commission with the command:

"That repentance and remission of sins should be preached in His name *to all nations, beginning at Jerusalem" (Luke 24:47, NKJV).*

Two verses later, Jesus said:

"Behold, I Myself *[literal Greek] am sending the promise of My Father upon you; but remain in Jerusalem until you are clothed with power from on high" (Luke 24:49).*

As in other passages of Scripture, Jesus here again revealed Himself to be the Father; and as the heavenly Father, our risen Savior *Himself* would empower His disciples with His Spirit later in Jerusalem. After Jesus spoke in the role of a Son, referring to the coming Holy Spirit as the promise of His Father, the risen, glorified Christ immediately revealed that He Himself would be the One who would send this promise upon His disciples. Therefore, it is not surprising that Jesus only two verses earlier declared that repentance and forgiveness of sins should be preached to all nations "in *His* name" (verse 47). And His name is, of course, "Jesus," the same name that He referred to in Mark 16:17 and Matthew 28:19.

Like the three other Gospels, John also closes with an emphasis on believing in the name of Jesus. The risen Messiah revealed Himself to His apostles, with even the doubting Thomas finally confessing, "My Lord and My God!" (John 20:28). Then, after John related that the risen Savior did many other signs in the presence of His disciples that he did not write about, he added:

"But these are written that you may believe that Jesus is the Christ, the Son of God, and that believing you may have life in His name" *(John 20:31, NKJV).*

Although some may be confused and misled because of a long-standing, distorted, and pervasive misinterpretation of Matthew 28:19, our Lord has not left us without witness. Matthew, Mark, Luke, and John *all* agree that the risen Christ emphasized salvation in His own name and in His own authority! In this regard, it would be wise for us never to forget that Jesus once declared, "*All* things that

the Father has are Mine" (John 16:15). This majestic declaration identifies Jesus with the Father in the clearest
language possible. If Jesus possesses all things that the
Father has, then this includes the Father's name, and that
is exactly what Jesus claimed in John 17:11 when He
revealed that the Father had given Him His own name.
The name of the Son is the name of the Father, just as it
is the name of the Holy Spirit—simply because "Jesus" is
the name of one God.

In His profound wisdom and divine foresight, God has
also left us the consistent testimony of the apostolic
church. In the Book of Acts the apostles and the other disciples *always* baptized in the name of our Lord Jesus. On
the day when the church was born with the coming of the
Holy Spirit, by inspiration Peter commanded:

"Repent, and let every one of you be baptized in the
name of Jesus Christ *for the remission of sins; and you
shall receive the gift of the Holy Spirit" (Acts 2:38,
NKJV).*

The Book of Acts repeatedly associates the name of
Jesus with water baptism. In Samaria, believers were likewise baptized "in the name of the Lord Jesus" (Acts 8:16).
In the city of Caesarea the Roman centurion Cornelius,
the first Gentile to be converted, called together his relatives and close friends so that they could hear Peter
preach the gospel (Acts 10:24). When the Holy Spirit fell
upon these Gentile hearers, the apostle Peter commanded
them to be baptized in the name of our Lord Jesus Christ
(Acts 10:48).

While most English versions have "in the name of Jesus

Christ" in this verse because of strong manuscript evidence, both the KJV and NKJV have simply "in the name of the Lord" because of other manuscript evidence. However, even the latter reading itself, "the Lord," also refers to Jesus, which the context confirms. Only a few verses before verse 48, Peter identified the Lord to *be* Jesus when he informed Cornelius and his household that "Jesus Christ" is "Lord of all" (Acts 10:36). And in the same context, Peter certainly spoke of Jesus when He proclaimed that "through *His* name" our sins are forgiven (Acts 10:43). In fact, Peter's entire sermon in Acts 10 was about our Lord Jesus Christ and what God did in Him to bring us salvation from our sins.

In the city of Ephesus, Paul learned that some disciples had not yet received the Holy Spirit because they had only been baptized "into the baptism of John" (Acts 19:1-3). On learning this, Paul immediately taught them that they should believe on Christ Jesus (verse 4):

"When they heard this, they were baptized in the name of the Lord Jesus" (Acts 19:5, NKJV).

As a matter of fact, there is no record in the Book of Acts of Christians being baptized in *any* divine name other than the name of the Lord Jesus Christ! The name of Jesus represents the *being* of our Lord Jesus. Therefore, whenever converts were baptized in His name, they were actually baptized in the authority of His divine being—"the true God." (See I John 5:20.)

When the apostle Paul wrote to Christians in Corinth, he asked these thought-provoking questions:

"Is Christ divided? Paul was not crucified for you,

was he? Or were you baptized in the name of Paul?"
(I Corinthians 1:13, literal Greek).

Of course, Paul had *not* been crucified for them, and they had *not* been baptized in the *name* of Paul. The inspired author used the Greek negative particle *me* in his second question because this particle was always used if a writer expected a negative response to a rhetorical question: "You were not baptized in the name of Paul, were you?" What the apostle emphasized was that we should not be baptized in the name of anyone other than the One who *was* crucified on our behalf.

Water baptism is the very picture of the death, burial, and resurrection of Jesus (Romans 6:3-6). And the Word of God explains to us that when we are "baptized into Christ Jesus," we are "baptized into His death" (Romans 6:3). Our baptism in the *name* of Jesus shows our Lord— and others—that our faith is in *Him*. Our immersion in water is an expression of our faith that Jesus was crucified, was buried, and rose again as the living Savior (Colossians 2:12). Our immersion in water and coming up out of the water is an expression of our faith that we *have* a new life now and eternal life later because our Savior, the Lord Jesus, rose from the grave Himself (Romans 6:3-5).

Some have mistakenly suggested that the baptismal passages in Acts do not refer to an actual baptismal formula because of the use of different Greek prepositions. For example, Matthew 28:19 uses the preposition *eis*, while Acts 2:38 uses the preposition *epi*. This argument wrongly claims that the Matthew 28:19 means "into the name of," but the references in Acts mean only "in the authority of"—in other words, something supposedly altogether different. This argument is the unfortunate result of refusing to identify the three titles in Matthew 28:19 with the name "Jesus" in the Book of Acts.

Greek scholarship has demonstrated that this approach is completely invalid. Let us consider these facts: (1) The eminent Greek scholar A. T. Robertson confirmed long ago that the Greek New Testament uses the prepositions *epi*, *eis*, and *en* interchangeably before the noun *name*.[3] (2) Therefore, while Peter did mean "in the authority of" in Acts 2:38, Jesus meant the same thing in Matthew 28:19.[4] (3) In fact, both Acts 8:16 and Acts 19:5 use *eis*, the same preposition in Matthew 28:19!

So these verses all make the same point. The believers who were baptized "in the name of Jesus" in the Book of Acts were baptized in His authority, just as in Matthew 28:19 the disciples who were commanded to baptize all converts in the name of the Father, the Son, and the Holy Spirit were instructed to baptize in the *authority* of the name that those titles represent. In other words, the apostles and all the disciples in Acts naturally followed Jesus' commandment of Matthew 28:19 when they consistently baptized others in His name and in His authority.

It is just not logical to conclude that *all* the apostles and disciples in the Book of Acts were disobeying Jesus' commandment in Matthew 28:19 by refusing to baptize according to a trinitarian formula. It *is* logical to conclude that the name in Matthew 28:19 refers to the same name, "Jesus," in which all believers were baptized in the New Testament. And as we noted earlier, four areas of proof verify this: (1) the wording of Matthew 28:19 itself, (2) the context of the verse, (3) the post-resurrection parallel passages in the three other Gospels, and (4) the baptismal texts in the Book of Acts.

All of these passages of Scriptures consistently agree that "Jesus" is the name that Christ referred to in the great commission of Matthew 28. However, in spite of this powerful Biblical testimony, some Christians may still find it difficult to see Matthew 28:19 as anything other than a trinitarian statement simply because Christendom has been conditioned to this interpretation for so long. As a former trinitarian, I have empathy for many believers' plight; it is just difficult for some to think of Jesus as their heavenly Father because they have always thought of Him only as the Son. The problem with this is that as long as one refuses to accept the Biblical evidence that identifies Jesus with the Father, it will always be impossible for him or her to reconcile Matthew 28:19 with the parallel passages in the other Gospels and the baptismal accounts in Acts.

In addition to the many Biblical verses we have already discussed that reveal Jesus to be our God and our Father, such as John 14:7-9, because of His marvelous grace, our Lord has given us yet another passage of Scripture that substantiates this great truth. Like Matthew 28:19, it is a post-resurrection text, occurring in the last chapter of the Gospel of John. The risen, glorified Christ suddenly appeared on the shore of the Sea of Galilee, near where the apostles were fishing. When Jesus appeared, He called His disciples one word which revealed that He was more than the Son of Man. That one word is found in John 21:5 and is the Greek term *paidia*, which literally means "little children" and is normally translated as "children." By calling His disciples by the affectionate term "little children," the risen Jesus demonstrated in unmistakable language that He Himself was their spiritual Father, shortly before He returned to heaven as their Lord and Savior!

The Lord Jesus Christ still wants us to be His "little children," just as His disciples were in the New Testament. He still wants us to consider Him as our Father and to be baptized in the *name* of the Father—His name, "Jesus," as He commanded in Matthew 28:19.

Because of the weight of the Biblical evidence, scholarship is rightfully speaking out. The editors of the highly respected *New American Standard Bible* undoubtedly realized that Matthew 28:19 refers to the name "Jesus," for as the cross references to this verse, they give Acts 2:38; 8:16; Romans 6:3; and I Corinthians 1:13, 15, all of which deal with water baptism in the name of Jesus Christ. Similarly, the distinguished minister and Christian author John Stott has stated: "The minister baptizes the professing believer . . . in water, into the one name (Matthew 28:19), or more precisely, into the name of the Lord Jesus (Acts 8:16; 19:5).[5]

Jesus: Yahweh-Savior

The name *Jesus* is powerful but not because the name itself is some kind of oral, magical formula for us to pronounce. On the contrary this name has power for those who *believe* in the One who owns it. In the New Testament, it is in this name that demons are cast out of human beings. In this name the sick are healed. In this name sins are forgiven. And in this name eternal life is offered. All of these things occur because of living faith in the Lord Jesus Christ, whom this name represents.

Shortly before Peter baptized the first Gentile converts "in the name of Jesus Christ" (Acts 10:48), this apostle testified of Jesus:

> *"To Him* all the prophets bear witness *that everyone who believes in Him receives forgiveness of sins* through His name" *(Acts 10:43).*

The prophets in the Old Testament did promise that the time would come when Yahweh would have one name and that this name would be made known (Zechariah 14:9; Isaiah 52:6). Yahweh predicted through His prophet Zechariah:

> *"And the* LORD *[Yahweh] shall be king over all the earth. In that day it shall be—'The* LORD *is one,'* and His name one" *(Zechariah 14:9, NKJV).*

Zechariah 14 is a prophecy of the LORD'S descent on the Mount of Olives, and the context of Zechariah 14:9 is the *second* coming of our Lord, when Jesus descends to the Mount of Olives (verse 4), the very mountain *from* which He had ascended into heaven following His resurrection (Acts 1:9-12). Zechariah 14:9 is obviously about the one name "Jesus," which Yahweh would have as a divine Messiah who is king over all the earth.

A similar prophecy is found in the Book of Isaiah, where the Lord God predicted:

> *"Therefore* My people shall know My name; *therefore they shall know in that day that I am He who speaks:* 'Behold, it is I'" *(Isaiah 52:6, NKJV).*

Yahweh is speaking here (verses 3 and 4), and this prophecy is concerned with the Christian age. Paul quoted the very next verse (Isaiah 52:7) in Romans 10:15 as a fulfillment of Messianic prophecy. Here is the verse as it is in Isaiah: "How beautiful upon the mountains are the feet of him who brings good news [the Gospel], who proclaims peace, who brings glad tidings of good things, who proclaims salvation, who says to Zion, 'Your God reigns!'" (Isaiah 52:7, NKJV). (Compare with Romans 10:15.)

Only a few verses later is Isaiah 53, a chapter of prophecies that Jesus definitely fulfilled in detail as the Messiah. Therefore, we can be certain that Isaiah 52:6 is a prophecy about "Jesus" as the Lord's name that His people "shall know."

Christ Himself once promised: "Where two or three are gathered together in My name, I am there in the midst of them" (Matthew 18:20). Whether we are baptized in that name or are gathered together for worship in that name—whatever we do in the magnificent name of Jesus—we are expressing our faith *in* Him and our dependence *upon* Him. An article in the Churches of Christ's religious periodical, *The Firm Foundation*, has properly stated: "To be baptized in the name of Jesus, as Peter commanded (Acts 2:38) . . . signifies reliance upon Jesus. . . . So the person being baptized in Jesus' name realized that Jesus is the one with the power to save him."[6]

In fact, Jesus Christ is the *only* One who has the power to save us because He *is* "far above all principality and power and might and dominion, and every name that is named, not only in this age but also in that which is to come" (Ephesians 1:21).

The New Testament repeatedly exalts the name of

Jesus, and among the many texts in Acts which demonstrate that water baptism was always in the name of the Lord Jesus Christ, one verse deserves detailed attention because of its special revelation: Acts 22:16. Here, Paul recounted his Christian conversion before his Jewish countrymen in Jerusalem, and this verse gives the instructions that Ananias had for the repentant Saul of Tarsus:

"And now why do you wait? Rise and be baptized and wash away your sins, calling on His name" (Acts 22:16).

Both the KJV and NKJV have "the name of the Lord" in this verse, while most English versions have "His name," which is what the Greek literally says. Actually, the context confirms that it is the name of the Lord Jesus. Whether He is called "the God of our Fathers" (verse 14), or "the Just One" (verse 14), or "the Lord" (verses 8, 10), or simply "Jesus" (verse 8), the context shows that "His name" in verse 16 is the name of our Lord Jesus Christ.

In Acts 9, where Saul's supernatural encounter with the Lord is first related, Ananias explained in verse 17 who was really involved. Here, he stated that "the Lord *Jesus*" not only appeared to Saul but was also the One who had sent Ananias to guide Saul in his conversion. So the Lord Jesus of Acts 9:17 is the same Lord that Ananias referred to in Acts 22:16 when he told Saul to rise and be baptized, "calling on His name." In addition, it is interesting that preceding Acts 9:17 are three consecutive verses that refer three times to the importance of the name of the Lord Jesus (verses 14-16)!

What makes Acts 22:16 so revealing is that it mentions "calling on" the name of the Lord Jesus at baptism. In chapter 6 of this investigation, we learned that the New Testament Christians were "calling on" or "invoking" the Lord Jesus in their prayers. In this regard, Acts 9:14 refers to "all who call on" the name of Jesus. This verse appears to discuss prayer in general, since the Greek has "call on" as a present tense participle, indicating continuous or repeated activity. In contrast, Acts 22:16 specifically has Ananias commanding Saul *himself* (literal Greek) to "call upon" or "invoke" the name of the Lord Jesus at his baptism. This is an indication that when the New Testament Christians were baptized, they orally "called upon" or "invoked" the name of Jesus in a prayer of praise and thanksgiving.

Besides this example of Paul's conversion in Acts 22:16, the Book of James confirms that the name of Jesus was called upon at water baptism. In talking about the wealthy who persecute Christians (James 2:6), the writer asked:

"Do they not blaspheme that noble name by which you are called?" (James 2:7, NKJV).

It has been customary for the English versions to translate this verse similar to the wording of the NKJV. However, the literal Greek is more precise:

"Do they not blaspheme that beautiful name which was invoked [or "called upon"] over you?"

David Bernard was absolutely correct when he stated

that the Greek phrasing in the verse indicates that "the name was invoked over the Christians at a specific time."[7] A unique characteristic of Hellenistic (Biblical) Greek is that its verbal tenses have an exactness that are unequaled in any other language. In James 2:7 the writer used an aorist passive participle in the neuter gender, confirming that the participle refers to the neuter noun "name." As we noted earlier in this study, the aorist tense in Greek shows "point action," normally at some time in the past.

The adjective before "name" in James 2:7 is the Greek word *kalon*, which basically means "beautiful." That "beautiful name" is, without a doubt, the name of our Lord Jesus Christ because He is mentioned *by* name only a few verses earlier as the One in whom we hold our faith (James 2:1).

Because James used the *aorist* tense for "invoked," or "called upon," it is obvious that he referred to water baptism as that special, one-time experience when the Lord Jesus was called upon by name. And it is significant that just as James 2:7 uses the "point action," aorist tense for "invoked," Acts 22:16 uses the *same* Greek word and the *same* Greek aorist tense when Ananias encouraged Paul to be baptized, "invoking" or "calling on" the name of the Lord Jesus! The latter verse uses the middle voice, emphasizing that Paul himself was to call upon the name of his Lord.

In summary, Acts 22:6 informs us that Ananias told Paul to *personally* "invoke" or "call on" the name of Jesus at his baptism, while James 2:7 informs us that the "beautiful name" of Jesus was *customarily* "invoked" at water baptism. And the wording of James 2:7—"invoked *over* you"—indicates that the name of Jesus may have been invoked also by others present, and not just by the convert himself who was being baptized. Water baptism is not only a special, personal experience between the new Christian and the Lord Jesus; it can also be a public experience that is joyfully shared by the community of believers.

Throughout the Book of Acts the name of Jesus is constantly uplifted and glorified. Besides the verses concerning water baptism, there are many other passages that exalt His name: Acts 3:16; 4:12, 18; 5:40-41; 9:29; 15:14, 17, 26; 16:18; 19:17; 21:13; 26:9.

Jesus' name is likewise honored throughout the New Testament. In John 17, Jesus, the Son of Man, glorified His name as He prayed to God the Father. As we have already explained, Jesus of Nazareth could sincerely pray to God because He was fully human. Since Jesus had a *dual* nature, He was both fully man and fully God. And it was through His humanity that He ate food when He was hungry, slept when He was tired, and prayed when He had the spiritual need. If Jesus Christ did not need to pray as a man, then He would not have been fully human.

On the other hand, the Son of Man also had the divine nature, since He was also the Son of God and not only the Son of Man. The divine nature, the eternal Spirit that was in Jesus, was also beyond Him as an omnipresent Spirit. We must remember that although God was *in* Jesus the Son (II Corinthians 5:19), God was also in heaven as the Father. Because it is not possible for the human mind to comprehend the different roles of God in the incarnation of God in Jesus, the apostle Paul called it "the mystery of godliness" (I Timothy 3:16). As we noted earlier, the Bible says nothing about the Godhead being a mystery; we know from the Scriptures that God is one eternal Spirit who created and rules the universe. However, according to I Timothy 3:16, the mystery of godliness is what God did in Jesus: "And without controversy great is the mystery of godliness: God was manifested in the flesh, justified in the Spirit, seen by angels, preached among the Gentiles, believed on in the world, received up in glory" (I Timothy 3:16, NKJV).

Therefore, let us appreciate this mystery of godliness when we read about the two roles of one God, Father and Son, in passages of Scripture like John 17. In this chapter, two verses of Jesus' prayer are particularly worthy of note at this point in our study since they refer to the Father's name. The two verses are John 17:11-12, and they have been translated differently in a significant way by the English versions. According to the New King James Version, Jesus prayed:

"Now I am no longer in the world, but these are in the world, and I come to You. Holy Father, keep through Your name those whom You have given Me, that they may be one as We are. While I was with them in the world, I kept them in Your name. Those whom You gave Me, I have kept; and none of them is lost except the son of perdition, that the Scripture might be fulfilled" (John 17:11-12, NKJV).

The King James Version's translation of the above passage is very close to the New King James Version; however, almost all other English versions have a very different translation of the two verses at an important point, generally agreeing with the New International Version, which has:

"I will remain in the world no longer, but they are still in the world, and I am coming to you. Holy Father, protect them by the power of your name—the name you gave me—so that they may be one as we are one. While I was with them, I protected them and kept them safe by that name you gave me. None has been lost except the one doomed to destruction so that Scripture would be fulfilled" (John 17:11-12, NIV).

According to the KJV and the NKJV, it is the *apostles* that the Father had given to Jesus. According to almost all other English translations, it is *the Father's name* that the Father had given to Jesus. Which is correct?

The accepted, modern Greek editions of the New Testament agree with the NIV and most versions that Jesus referred to the Father's name, which the Father gave to Him. This is because of the strong testimony of the most ancient manuscripts that have survived. These ancient sources consistently have a singular, neuter, relative pronoun, which would refer to the neuter noun "name." Another reason why most scholars and translations accept these ancient manuscripts here may be because the relative pronoun is found *immediately after* the phrase "Your name" in both verses. This indicates that the relative pronoun would most likely refer to "name" in verses 11 and 12.

On the other hand, in verse 12 the Greek Byzantine manuscripts and some other ancient sources do have a plural relative pronoun, which would refer to the apostles that the Father gave to Jesus and not to the phrase "Your name." This is probably why the KJV and the NKJV translate John 17:12 accordingly. On several occasions in this study, we have pointed out that the Byzantine family of manuscripts is generally a consistent and reliable source and that both the KJV and NKJV almost always follow these manuscripts (with a notable exception being I John 5:7-8, where a trinitarian tradition led to the addition of a so-called trinitarian statement supported by *no* ancient Greek sources).

What is interesting is that the KJV and NKJV did not follow the Byzantine manuscripts in John 17:11. Unlike verse 12, verse 11 does *not* have the support of *either* the Byzantine manuscripts *or* the most ancient manuscripts. In fact, the translations of John 17:11 by the KJV and NKJV have the support of only a few late manuscripts.

Before we look at the Greek evidence of verse 11 in detail, it is appropriate to mention comments in footnotes on verses 11 and 12 in some editions of the New King James Version. For example, it is enlightening that the editors of the Open Bible of the New King James Version acknowledged in footnotes to John 17:11-12 that the *singular* relative pronoun, which would refer to "name," is accepted by the modern Nestle-Aland Greek New Testament (N) and by the United Bible Societies' Greek New Testament (U). Perhaps, the editors of the NKJV noted these two verses not only because the strong, ancient evidence gives a singular relative pronoun, but also because the Greek syntax indicates a relative pronoun that would refer to the noun "name."

Returning now to the manuscript evidence of John

17:11, it is particularly interesting that even the Byzantine manuscripts do not support the translations of the KJV and NKJV for this verse. The editors of the NKJV Open Bible acknowledge in a footnote to verse 11 that the Majority Text (M), which includes the Byzantine manuscripts, has a singular, neuter relative pronoun that refers to the neuter noun "name." Therefore, it is perplexing that the KJV and NKJV did not follow the Byzantine sources when they translated John 17:11 the way they did.

In summary, the translation of the NIV and most other English versions for verse 12 is supported by (1) strong manuscript evidence and (2) the internal evidence of the syntax (grammar), for having, "Your name which You have given Me." However, there is still a certain measure of doubt for this translation, since the normally reliable Byzantine manuscripts have Jesus referring to the apostles, and not the Father's name, as having been given to Jesus. On the other hand, *there is absolutely no doubt* that in verse *11* the correct translation is: "Your name which You have given Me." This translation is supported by (1) the internal evidence of the syntax, (2) the most ancient manuscripts, and (3) the Byzantine manuscripts. As a matter of fact, the certainty of this translation in verse 11 indicates that Jesus may have said the same thing in verse 12 to emphasize His reference to the Father's name.

In any case, the Man from Nazareth definitely stated in John 17:11 that He had the Father's name, which the Father had given to Him! This means that, according to Christ Himself, the name of Jesus was not only the name of the Son but was also the name of the Father and had been the Father's name that He had transferred to the

Son. And this agrees with what Jesus expressed in Matthew 28:19 when He told His disciples to baptize in the name of the Father, the Son, and the Holy Spirit— which is the name of Jesus.

Even if one does not know Greek, it is still obvious that Jesus emphasized the Father's name in John 17:11-12, no matter which English translation one reads. Also, in this same prayer Jesus associated Himself with that name again, not once, but twice; and all major translations bring this out. Near the beginning of His prayer, Jesus prayed to the Father: "I have manifested [revealed] Your name (John 17:6, NKJV; see also KJV). And again at the close of His prayer, Jesus emphasized: "I have declared to them Your name" (John 17:26).

It would only be natural that the Father's name would be transferred to the Son at His human birth since the Messiah came into the world as a divine Messiah, Emmanuel, "God with us" (Matthew 1:23). And it is only logical that the angel from the Lord would instruct Joseph to name the Son of God "Jesus" since He would "*save* His people from their sins" (Matthew 1:21). Therefore, it is no coincidence that the name "Jesus" means "Yahweh-Savior," "Yahweh Saves," or "Yahweh is Salvation." Because "Yahweh" was the name of God the Father in the Old Testament, it is only consistent for God to make His name "Yahweh" a part of His name "Jesus" when He came into the world as a Son to save His people from their sins. For those who have been conditioned by tradition not to identify the name of Jesus with the Father, it is helpful to remember that the name "Yahweh" is a part of the name "Jesus" because God the Father *wanted* us to associate Him with that name. Passages of Scripture like John 17:6,

12, 26; Matthew 28:19; and other similar New Testament texts, specifically associate the name of Jesus with both the Son and the Father because it is the marvelous name of one wonderful God. This is why the Son glorifies the Father when the Father glorifies the Son. The two roles of Father and Son glorify one God who has one name, Jesus: "Yahweh-Savior."

The New Testament also identifies the name of Jesus with the Holy Spirit since God is one Spirit (Ephesians 4:4). We saw earlier in this study that Jesus revealed to His disciples that He Himself would become "the Spirit of truth" who would come to His followers after His physical departure from this world, for He stated that He who then dwelt "with" them (as the Son of Man) would later be "*in*" them (as the Holy Spirit) (John 14:17-18). Shortly afterward, Jesus declared:

> *"But the Comforter, the Holy Spirit, whom the Father will send* in My name, *He will teach you all things, and bring to your remembrance all things that* I Myself *[literal Greek] said to you" (John 14:26).*

According to Christ in this verse, "the Father" will send "the Spirit" in the name of the Son! Like Matthew 28:19, this is another verse that, in itself, associates the Father, the Holy Spirit, and the Son with the *name* of the Son, which, of course, is Jesus.

In this same chapter Jesus promised:

> *"And whatever you ask in My name, I will do it, that* the Father *may be glorified in the Son. If you ask anything in* My *name, I Myself will do it" (John 14:13-14).*

This is another passage in which Jesus explained that the Father is glorified "in the Son." (Compare John 14:13-14 with John 16:26.) If Christians want to glorify the Father, they will do so by glorifying the Son. It is not possible to give "too much glory" to the Son and His name, for "God has highly exalted Him and given Him the name which is above every name, that at the name of Jesus every knee should bow" (Philippians 2:9-10). And the time will come when every tongue will confess that "Jesus Christ is Lord, to the *glory* of God the Father" (Philippians 2:11).

Whenever the Christians in Corinth gathered together for worship, they did so "in the name of our Lord Jesus Christ" and "with the power of our Lord Jesus Christ" (I Corinthians 5:4). As followers of Christ, we are all "justified in the name of our Lord Jesus Christ and by the Spirit of our God" (I Corinthians 6:11). Whatever we do in word or in deed, we are to do "everything" in the name of the Lord Jesus Christ (Colossians 3:17). We are to give thanks "always for all things" to God the Father in the name of our Lord Jesus Christ (Ephesians 5:20). This means far more than simply attaching Jesus' name at the end of our prayers, for the New Testament writers consistently called Jesus "our *Lord* Jesus Christ," as in the foregoing references. To pray to our Lord Jesus *is* to pray to God the Father. And to pray in the *name* of Jesus means to approach God in the *authority* of Jesus Christ as our Lord and divine Savior.

It is good and right for us to honor and glorify the name of Jesus, but may we do so through the activity of our lives and not only by the speech of our lips. To honor the name "Jesus" in the Biblical sense means far more than just honoring a name. It means honoring Jesus Christ Himself, the Creator and Lord of the universe!

When the God of the Old Testament identified Himself to Moses as Yahweh, God informed him that "Yahweh" was His eternal name (Exodus 3:15). Is it not significant that the name "Jesus" means in the Hebrew language "Yahweh-Savior"? For that name is a constant reminder that, in Jesus, Yahweh has *become* our Savior. Yahweh of the *Old* Testament became Jesus—"Yahweh-Savior" of the *New* Testament.

A Mark and a Name

We will now discuss several passages of Scripture that associate a *mark* and a *name* with Jesus in a profound way. Old Testament texts speak of a special mark, and Christians are aware that the account of the Passover lamb and a mark in Exodus 12 was prophetic of Jesus Christ, whom the New Testament identifies as the Lamb of God. Exodus 12 informs us that if the Israelites were to escape the judgment coming over the land of Egypt from the angel of death they had to sacrifice a *male lamb* "without blemish" (verse 5). According to the Lord's command, each household was to roast and eat the lamb that night; but before they did so, they were to take some of the lamb's *blood* and mark it as a *sign* on the two door posts (right and left) and on the lintel (the horizontal beam over the doorway). Thousands of Israelites' houses had this mark of the lamb's blood on their door posts and on their lintels as a demonstration of their faith in Yahweh to deliver them from the judgment of Egypt and from the bondage of Egypt.

We should note that this marking of the lamb's blood

was probably on wood, very likely a divine portrait of the cross of Jesus where the blood of the Lamb of God was marked on a *wooden* cross for the sins of humanity. Some commentators have suggested that this mark in Egypt may have been in the shape of a *cross*; and this is very possible, especially in light of other related passages of Scriptures that we will discuss shortly.

The ancient Hebrews were told that the blood of the lamb would be a "sign" for them (Exodus 12:13). The Lord informed them that when He saw the blood on the doors of their houses, He would "pass over" them and spare them from the judgment of God (verse 23). Each Israelite household demonstrated their faith in the Lord by sacrificing an unblemished male lamb. As a result, their lives were saved, and they were liberated from the slavery of Egypt.

In like manner, Christians today believe that "Christ our Passover lamb [literal Greek] was sacrificed for us" (I Corinthians 5:7). We demonstrate *our* faith in the Lord by repenting of our sins and being baptized in the name of Jesus (Acts 2:38). As a result, *our* lives are saved, and we are liberated from the slavery of *sin* (Romans 6:3-6).

Biblical prophecy is often general in the beginning and becomes consistently more revealing as time progresses. Because of this, the sacrifice of the Messiah on a cross is the focus of more detailed prophecies that come after Exodus 12. One of these prophecies shows that the *sign* of the blood of the Lamb of God would be a specific "mark." This "remarkable" passage of Scripture (to use an appropriate pun) appears in the Book of Ezekiel, where a prophet of God wrote about a coming vision of judgment in Jerusalem:

"Now the glory of the God of Israel went up from above the cherubim, where it had been, and moved to the threshold of the temple. Then the LORD called to the man clothed in linen who had the writing kit at his side and said to him, 'Go throughout the city of Jerusalem and put a mark on the foreheads of those who grieve and lament over all the detestable things that are done in it'" (Ezekiel 9:3-4, NIV).

What is profound about Ezekiel 9 is that the Hebrew word for "mark" in verses 4 and 6 is *tau*. The inspired writer could have used a general Hebrew term like *oth* (as in Exodus 12), which is commonly used either for "sign" or "mark" in the Old Testament. Or he could have used the Hebrew word *shem*, which means "name" as well as "sign" or "mark." But under the guiding hand of "the Spirit of Christ" (I Peter 1:11), this Old Testament prophet used *tau*, which is a much more specific word than either *oth* or *shem*. For *tau* has a particular meaning that the other two general words do not have. *Tau* is both a letter of the Hebrew alphabet and a word in the Hebrew language, and it means "mark," or more exactly, "cross"!

As just mentioned, early Biblical prophecy is often general, and the Hebrew word for "sign" in Exodus 12 is *oth*, a general word. Some Bible commentators have properly suggested that the sign that was marked on the door posts and lintels of each Israelite house in Egypt may have been a *tau*, a cross, because of (1) the revelation in Ezekiel 9:4, 6, (2) the piercing prophecies (Psalm 22:16; Isaiah 53:5; Zechariah 12:10) and related passages in the Old Testament, and (3) the historical record in the New Testament of the Lamb of God dying on a cross.

In any case, the word in Ezekiel 9:4, 6 is *tau*, the classical Hebrew word for "cross," which is a figure or mark formed by two, straight, intersecting lines. The classical Hebrew alphabet of Old Testament Hebrew, like modern Hebrew, has been preserved in the Aramaic square script. However, the earlier Hebrew letters had different shapes, as shown in various ancient inscriptions. In the early Hebrew script, each letter not only represented a word, but the letter was originally in the *shape* of the object that it represented. Even several letters in the modern script are still written in a similar shape as the objects which those letters represent. Hebrew dictionaries and lexicons state that the ancient Hebrew letter *tau* not only means a "cross," but that it was also written in the *shape* of a cross as the letter *t* (or an *x*, which is a *t* on its side). *Tau* is the Hebrew letter for *t* and is pronounced like the modern English *t*. In fact, the Hebrew *tau* is the ancestor of the *t* in later languages, including English. And in many modern languages, including our own, the letter *t* is still *shaped* like a cross, as it was in early Hebrew.

What is particularly interesting is that in Greek, the language of the New Testament, the letter *t* is also shaped like a cross. The Greek letter even has the same *name* as the Hebrew letter, *tau*. As a matter of fact, there is an amazing linguistic relationship between (1) *tau*, the Hebrew letter for *t*, (2) *tau*, the Greek letter for *t*, (3) *tau*, the Hebrew word for "cross," and (4) the Greek word for "cross," *stauros*, which has *tau* as its root letters!

Stauros is the Greek noun used in the New Testament whenever it discusses the cross of Jesus. When the verb "crucify" is used, the Greek verb is *stauroo*. The central message of the New Testament is that Jesus, the perfect Man who was the Son of God, reconciled us to God through the cross—the *stauros*.

Returning now to the prophecy of Ezekiel 9, verse 4 not only has the noun *tau*, "the mark of a cross," but the verse also has a verb with the same root, which is *tawah*. It was not unusual for the Hebrew writers of the Old Testament to use the same Hebrew root more than once in a sentence in order to show emphasis, and this is what we see in Ezekiel 9:4. The inspired prophet emphasized that Yahweh commanded the messenger of judgment to go through Jerusalem and "mark a mark," or more literally in the Hebrew, "cross a cross" on the foreheads of the saints!

It is also interesting that the verb of *tau* means in the causative stem of Hebrew grammar (the *Hiphil*) not only "to mark" or "to cross" but *also* "to grieve." Because the verb in Ezekiel 9:4 *is* in the *Hiphil* stem, it has the dual meaning in this verse of "to mark a cross" on the foreheads of saints who are "grieving" in the process. In fact, in verse 4 Ezekiel also used two other Hebrew verbs that mean "to grieve" in order to emphasize his point—*hanne'enachim* and *hanne'enaqim*. In these two additional verbs of grief, the inspired writer used *another* poetic device to express emphasis by verbs that are similar in both meaning and sound. In fact, the verbs are identical in sound and spelling except for one letter, and even here the "ch" sound in the first verb is very close to the "q" sound in the second verb. Thus in an ingenuous, linguistic manner, Ezekiel emphasized the great grief that the saints in Jerusalem felt—

first by using *tawah* in the *Hiphil* or causative stem, and then by adding the two related verbs of grief that mean and sound alike.

According to this passage of Scripture, the saints grieved over the sins that were being committed in the city of Jerusalem. And much is written in both Testaments about the grief associated with the sacrifice of the Lamb of God (Isaiah 53; Zechariah 12:10; Luke 22:42-45; Acts 2:37; Revelation 1:7). Jesus went to the cross with great grief for the sins of humanity. This divine act was accomplished with enormous personal sacrifice in order to help us human beings understand that *our* sins made the cross of the Holy and Just One necessary. And when the gospel of Christ is proclaimed, receptive hearts repent *because of* grief for their sins (Acts 2:37-41), but it is a grief that soon turns to joy when faith in Jesus leads to a comprehension that those sins have been forgiven because of His death on the cross.

Grief is not the only thing that the saints in Ezekiel 9:4, 6 and the saints of the New Testament age have in common. We can be confident that this passage in Ezekiel is a prophetic picture of the gospel age: Just as the saints of Jerusalem in Ezekiel 9:4, 6 had the mark of a cross "on their foreheads" to show that they were redeemed and saved, Christians of the gospel age have the cross of Jesus *in their minds* because they are the redeemed and saved. To summarize, the passage in Ezekiel is a profound prophecy of the gospel of the cross in general. But in addition, it is a prophecy that relates to specific passages in the Book of Revelation that deal with the name of Jesus. The following are two passages from Revelation that are reminiscent of Ezekiel 9:

"Then I looked and behold, the Lamb standing on Mount Zion, and with Him one hundred and forty-four thousand, having His name, even [kai] His Father's name, written on their foreheads" (Revelation 14:1, literal Greek).

"And he showed me a river of living water, clear as crystal, proceeding out of the throne of God, even [kai] of the Lamb. . . . And there shall be no more curse, but the throne of God, even [kai] of the Lamb, shall be in it ["shall be" is a singular Greek verb in order to agree with the one "throne"]. And His servants shall serve Him. They shall see His face, and His name shall be on their foreheads" (Revelation 22:1, 3-4, literal Greek).

The prophecies in Ezekiel 9, Revelation 14, and Revelation 22 have much in common. The saints in Ezekiel's vision are in Jerusalem. The saints in Revelation 14 are on Mount Zion (verse 1), which is in Jerusalem; and the saints in Revelation 22 are in "New Jerusalem" (Revelation 21:2-22:5; see 21:2, 10). The believers in both books are faithful, redeemed, and saved. Just as the faithful in Ezekiel receive the mark of a *cross* on their foreheads, the faithful in Revelation receive the mark of the Lamb's *name* on their foreheads. And it is self-evident that the cross in Ezekiel 9 is related to the name of the Lamb, Jesus, who was crucified on a cross.

The central message of the New Testament is that Jesus, as the Lamb of God, died on a cross for our sins (I Corinthians 1:18-25). And this message of a perfect sacrifice on a cross is the fulfillment of numerous Old Testament prophecies (Psalm 22; Isaiah 53; Zechariah 12:10; compare Galatians 3:13 with Deuteronomy 21:23).

Both Revelation 14:1 and Revelation 22:3-4 show that the name of the Lamb is the name of the Father, and this agrees with earlier passages that we have examined. If the name of the Father is the name of the Lamb in Revelation 14 and Revelation 22, then the Father's name is also Jesus—the same name that our Lord referred to in Matthew 28:19 and in many other passages (e.g., Luke 24:47; John 14:13; 17:6, 11-12, 26).

Revelation 22:3-5 reveals that "God" (verse 3), "the Lamb" (verse 3), and "the Lord God" (verse 5) are the same. Let us notice the singular pronouns in these verses: "His" servants shall serve "Him" (verse 3). They shall see "His" face, and "His" name shall be on their foreheads (verse 4). As we pointed out earlier in the quotation of Revelation 22:3, the Greek verb for "shall be" is singular in order to agree in number with the singular subject, "the throne." This confirms that the throne of the Lamb *is* the throne of God. The singular verb also shows that we must take the Greek word *kai* in the sense of "even" in the phrase "the throne of God, even [*kai*] of the Lamb" (with *kai* having the same meaning in verse 1). In addition, may we observe that the relevant nouns in verses 3, 4, and 5 are also all singular. There is one throne, one God, one Lord God, one Lamb, one face, and one name!

Revelation 22:3-5 establishes beyond any doubt that the parallel passage in Revelation 14:1 also declares that the name of the Lamb is the name of the Father. Therefore, as in Revelation 22:3, we are to understand *kai* in Revelation 14:1, too, as "even" or "that is" in the phrase "His name, even [*kai*] His Father's name."

The context in Revelation 14 itself shows the same

thing. The focus on this chapter is the Lamb. *He* is the One who stands on Mount Zion (verse 1). It is with *Him* that 144,000 redeemed followers stand (verse 1). One name is on their foreheads, and it is the name of the Lamb, which is His Father's name as well (verse 1). The 144,000 (probably a symbolic number) sing a song that no one else can learn because only they are "redeemed" from the earth (verse 3). These are the ones who "follow the Lamb" (verse 4). A few verses later, the saints are identified as those who keep "the commandments of God and *the faith of Jesus*" (verse 12). But those who worship a false god, instead of the true God, are condemned by "the Lamb" (verses 9-11). The Lamb is then referred to as "the Son of Man" with a golden crown who will reap the harvest of the earth (verses 14-20).

Revelation 14 not only talks about Jesus the Lamb but also about *another* who gives a mark and receives worship from millions who have *rejected* the Lamb. The Book of Revelation calls this object of false worship "the Beast," and several chapters describe the Beast as a great, false, worldwide, religious-political system that deceives many nations of the earth (Revelation 13-20). The Beast also appears, at least sometimes, to be a person (possibly an influential leader representing and personifying this worldwide system) who, along with "the false prophet," is cast into the lake of fire when the Lamb brings judgment on this world (Revelation 19:20).

As a matter of fact, *all* who follow and worship the Beast and who receive the mark of the Beast will be cast into the eternal lake of fire in the presence of the holy angels and "the Lamb" (Revelation 14:9-10).

No Other Name

As we conclude our investigation, it is hoped that all will continue to study the Word of God concerning Jesus. In the meantime, let us note five declarations from the Bible that ring down through the centuries to our own day:

1. "And this is His commandment: that we should believe on the name of His Son Jesus Christ" (I John 3:23, NKJV).

2. "He who has the Son has life; he who does not have the Son of God does not have life. These things I have written to you who believe in the name of the Son of God, that you may know that you have eternal life, and that you may continue to believe in the name of the Son of God" (I John 5:12-13, NKJV).

3. "Now all things are of God, who has reconciled us to Himself through Jesus Christ . . . that is, that God was in Christ reconciling the world to Himself" (II Corinthians 5:18-19, NKJV).

4. "For no other foundation can anyone lay than that which is laid, which is Jesus Christ" (I Corinthians 3:11, NKJV).

5. "Nor is there salvation in any other; for there is no other name under heaven given among men by which we must be saved" (Acts 4:12, NKJV).

These are sobering words, and yet they are also comforting words. They are both sobering and comforting because they come from the authoritative source of inspired apostles. These words clearly and majestically testify that, apart from Jesus, there is no other name—there is no other God—through whom we can be saved.

Who is Jesus? He is what His very name identifies Him to be: "Yahweh-Savior." Who is Jesus? He is what the Bible, from beginning to end, reveals Him to be: the God of two Testaments.

NOTES

Chapter 1

[1]*Encyclopedia Judaica* (1972) 7:642.

[2]Matthew Henry, *Commentary* 1:10.

[3]Ephraim A. Speiser, *The Anchor Bible: Genesis*, 7.

[4]Ibid., 4.

[5]A. T. Robertson, *A Grammar of the Greek New Testament in the Light of Historical Research*, 407.

[6]J. H. Hertz, *The Pentateuch and Haftorahs*, 5.

[7]*The Oxford Annotated Bible*, Revised Standard Version, 2.

[8]II Kings 19:20-37.

[9]Henry, 2, see also Nathan Stone, *Names of God*, 11-12, and V. E. Howard, "The Godhead: One or Three?"

[10]Francis Brown, S. R. Driver, and C. A. Briggs, *Hebrew and English Lexicon of the Old Testament*, 43.

[11]William Smith, *Bible Dictionary*, teacher's edition, 220.

[12]Hertz, 2.

[13]Smith, 220.

[14]Ibid.

Chapter 2

[1]Norman Geisler, *Christ: The Theme of the Bible*, 49.

[2]Ibid., 50.

[3]Some Greek manuscripts read "the Lord," but note the context (verses 1-5).

[4]Isaiah 50:1; Hosea 2:7-8.

[5]Revelation 19:7-8; Ephesians 5:21-32.

[6]Harry Rimmer, *The Magnificence of Jesus*, 35.

[7]Smith, 284.

[8]Ibid., 220.

[9]*Oxford Annotated Bible*, 1298.

[10]Matthew 21:45-46.

[11]Leon Morris, *The First Epistle of Paul to the Corinthians*, 141-42.

[12]Luke 15:1-7.

[13]Dr. John Shakeshaft and Dr. Peter Scheuer of the Mullard Radio Astronomy Observatory of Cambridge, England, BBC interview.

[14]Carl Henry, *Answers for the NOW Generation*, 19.

[15]*Oxford Annotated Bible*, 1172.

[16]See *The Prophecy Edition* of the New Testament, x.; Smith, 307; William Barclay, *Commentary on Matthew* 1:10.

[17]See Psalm 68:4; 104:35; 105:45; 106:1, 48; 113:1; 115:18; 116:19; 117:2; Isaiah 12:2; 26:4.

[18]It is true that Semitic names in the Bible were often theophonic (carrying God's name), but of course, as this chapter has demonstrated, the identity of Jesus as Yahweh does not depend upon that name alone.

Chapter 3

[1]Fritz Rienecker, translated and revised by Cleon L. Rogers, Jr., *A Linguistic Key to the Greek New Testament*, 604. For the Greek word for "radiance," this source refers to the following (among other works): A. T. Robertson, *Word Pictures in the New Testament*, 6 vols. (New York: Harper & Brothers, 1930; Gerhard Kittel and Gerhard Friedrich, eds., *Theological Dictionary of the New Testament*, 9 vols. (Grand Rapids: Eerdmans, 1973).

[2]William F. Arndt and F. Wilbur Gingrich. *A Greek-English Lexicon of the New Testament and Other Early Christian Literature*, 173.

[3]Oscar Cullmann, *The Christology of the New Testament*, 293-94.

[4]Romans 8:9, 14.

[5]Galatians 4:6.

[6]Romans 8:9.

[7]Cullmann, 224.

[8]John 1:14.

[9]John Stott, *Basic Christianity*, 35.

[10]John 10:11, 14; a different Greek word for "good," but with the *same* basic meaning.

[11]John 1:14.

[12]William Barclay, *The Mind of Jesus*, 190-91.

[13]The first-year Greek student soon learns that *ginomai* means "become," "come into being," etc. The rendering of "made" by the King James Version in Romans 1:3 and Galatians 4:4 has the support of the Greek lexicons, and the use of the word in texts like John 1:1 and Hebrews 11:3 shows why.

[14]Cullmann, 294.

¹⁵Ibid., n. 5.

¹⁶Some English translations have "the only begotten God" or similar terminology, following certain manuscript evidence. The RSV has "the only Son," and both the KJV and NKJV correctly have "the only begotten Son" in following the reliable Byzantine family of manuscripts and other ancient sources. Although the Bible nowhere teaches that *God* was ever begotten, since He is revealed to be eternal and immortal, the Scriptures do teach that the "only begotten Son," Jesus, was begotten when He was conceived in the virgin Mary by the Holy Spirit of God.

¹⁷Alexander Souter, *A Pocket Lexicon to the Greek New Testament*, 23-24. My second-year Greek professor at Abilene Christian University, Robert Johnston, once pointed out to me the value of this little lexicon.

Chapter 4

¹Theodore Pitcairn, *My Lord and My God*, 52.

²V. E. Howard, "The Godhead: One or Three?," 13.

³The apostle Paul's salutations are in Romans 1:7; I Corinthians 1:3; II Corinthians 1:2; Galatians 1:3; Ephesians 1:2; Philippians 1:2; Colossians 1:2; I Thessalonians 1:1; II Thessalonians 1:2; I Timothy 1:2; II Timothy 1:2; Titus 1:4; and Philemon 1:3. In this study we are dealing with the portion of the greetings that mentions the divine titles and the name "Jesus."

⁴In addition to our comments in this chapter, an excellent discussion of the salutations and related verses of Scripture can be found in David K. Bernard, *The Oneness of God*, 207-15.

⁵Another acceptable rendering is to have the same translation but without commas. It is commendable that many English translations now translate the salutations without the use of commas. Unfortunately, they fail to associate the personal possessive pronoun "our" with *both* "Father" and "Lord Jesus Christ," unlike the Greek, thus making the two divine titles seem to indicate an unwarranted separation of being. The Greek does have "our" *between* "Father" and "Lord Jesus Christ," and it does *not* have "the" before "Lord Jesus" (even though it was commonly used before "Lord" in the New Testament).

⁶H. E. Dana and Julius R. Mantey, *A Manual Grammar of the Greek New Testament*, 250.

⁷Consult also the following verses in the King James Version:

Philippians 4:20, I Thessalonians 1:3; II Timothy 4:1; James 1:27. It is interesting that the King James Version itself renders *kai* as "even" in James 3:9 ("God, *even* the Father").

⁸Cullmann, 313.

⁹Dana and Mantey, 137, quoting Robertson, 776.

¹⁰Dana and Mantey, 137.

¹¹Ibid., 149.

¹²Geisler, 27, n. 10.

¹³Rimmer, 60-61.

Chapter 5

¹Bruce Metzger, *The Text of the New Testament*, 101-2.

²Metzger, *Theology Today* (April 1953), 73.

³Bernard, *The Oneness of God*, 140.

⁴Howard, 5.

⁵In this verse the Revised Standard Version capitalizes "Spirit" but not "holy."

⁶Acts 7:51.

⁷Isaiah 6:1-13.

⁸Acts 28:25-27.

⁹Isaiah 6:1-5.

¹⁰Acts 28:25.

¹¹Exodus 17:1-7; Psalm 95:6-10.

¹²Hebrews 3:7-9.

¹³Matthew 1:18.

¹⁴Mark 3:28-30.

¹⁵John 14:26.

¹⁶I John 2:1.

¹⁷Compare Hebrews 12:9 with verses 2, 3, 5; the theme is Jesus.

¹⁸*Oxford Annotated Bible*, 1380, note to I Corinthians 2:16.

¹⁹David K. Alexander and C. W. Junker, eds., *What Can You Believe?*, 23.

²⁰John Stott, *The Baptism and Fullness of the Holy Spirit*, 53.

²¹Acts 11:15-18.

²²*New Catholic Encyclopedia* 2:62.

²³Ibid. 2:58.

²⁴Revelation 1:5; Colossians 1:18; I Corinthians 15:42-54.

²⁵Romans 8:9. The entire eighth chapter of Romans empha-

sizes the importance of accepting Jesus Christ and His Spirit.

[26]I Corinthians 2:16.
[27]Luke 11:9-13; Acts 2:38.
[28]Matthew 3:1-2.
[29]Matthew 4:17.
[30]Acts 2:4.
[31]Acts 2:16-18.
[32]Acts 8:16; 10:44.
[33]Acts 10:45.
[34]*Oxford Annotated Bible*, 1295-96.

Chapter 6

[1]Rienecker and Rogers, 411.
[2]Cullmann, 202.
[3]Morton Scott Enslin, *Christian Beginnings*, 192.
[4]Alexander and Junker, eds., 16.
[5]Matthew 6:24.
[6]John 12:41.
[7]Acts 2:47.
[8]Revelation 14:14-16; Matthew 13:36-43.
[9]Cullmann, 215.
[10]Rienecker and Rogers, 385. See also Charles Hodge, *Commentary on the First Epistle to the Corinthians*, 1953.
[11]*Oxford Annotated Bible*, 1395, note to I Corinthians 16:22, 1395.

Chapter 7

[1]Matthew 8:1-2.
[2]Matthew 9:18.
[3]Matthew 14:33.
[4]Matthew 15:22-28.
[5]*Oxford Annotated Bible*, 830.
[6]Hugh Schonfield, *The Passover Plot*, 33.
[7]C. S. Lewis, *Mere Christianity*, 55-56.
[8]William Barclay, *The Letter to the Hebrews*, 134.
[9]Stott, *Basic Christianity*, 30.
[10]Adapted from Oliver F. Fauss, *Buy the Truth and Sell It Not*, 48-49.
[11]Albert Barnes, *The Prophet Isaiah* (1867) 1:209.
[12]*Oxford Annotated Bible*, 1198-99.

[13]William Barclay, *The Gospel of Luke*, Luke 19:44, 250.

[14]*The Amplified New Testament*, Luke 19:44.

[15]*The New Testament in Modern English* by J. B. Phillips, Luke 19:44.

[16]Hugh Schonfield, *The Authentic New Testament*, 117, note to Matthew 18:20.

[17]Carl Henry, *Answers for the Now Generation*, 46-47.

[18]Bruce Metzger, "Jehovah's Witnesses and Jesus Christ," *Theology Today* (April 1953), 78-79.

[19]Dana and Mantey, 147.

[20]Ibid.

[21]Robertson, 786. Compare Titus 1:3 with 2:13, and Titus 3:4 with 3:6. Jesus, as God, is our Savior.

[22]Schonfield, *Those Incredible Christians*, 257.

[23]Clark Pinnock, *Set Forth Your Case*, 88.

[24]Metzger, in *Theology Today*, 77-78.

[25]Charles B. Williams, *The New Testament*, 14, note to Matthew 2:23.

[26]*Oxford Annotated Bible*, 1428, note to Colossians 2:9.

[27]Eugene Van Goetchius, *The Language of the New Testament*, 47.

[28]Ernest Colwell, "A Definite Rule for the Use of the Article in the Greek New Testament," *Journal of Biblical Literature*, 52 (1933): 12-21.

[29]Cullmann, 312.

Chapter 8

[1]Wayne Jackson, *The Godhead: One or Three?*, 4.

[2]Robertson, 785.

[3]Ibid., 525.

[4]Ibid., 649.

[5]John Stott, *The Baptism and Fullness of the Holy Spirit*, 25.

[6]Allen Holden, Jr., "In Jesus' Name," *The Firm Foundation*, 23 January 1973.

[7]Bernard, 137.